Unjustly Accused:

The true story of one man's experience in, and escape from, a Dominican Republic prison

. . . .

SUSAN L STEWART

Additional Books
by Susan L Stewart

Non-fiction E-books

- *How to pack for a 3-week vacation with only one carry-on*
- *Stop Dieting Forever! A natural, healthy way to lose weight*

Memoir available in E-book and Paperback

- *Unjustly Accused: The true story of one man's experience in, and escape from a Dominican Republic prison*

Regency Romance

- *To Wed the Devil* (out early 2018)

Unjustly Accused:
The true story of one man's experience in,
and escape from, a Dominican Republic prison

Take Flight Press • Littleton, Colorado
1st Edition
ISBN-13: 978-0-9996222-0-9

Printed in the United States of America

I love to hear from readers! You can write to me directly at
Susan@SusanLStewart.com or visit my author website at
SusanLStewart.com

Dedication

I want to dedicate this book to my loving husband, Tom, who supports me whenever I decide to try something new.
And, to Corey. Without his words there would be no book.

Author's Note

This is the true story of how two young men with completely different personalities dealt with their unjust arrest, conviction and sentence to a Dominican Republic prison on drug trafficking charges.

Corey and I spent more than six weeks talking about what happened while he and Jeff were on vacation in the Dominican Republic. The result was 65+ hours of digital recordings. I have used his words throughout the book. I changed the names of the people involved and a few other small details to protect their privacy, but in no way has this affected the facts of the story.

Najayo prison is real. Although built to house 950 prisoners, Najayo's population was approximately 2,500 when Corey and Jeff were there. Prison conditions are described as Corey experienced them at the time of his incarceration.

Corey worked hard to learn Spanish from the moment he and Jeff were arrested. By the end of their prison experience, he was only speaking Spanish. I know a little Spanish and as Corey said things, I did the best I could to write them down accurately. Even so, I know there are errors in spelling, word choices and phrases that I couldn't find in dictionaries or translation apps. I hope you will forgive these errors. In addition, some words may be specific to the Dominican Republic. For example, the word *fue* means "it was" in Spanish but in the DR it is the word they use for "free" as in "free to leave or go."

Las puertas de conseguir en prisión son muy, muy grande
pero las puertas para salir son muy, muy pequeña.

The doors to get in prison are very, very large
but the doors to get out are very, very small.

Contents

Thursday morning, June 18

Corey wakes up slowly, holding on to sleep as long as he can. He and Diego are sharing a thin mat on a narrow, concrete bunk designed for one. Then Diego, snoring like a bull on steroids, rolls over and sighs heavily sending his hot, rancid breath toward Corey's face.

He rolls over with a groan and stares through the bars holding them in.

"How did I get myself into this? I let my guard down one time! One time and here I am," he thinks. "We had a deal, God! Remember?"

Jeff, a friend from work, is on the top bunk. Corey can see his feet hanging over the end. Dominicans as a whole are relatively short and at six foot two inches there's no way Jeff will ever fit into anything the Dominican Republic has to offer. He lets out a snore that's nearly as loud as Diego's.

So how did Corey get into this? It started out innocently enough, as most things do. Corey worked as a consultant on a U.S. government project in the Caribbean for about two years and his contract was up. The original plan was for Corey, Jeff, and two other guys from work, Victor and Lucas, to fly to the Dominican Republic (DR) on Thursday for one last weekend party before Corey headed back to the States.

At the last minute, Jeff asks Corey if he'd like to leave two days earlier than planned so they can do some sightseeing in Santo Domingo, the capitol of the DR. Once Victor and Lucas arrive they're going to be in a resort so this would give them a chance to experience the real Dominican culture. Corey agrees to go.

Jeff makes all the plans. He does some research and creates a list of things to see. He asks around, and someone at work recommends this guy, Diego, to be their taxi driver and tour guide. These guys used him the last time they were in the DR and they didn't have any problems. Jeff gets Diego's name and information, contacts him and gets him set up for their time in Santo Domingo. He makes the flight and hotel reservations and they're ready to go.

Except for Jeff, who is married with two children, spending a long weekend on a Caribbean island is something Corey and his friends have done many times. They hang out at the beach, surfing and drinking, and if they connect with some beautiful women well, that's fine, too. This is supposed to be one last fling in paradise, except paradise doesn't usually include a cell with two concrete bunks.

As the morning crawls on, people walk back and forth in front of the iron bars trying to look like they aren't looking, but they are, and Corey knows it. All of his senses are heightened. He's alert to anything that may be a clue to where they are or why they are there or, better yet, how they can get out. The people passing by are young, dressed in regular street clothes, and are carrying files and briefcases instead of guns like the night before. This appears to be an office of some sort–an office with cells designed for two. It doesn't make sense.

Time passes slowly as time does when you have nothing better to do than to wonder what time it is. Corey sits, motionless, watching the door, while his thoughts race over probabilities and outcomes. He balls his hands into skilled boxer's fists. He wants to beat up the bastard that got them into this mess. The only problem is that since flunking Spanish in high school–twice–he needs the bastard to translate. Besides, he's the one who let his guard down, he's the one who trusted someone he didn't know, and he feels responsible for getting himself and Jeff into this situation. And he knows one thing as clearly as he has ever known anything else in his life; he is going to have to be the one to get them out.

If he could speak the language, he could explain who they are, and what happened–without the need for Diego's questionable translation–and get them out of there. It's all a big misunderstanding.

After all, they were just passengers in a taxi and knew nothing about any cocaine.

Tuesday, June 16

Two days earlier...

Me and Jeff step out of the Santo Domingo airport and into a cloud of humidity and bugs. A large crowd of men in white shirts with the sleeves rolled up are ready to sell us a timeshare, book us on a sightseeing trip or take us anywhere we want to go. We pass through them, find a taxi, and climb in. We're traveling light. Each of us has a carry-on and Jeff brought his laptop. He's planning to do some work during the weekend.

We're on our way to *La Perla Hotel and Casino* in the heart of Santo Domingo. It's a forty-five minute drive and as we leave the airport, we pass by less populated areas. There are stretches of road that are obviously being used as trash dumps. Straggly grass and half-starved cows are scattered on land that has been overgrazed.

When we reach the city, one of the first things that stand out are the mopeds. Watching the mopeds and what people manage to carry on them is hysterical. A family of five rides by on one with a baby shoved between the man, who is driving, and the mother. The other two kids are hanging on behind her. Another one has a load of live chickens on the back. A man is riding a moped with stacks of bread as wide as a car strapped all around it.

As we get farther into the city, the traffic becomes heavier and more difficult to maneuver. The smog makes it hard to breathe. Although there are probably rules governing driving, you'd never know it. There are no lanes painted on the street so people drive wherever they want to. Mopeds have the advantage of being smaller, so they can weave through the cars that are weaving through the rest of the traffic. Stoplights are a suggestion, not a rule, as no one pays any attention to them. If you're lucky, a taxi driver approaching an intersection might slow down for ten seconds before taking a chance with his, and your, life and shooting the gas.

There are people everywhere on the sidewalks selling anything a person could possibly need or want. There's a pickup truck half full of oranges; the other half has been dumped on the ground. A guy sits on the tailgate waiting for customers. I see a donkey pulling a cart filled with bananas. I can buy a watch, cell phone, car parts, bandanas, piñatas, chickens–alive or dead–plantains, limes, fruit, burritos, children's shoes, dresses, underwear, socks, t–shirts, clay pots, bread, beer and anything else right from my window in the taxi. Very convenient.

It looks like the shop owners opened their doors this morning and threw everything to the curb. Dozens of shops fill the blocks selling all kinds of tourist crap. Three t–shirts for $10! Across the street, it's three t–shirts for $9. There's trash everywhere. It's filthy. It's a typical third–world country. Me and Jeff can't stop laughing.

Merengue or *Bachata*, a slower version of *Merengue* with more guitar, is playing on every block. Both *Merengue* and *Bachata* originated in the DR and then spread throughout the Caribbean. Music is important to me. It helps me relax and remove myself from stressful situations. There are very few places or times when I can't listen to music. Unfortunately, I hate Caribbean music.

Every time we come to a stop, or even slow down, people selling food and *Presidente* beer bombard us. *Presidente* is made in the DR and is one of its very few exports besides drugs. And baseball players. For many, Presidente represents the DR.

We drive through the city and it's awesome. We're seeing it; we get a feel for it. It's loud. It's noisy. I can smell the city. Exhaust fumes fill the air because no one has mufflers on their cars. People are constantly whistling, yelling at each other, trying to get each other's attention.

We're seeing wild, crazy stuff. We're cracking up. There's a guy with a bunch of dead goats piled up on the back of his moped going down the middle of the traffic. It's stuff like that.

By the time we reach the hotel, Diego is waiting for us. We get out of the cab and introduce ourselves. I peg Diego as a hustler right away. I feel uncomfortable in this situation. I get a vibe. I pick up on stuff. My instincts kick in and I'm not feeling too good about this guy. I knew it and I didn't act on it. I chose not to act on it.

As time goes on, we learn more about Diego. He moved to New York when he was about 14. He says he made a living driving Italian mobsters around and that's where he picked up an Italian accent. When he got in trouble with the law, he moved back to the DR.

Diego is short, about 5' 5". He's a loudmouthed guy who talks non–stop while waving his hands around. He speaks Spanish with a New York Italian accent. He acts and sounds exactly like the characters Joe Pesci played in the *Lethal Weapon* and *Goodfellows* movies.

The girl at the front desk doesn't speak very much English, so Diego helps us get checked in. It's safe to assume he has some kind of relationship with the management there and gets a kickback every time his clients stay there.

The girl at the front desk gives us the nicest rooms in the hotel for $50 a night. We pay with credit cards, take our things up to our rooms and get settled in.

When we go back downstairs, Diego says, "What would you like to do?"

"No plans, we just want to see the city."

"Let's go then."

We slide into the back seat of Diego's Volvo. The Volvo is pretty nice on the outside and inside. Most people in the DR don't have anything, so if someone has something like a car that can provide a means to make a living, they take care of it. Diego drives us through town, pointing out the sights as we go along.

Jeff has done a lot of research for the trip. He knows where he wants to stop and what he wants to see. He has plans for the whole time we'll be here before Victor and Lucas arrive on Thursday.

I mostly work on government projects. I also do some work in third-world countries. Most of my day is spent with the people working in the field. They're the ones getting the job done. I have a great ability to relate to them and motivate them. Over the years, I've supervised people from many countries, customs and backgrounds. Because of that, I have a serious interest in different cultures and am very interested in seeing and experiencing life in the Dominican Republic.

I tell Jeff, "Whatever you want to do, man, I'm cool with it."

Diego's first stop is at a huge mall that looks like it's straight out of the 1980s. We see a Taco Bell in the food court! Imagine eating at a Taco Bell in the food court of a mall in a Spanish-speaking country where you can probably get homemade tacos on any corner. We start to crack up. I love to laugh and can usually find something funny in any situation. I tell people, if it isn't funny or important, don't waste my time.

We pass on Taco Bell, and buy a 32-ounce bottle of Presidente beer. It comes with some plastic cups and me, Jeff and Diego do beer shots as we walk around, talking and getting to know each other.

A beautiful woman walks up to us and speaks with Diego for a moment. Then she walks away.

"What's all that about," I say.

"She wants to hang out with you."

"What?"

"She wants to sleep with you. You can have anything you want here, as long as you have money. See that guy over there? I guarantee you that you can take his wife home tonight if you want. He'll gladly give her to you."

"Do you mean...?"

"I mean that man will let you sleep with his wife for the money."

I say, "Just so we're straight, I don't sleep with strange women whether they're married or not."

I haven't cut my hair the entire time I lived in the Caribbean and after two years, it's past my shoulders. I'm 5' 10", about 180 pounds. I have no body fat. I spend hours at the gym every day, sometimes twice a day, lifting weights. My shoulders are massive. Together with my small waist, I come across as a body builder even though that is not my motivation to lift weights. Often, after my workout, I'll run five to seven miles until I'm so tired, or in so much pain, that I have to stop. People can be very intimidated by me.

Jeff is 6' 2", 220 pounds and wears his hair cut short. He's a goofy white kid. He's meek. He goes around with this sort of smirky smile on his face all the time. It looks like he thinks this whole thing is funny when, in fact, he's terrified. I try to get him to stop smiling, but he keeps doing it and there's nothing I can do to help him. It's tough. Although there's nothing physically impressive about him, he is a genuinely sensitive and caring person, and an amazing dad.

Most importantly, as far as I'm concerned, is Jeff's wild sense of humor. He and Diego are goofing around, telling jokes and the three of us spend much of our time laughing.

As we leave the mall and walk out to the car Diego says, "I need to drop something off at my father–in–law's house. Is that cool with you guys or do you want to go back to your hotel?"

We decide to see where Diego lives. We continue down the busy streets until we come to the neighborhood that Diego's father–in–law lives in. Diego lives a couple of streets over.

The street is in pretty bad shape with potholes here and there. Instead of sidewalks, there are dirt paths. The cement houses are connected in one long row down the block. Each house is painted a different bight color: yellow, blue, pink, purple. It looks like a paint store exploded and paint landed on houses no matter what color the house next door was painted.

There are no grocery stores close by but it doesn't matter. People selling fruits and vegetables, different breads and desserts, and household products like brooms, mops and cleaning supplies, set up stands along the street. A butcher shop is within walking distance and sometimes people riding bikes bring chicken and other meats into the neighborhood in an ice chest, or in an old bucket filled with ice hanging off each handle bar.

Everyone knows each other. That's the thing you get a vibe for. That's the thing that's authentic about it. There's a true sincerity from people there. All of the people we meet in the DR are really nice. It's their culture. They're caring people. We didn't have any bad experiences with the people themselves. Even the people we meet inside the jail were very nice people. They don't have much, but they'll share what they have with you.

Some of the people standing around on the street come up to us and try out their limited English:

"Where are you from?"

"It is nice to meet you."

I do what I can to reply and then I have to resort to Spanglish. It isn't working great, but at least I try to communicate and the people respond to that. They are very excited to see Americans other than family members in their neighborhood and they want to take pictures of me and Jeff.

We go into Diego's father–in–law's house and meet his family. This becomes very important to us later on.

Then we go outside and walk around. We're probably the only white people this neighborhood has seen. It feels semi–dangerous but I still look imposing with my huge shoulders. As a rule, Dominicans tend to be physically small so, next to me, it's even more dramatic.

People come out of their houses, stand in the doorway and watch us. Girls flirt with us. They smile and wave, "Hey, Americans!"

Kids run around all over the place. If you saw this neighborhood in the States, you would think it's part of an inner–city project, but in the DR, it's a decent place to live.

There's a little shop across the way with some guys hanging out. They're looking at us; they're not saying anything. I know when people are looking and they're not sure what to say, so I go over and say, "Hey, how's it going? What's up, man?"

They say, *"Bueno, bueno."*

They don't speak any English, so I use my best Spanglish. The guys are happy that I acknowledged them. That's the biggest thing. You acknowledge people and their presence.

Jeff doesn't know any Spanish and he just stands there.

I say, "Hey, man, say *hola*."

Jeff tries it and starts cracking up.

He says, "Dude, it works. Everyone says 'hi.' These are the friendliest people. When I say 'hi' back home, nobody says 'hi' back."

Jeff tells Diego that we want to try some authentic food here. Diego says, "Well, don't try that, it's going to make you sick. Don't drink anything unless it's in a bottle. Dude, don't drink that water."

Diego's doing that constantly. He's serving a purpose. The price that we're paying him, ($100US per day plus expenses) for all of his attention, strictly to us, is really a great deal. We're experiencing the life and culture because we're getting right in there; we go right into the city, he's looking out for our interests, and he's covering for us, speaking for us and everything like that. We really get to be part of that culture and that population.

Until we get arrested, this is the most fun I have ever had in 24 hours on any trip I've ever been on in my entire life. It's a blast. Part of it is Diego. He facilitates it. He knows everyone; he's talking to them and introduces us to them. Sometimes he wanders off to talk to someone and we stand around doing our best to communicate. Some of the people in the neighborhood know a little English and they want to practice it with us.

As we're leaving the neighborhood, Diego takes us by a small local police substation to meet the Colonel. He introduces us to him. Diego explains,

"I let him know that you guys are with me. These guys know my car. I pay, they provide protection." Diego pays a "tax" to these police so they protect him and his clients. I give the Colonel a few hundred pesos.

The concept of paying, or "tipping," police officers is foreign to Americans. In our culture, the job of the police to "Protect and Serve" needs no other incentive beyond the fact that they are paid and have benefits through whatever entity employs them.

In third–world countries, if the police pull you over for whatever reason, the majority of the time they are waiting for you to pay the tax. The difficulty arises when you try to do that and that particular police officer doesn't accept taxes from the public. Then you are facing charges of attempting to bribe a police officer. This is a position you don't want to be in.

Paying your taxes

An important concept to understand in the DR, and most third-world countries, is paying your taxes. This is not like the States where you pay taxes to the government depending on how much you earned that year. There is an expectation that if you have money–even a little bit–you will give some of it to someone who has none.

There's no racial segregation in the DR. From the beginning, people came here from many nations; it's a true melting pot. Instead of racial segregation there's a caste system similar to India. A person is born into a certain economic situation and it's very rare for anyone to rise above that. If you are born poor, you're going to suffer and you will spend your life begging people who have money to kick some down. It's accepted. That's your lot in life.

In a poverty-based society people will do whatever they can to simply survive. There's nothing wrong with committing a minor crime to get money when you're starving. You're at the bottom. You need money. The moral concept of right and wrong doesn't figure into it.

It's easy to understand the concept of the poor begging for money. It happens on street corners of every large city in America. The DR, and other third-world countries, is the opposite of America. We have welfare; we have free schools. We have organizations and people to turn to when our lives go to hell. In these countries, they don't have that. If you have nothing, you die.

People who do have money–other than tourists–are expected to share some of it. If you own a car, and I am starving, I know you have more money than I do. I will beg if I have to so you will share a little of your money. Then I–and possibly my children–won't starve to death tonight.

Now, if you hand some money down, that's great. You have a wonderful day. I will treat you like a king. I will get down on my knees and thank you for that. But if you don't, you're going to get a reputation that you don't pay your taxes, and then problems are going to happen because now you're not being a good person.

Here's an example. That afternoon me and Jeff are hanging out at a bar while Diego goes to talk to someone. We order a beer and share it with the guys that are sitting there.

I say, "Here you go, man." It cost me less than a dollar.

He says, "Thank you very much." It means something here. It's important.

I tell the bartender to keep the change and he says, "Oh, no, no. Here, have this as a gift from me," and it's a bracelet that he made.

It's kind of like that.

Tuesday, June 16, cont.

Around dusk, about 8:00 p.m., Diego says, "What else do you guys want to do? Do you want to go over by the college?"

"Yeah, man," Jeff says. "There's a college here?"

We drive over to the college neighborhood and that's when it starts getting dark. There are lots of young people, college age, walking around the streets with books and stuff like that. Again, little shops all over the place, a little bit cleaner and nicer. They aren't trying to sell a pile of shirts in a bag. So, we hang out there.

Diego says, "My cousin has a little shop over here. We can stop there and have a beer or whatever. You guys want to play some dominos?" It seems like that's all they do in the DR–play dominos on the sidewalk. Guys just sit down and start to play. We decline.

Here's what Dominicans like to do from what I've seen. They like to have sex and make as many kids as possible whether they can feed them or not. It doesn't matter. That's their lifestyle. You have your wife, you have your girlfriend, you have your mistress and you have your other girlfriend. It's accepted and that's how it is. And you have kids scattered out all over the place. They like to do that.

They like to play Dominos. They like to cock fight. Cock fighting is huge; it's the biggest sport in the country. They like baseball and drinking. That's it. That's all the people do there from what I've seen.

We stand on the street where the college is and beautiful women walk by. There are beautiful women everywhere. The Dominican women are the most beautiful women I've ever seen in my entire life. If they were in the United States, they'd be super models, every single one of them. It's such an ethnic mix. Their skin tone and hair and everything like that. They're very, very pretty. So, I'm talking to all the girls walking by. When they talk back, it only lasts so long before my Spanish runs out.

Diego comes over to us and says, "I have to go do something. I'll be back in 15 to 20 minutes," and then he leaves–without discussion or explanation. It's dark by now and we don't know where we are.

This is how it starts.

"OK, well, I guess," I say to no one in particular since Diego is already gone.

"I don't know, man, I don't feel too good about this," Jeff says.

"Well, we still have all of our money. We haven't paid him for the day yet. Who cares? We'll grab a cab and go back to the hotel."

This is how our experience with Diego goes. He comes up to us unexpectedly, tells us he has something he has to do and leaves us stranded before we can say anything.

"I need to take care of something."

"I have to drop this off."

"I have to see this person."

We say, "Whatever. We don't care."

It seems like Diego is connected to everyone. Everybody knows who he is. But he does this for a living. He has to pay his tax to everyone.

Diego tells us one of his friends says,

"If you have some Americans, bring them with you, tell them to stop by my shop and buy something from me. If other people see I have Americans coming to my shop, then I'll have more respect than the guy across the street that's selling the same stuff. Look, I have Americans coming in."

So, throughout the day, Diego's saying, "Yeah, I have to stop here and talk to this person." He sees someone, he talks to him for 20 to 30 minutes while we walk around, go over the area and look around. We're within eyesight of Diego the whole time, but we don't know what he's talking about or what kind of business he might be doing.

We don't want to sit there and listen to Diego talking to someone anyway. He's probably catching up with them, "Hey, what's your cousin doing? What about this?" He's waving to people as we're driving by, and we stop in the middle of traffic so he can talk to people.

He could be making drug deals; it's impossible to know. It's common when you go to any of the islands. I've been offered drugs before. Part of it's my appearance. That doesn't help. Many people from the States go down to the islands looking to do those kinds of things, except most of them don't have jobs like me and Jeff do where we get drug tested all the time.

That's the thing. To do what we do, we're required to take drug tests on demand. They do drug testing frequently. They take drugs and drug testing very seriously. They also do random breathalyzers for alcohol.

I don't do drugs. It's not my thing. I don't enjoy them. At a younger age, I tried a couple and they didn't work out for me. I've seen what happens with certain drugs and I've never gone near them. My friends that got heavily involved were never able to turn back.

What I really like is the feeling I get from alcohol. That's my thing. It's comfortable for me and it fits me. I drink beer. When I was younger, I used to drink a lot of hard alcohol but that became dangerous. I became angry and aggressive and liked to fight, especially with tequila. As you get older, you learn that the hard way.

I weaned myself off the hard alcohol until I was down to beer. The downside of beer for me is that to get to where I want to get, I have to drink like 20 of them and by the time I get done with that, I have to pee the whole time. It's a whole lot of work if you want to get a really nice buzz off of beer.

Diego comes back and says, "What do you guys want to do now? What are your plans for the night? Do you want to go out?"

"Yeah, I think I want to go out," Jeff says.

We need to get gas on our way back to the hotel. In the DR, they use liquid gasoline and natural gasoline. They run their cars off a cylinder of gas. Diego pulls up to a Shell station and we get out of the car.

There's a guy sitting in a lawn chair at each gas pump with a pump shotgun in his lap.

"What's that about?" Jeff says.

"Dude, to keep people from stealing the gas."

This is when we begin to understand how much the people are on their own in this country. If they have something valuable, maybe the police will care if something happens or maybe they won't. We begin to understand that there's a level of desperation in Dominicans.

"Do you guys want to give me payment for the day so far?" Diego says.

Jeff says, "Yeah. Well, we didn't do a full day. You didn't pick us up from the airport."

"Yeah, that's totally reasonable. We can negotiate that down. That's fine,"

"I don't know. What? Sixty, seventy bucks? Does that sound fair?"

Diego says, "That's fine, man. That's reasonable, seventy bucks. You didn't use me all day."

So, Jeff gives Diego the seventy bucks and he gets gas.

We tell Diego we want to go back to the hotel, take a shower and change clothes. The problem is that even though it's almost 8:30, it's still rush hour and we have to go back through the downtown area to get to the hotel.

"We're better off hanging out over here somewhere for another hour. We can go down to the ocean strip. That's where all the tourist stuff is. Whatever you do, don't go buying anything in any of those shops. It's like ten times over priced. They rape the tourists on everything over here."

So Diego takes us to a little sports bar with baseball on every TV. The men in the bar are betting on anything concerning the game: is this guy going to strike out, how many hits that one will get and things like that. Most of the guys in the bar are nicely dressed.

I'm chatting as well as I can with the pretty girls working there. The girl behind the bar speaks a little English. She wants to go to school in the States and become a dentist.

We go outside so Jeff can smoke a cigarette. We look over and there's another guy sitting in front of the bar/restaurant with a pistol grip pump shot gun. It seems odd. This restaurant is very nice. It has a courtyard in front with a water fountain; it's in a nice part of town. These shotguns aren't very accurate and they're hard to handle. If someone used it, it would make a lot of noise and spray some buckshot, but they wouldn't necessarily kill someone.

We talk the man into letting us take pictures on Jeff's Blackberry while we hold the shotgun. In one of them, I put the guy's hat on and sit in his chair. We take a picture of ourselves with our arms around him.

By now, it's around 9:30 and the traffic is clear so Diego takes us back to the hotel.

"What do you guys want to do? Do you want to go out some more?" Diego says.

I say, "I want to take a shower and change my clothes, stuff like that."

Jeff agrees.

I turn to Jeff, "Do you want to go see some more stuff?"

"Yeah, man. I think I do. I don't know yet," Jeff says.

Diego says, "Well, how about this. Why don't you guys change? I'll hang down here in the casino. Come back down, however long it takes and we'll do whatever you want."

When we come back to the lobby we decide we're hungry. I want a steak. We saw a Tony Roma's on the way back to the hotel but Diego says, "Oh, no, no.

You don't want to go there, man. They're going to charge you way too much. We'll go to this other restaurant I know."

When we get there, we find the staff cleaning up so they can close. Diego convinces them to stay open, and then negotiates the price down. The waitress arrives with a huge platter of meat for about five, six bucks. When we finish, I leave a one hundred peso tip. The girl is blown away.

Diego says, "No, man. Don't tip that much. I usually give about two pesos. She's going to get the wrong idea if you know what I mean."

"But she looks like she's twelve," I say.

Diego says, "She probably is."

I say, "OK. That's not good."

There are 32 pesos to a dollar so one hundred pesos are about three dollars. That's a lot of money in the DR.

The girls that work in the restaurant want to know what we're going to do for the rest of the night. Diego takes us, minus the girls, to a club he knows, but the music is pounding and we don't stay.

When we come back to the hotel after eating dinner, there's a line of people going around the building waiting to get into the club. That's what they do there. That's how they party.

We hang out in the bar. Three pretty girls approach us.

Jeff says, "Yeah, let's hang out with these girls. They know English. We'll have someone to talk to." Their English is very limited, though. This is the beginning of me trying to be Jeff's translator and it annoys the hell out of me.

Jeff says, "Corey, Corey, ask her if she's ever been to Florida and if she has, if she knows where such and such is."

I'm talking to one girl; he's over they're talking to this other girl. I'm saying it to her the best I can.

He's like, "What did she say?"

"She doesn't even know where Florida is, Jeff."

I have to work to keep up. This is the beginning of this translating thing. At this point, I don't know how miserable this is going to get. Diego's helping me out a lot because I don't understand most of what the girls are saying.

I tell Diego, "Help Jeff out."

Diego runs up a bar tab really quick when he's partying on someone else's money, not his. He keeps bringing more and more drinks back to the table.

Finally, I ask, "Who's paying for this?"

"I told him to put it on your tab."

"Oh no, no, no."

"Sorry, my fault."

I say, "Bring me the tab. Let me close it out. Nothing gets billed to my room."

I make sure the bartender knows that it's been paid. Then I give Diego another thousand pesos and say, "Here, this is yours. When it runs out, you guys are done. When the money's gone, there's no more."

At 11:00 the nightclub gets underway and the music quickly escalates to a deafening level. I'm having a blast flirting with the girls and dancing around. They're trying to teach me the Merengue.

Jeff wants to go to bed. He goes up to our rooms–which are directly over the nightclub–and comes back down telling me how loud it is. We all go upstairs. Although it isn't as loud as it is in the bar where we can feel the beat through the floor, it's still loud enough to keep us awake until 6:00 a.m. when it closes.

We party throughout the night, drinking and talking. The girls have a limited English vocabulary but with Diego's help, we enjoy ourselves.

We are pretty far gone when we come up with a plan for Thursday when we're supposed to pick up Victor and Lucas at the airport. Me and Jeff have this idea. We'll get one of those taxi vans we see driving around. We're going to have a bunch of girls in it.

I say to Jeff, "Yeah, dude, I want to get a big old fat cigar and big sunglasses."

We see these guys dressed up to go to the nightclub. I want to get a sports jacket like they wear with flames on the arms and a scorpion on the back in sequins, and glitter and stuff like that. I'll wear that with my board shorts and flip-flops, and I'll have that cigar. We're going to pick up our buddies at the airport like that and have all these girls with us.

I'll throw open my arms and say, "*Hola*! Welcome to the Dominican Republic!"

Jeff says, "I want to get a giant sombrero. I'll wear that. I want to get a six-shooter and the gun belt with the straps crossed over my chest and have it full of shots and I'll step out like that with a cap gun. Bang! Bang! Bang!"

It was going to be so funny.

Wednesday, June 17

Around 3:00 a.m., we're ready to call it a night. Diego and the girls leave. We aren't tired so we go down to the restaurant to get some breakfast. I'm not really drunk, but I haven't had any sleep, so I'm just hanging in there. We sit down at a table. There's no one there except an older white guy named Ned, in his fifties, who happens to be the manager. We have a little breakfast and talk with him.

Ned is American. He managed casinos in New Jersey for years. He wanted to come down to the DR, so now he's the manager of *La Perla Hotel and Casino*. We talk about the economy, and what it's doing to tourism right now and that gambling is on the down turn.

Ned says, "The thing that's been most successful is the nightclub we opened up."

"Yeah, that's kind of loud," I say.

"For the people that come here, the louder the music, the better. They'll make themselves deaf. That's what they love. We make tons of money. We charge them a ridiculous cover to get into the club. Which rooms are you in?" We tell him.

He says, "Oh, you guys are right next to me. Here, I'll give you a tour."

He takes us on a little tour of the hotel and casino. Along the way, he stops at the front desk and lets the girl know that we're with him, "Make sure these guys are taken care of."

Ned is talking about everything. It might have been awhile since he had an American to talk to, and then there's me and Jeff and what we do for a living.

Ned says, "Why don't you guys come back to the club tonight and I'll buy you a couple of drinks or something?"

"Sure, no problem, sounds great."

We continue to hang out and eventually Ned says,

"All right, whenever you're ready, come to the front desk. I'll send some security. We'll bring you guys in the back way to the nightclub. We'll put you in the VIP section where they have a door to keep the sound down. You don't have to wait in line or anything like that. I'll take care of you. All the drinks and everything you want are on me. What are you guys doing later on today?"

"We don't know."

"Do you guys have dinner plans?" Ned says.

I say, "No, not really. We're waiting for the rest of our buddies. But, we're going to *Puerta Plata* tomorrow."

Ned says, "Well, how about this. When you guys get back, do you want to eat here with me?"

"Sure, why not."

"OK. Whenever you guys come back, let the front desk know. They'll contact me. Is steak good with you guys?"

"Sure."

He says, "All right. How about 7:00, 8:00 or so? Does that work?"

Ned is making all these arrangements and Jeff says, "This is awesome, man."

By now it's about 8:00 a.m. and we decide to take a walk instead of trying to sleep. When Jeff spoke with Diego the night before, he said he had some things to do in the morning but would call when he was free. Jeff needs contact solution so we walk up the street to a drug store. It wasn't open yet so we stand around watching the cars and people go by.

La Perla is in the middle of the city; it's all hustle and bustle. We're the only white people we see. Jeff is a little hesitant because he doesn't speak any Spanish.

I'm comfortable with the following "conversation." It's short, but it doesn't lead me into a more difficult dialog, so it's perfect, and polite, for where my Spanish skills are at this point.

"*Hola! Cómo está usted?*" (Hi, how are you?) I start.

"*Bien, y usted?*" (Good, and you?) Hopefully the person replies something close to that or I won't know what he says.

"*Bueno, bueno*" (Good, good) I say, and at that point, my Spanish runs out and the discussion is over.

As we're walking down the street, we see a giant sign on a building:

Learn English in Three Months–Guaranteed!

There's a line in the parking lot to get into the class. Knowing English is very important. Someone who is bilingual can work in the resorts, some of the very few jobs on the island. They can also work in the Free Zone, an area of the Dominican Republic that the government leases to outside corporations for free, or very cheaply. On top of that, they get tax credits and other incentives to move there. When big corporations relocate their operations from the US to a foreign country, this is the common set-up.

We wait for the pharmacy to open, Jeff gets his contact solution and we walk back to the hotel. Eventually, Diego shows up and he has a girl in the front

24

seat of the car. She's in her early twenties, black, attractive and very quiet. He says she saw us the day before when we were walking around his neighborhood. She lives near him and wants to hang out with the Americanos. She doesn't know any English.

He goes into detail about what he has already done with her and then offers her to us. We decline. Diego is a disgusting human being, and now he's a pimp, too. He talks non-stop with a New York accent and it's getting on my nerves big time. He eats like a pig and talks with his mouth full. We decide this is the last time we'll see him. Instead of more sight-seeing with Diego tomorrow, we'll leave early for the resort and hang out there until it's time to pick up Victor and Lucas.

Jeff has a list of what he wants to see and do. I'm fine with it; I'm along for the ride. I'm not much of a planner. I don't like to make things happen. We get in the Volvo and Jeff tells Diego we want to see Christopher Columbus' tomb that Columbus' brother started building in 1521, and the First Church of the Americas, the first church built in the Caribbean.

We drive along until we come to this monstrous, concrete building that looks like a power plant. Diego stops the car and we go in. It's the tomb of Christopher Columbus and a museum. The building is in the shape of a giant cross almost seven football fields long and a football field wide. It's three or four stories tall and all made of concrete. Supposedly, when it's lit up, it can be seen from outer space. They don't run the lights anymore because they don't have enough electricity to keep it going.

Diego finds a tour guide who can speak English and arranges a private tour for us. The guide does a good job and we get a better understanding of the island and its history. Pope John Paul II visited the DR in January 1979. There are little Pope mobiles parked in front of the monument.

We visit *Parque Colon*, Columbus Park. It has a skateboard park made of concrete with ramps and sloped walls. Apparently skateboarding is very big in the DR, too.

We finish there and Diego takes us to see where he grew up. It's a nice neighborhood. He knocks on the front door of the house he lived in and a lady opens it, obviously cautious. We stand by the car. Diego speaks with her for a few minutes and then comes back.

Close to the house is a large building. "What's that giant building over there?" I say.

Diego says, "That is *La Casa de Justicia*, the Justice Palace. My friends, we do not want to go anywhere near that place. We want to stay as far away as possible. That is what I am here to do, to keep you away from there."

Even so, we will be there, awaiting trial, within 48 hours.

If I was back in the States, I wouldn't hang out with someone like Diego. Absolutely not. He's shady; he's a hustler. He has ulterior motives all the time. Throughout the day, he's always asking for more money like,

"Hey, man. Can I get forty of those bucks now? One hundred for the day? I need to get gas in the car."

There are several incidents where he says, "Well, gas isn't included as far as the trip goes. All expenses paid except for that."

It's always something like that. Me and Jeff plan on ditching Diego later that day but we don't say it out loud in front of him. We head over to the First Church of the Americas. Across the courtyard is a Hard Rock Café. It's a touristy spot with all kinds of different stores selling tourist crap.

Jeff says, "I'm hungry. Let's get something to eat."

We have lunch at the Hard Rock Café. We can use our credit cards there. At most places we can't; it's cash only. We split the tab on our credit cards. After lunch, we go across the street to the *Catedral Primada de America*, the First Church of the Americas. There are cardinals and bishops, people who are significant in the Catholic Church, buried there, too.

It's around 4:00 or 5:00 p.m. and I've had enough of Diego. I say, "Let's go back to the hotel."

"Yeah, well traffic is going to be very bad again. We can hang out here or go someplace else," Diego says.

Jeff says, "Let's hang out here," and we walk around and look at the shops. I'm looking for a jacket with sequins to wear when we pick up our buddies but I don't find anything.

Diego decides it's time to leave. We get in the car and, of course, along the way Diego's stopping the car, bumping into people left and right, talking to God knows who. He knows everyone. He's a talker, like Joe Pesci. Non-stop. Talk, talk, talk, talk.

We're supposed to be heading back to the hotel but the girl needs to get home to her baby. Diego says, "Let me drop her off first before I take you guys back. It's on the way."

This doesn't sound right; she lives near Diego. But I'm not sure where his neighborhood is in relation to where we are. Besides, do we even have a choice in the matter? He's driving.

I say, "OK. Well, sure. Whatever."

Diego drives us through various neighborhoods. He stops and says "hi" to some people. We keep on driving.

I'm still taking everything in. It has only been 24 hours since we landed in the DR and so much has happened. Along the way, we call our buddies who are coming over to meet us. Jeff talks to his wife. She and the kids are back in Florida, visiting family. We're looking at stuff, talking about it.

At one point Diego says, "I gotta make a stop."

He stops in this place that looks like the worst thing I've ever seen in my life. It looks like it's somewhere in Africa that got bombed. It's ghetto. The whole 'hood. I can travel anywhere in the world, I think, and I always know when I'm in a bad neighborhood. I get the gut feeling of all gut feelings. I've seen this before. This isn't a good place to be.

Diego says, "Yeah, I gotta run an errand. I'll be right back." He gets out of the car and goes into a house. I'm looking around.

As soon as we get to that neighborhood, I'm thinking, "God damn it, Corey. Damn it. Fuck you, Corey. You stupid mother fucker."

I say this to myself because I know better. I've had this feeling before. Something isn't right. I know it. I also know we're in too deep now. There's no way out except wait for Diego to come back. I can't get out of the car and walk down the street; I'm dead.

We allowed Diego to put us in a very, very compromising spot. I hated it. I knew it. I hated it. I've felt this way before in my life and I don't get that feeling unless I know something isn't right. I know I need to get us the hell out somehow. Diego took the keys.

Babies in diapers are wandering down the street; there are giant holes in the road, broken down cars everywhere. It's probably a project. There are two- and three–story concrete buildings, apartments, and people wandering around doing nothing. It looks total ghetto. It feels like that. People are staring at the vehicle, staring at us. It's a nice car, much nicer than anything they've ever had. Men are staring at the girl and I can tell she's not happy about being there. She's crying quietly. These guys are hardcore. They're big, mean and aggressive and they're just looking for an excuse to start–and finish–a fight.

There's nothing friendly about it. We don't belong here. I know that. Time goes on and Diego doesn't come out of the house. Some of the guys on the street start moving, never taking their eyes off the car and the girl. It looks like they're ready to start walking over to the car. I have a really bad feeling.

I start looking around taking things in and looking at our options. I go through different scenarios–if those guys do this, I'm going to do that–stuff like that. I don't have anything on me to protect the girl other than my fists and I don't want to get into a fight if I don't have to. Jeff is very quiet.

Just when I'm about to get out of the car, go into the house and drag Diego out of there, he comes out and gets into the car.

As he's driving away, I say, "Dude, that was not cool."

Jeff says, "Yeah, man."

I tell him, "Dude, you never fucking take us there again."

He says, "Oh, no, no."

I'm thinking, "We need to get to our hotel. We're going to pay this guy and drop him. We're done. We're never going to be around this guy again." It's all in my head. I'm not saying it out loud or anything like that. I know this is bad.

Diego drives about 20 minutes until we come to an enormous bridge with a slope to it so it's higher in the middle. It's rush hour and traffic is stop-and-go, mostly stop. The bridge is wide with four lanes of traffic going in each direction. It looks like it's a major artery Dominicans use to get from one part of the city to another. There's a concrete median in the middle of the bridge to divide the traffic. It's long and spans a deep ravine. The bridge takes us from the bad neighborhood–where we never should have been in the first place–back to safety.

We're asking questions about what's underneath the bridge. We're in the far right lane and I lean across Jeff to look at what's down there. The cars are moving so slowly that I get a long look and say, "God, that looks like shit down there."

There are tiers cut out of the sides of the ravine. A rough, pothole-filled dirt path switchbacks from the top to the bottom. Here and there along the tiers are one-room concrete boxes that are posing as homes. Some of them were once painted in bright colors but now the colors are faded and much of the exterior is chipped off.

People are also living in one-room shacks made out of anything they can find. A lot of them lean one way or the other. Walls are constructed out of old wooden pallets, cardboard boxes and discarded pieces of wood. The roofs are made out of corrugated tin or cardboard; some of the structures don't have any roof at all. Given the DR's rainy season, which lasts six months, cardboard is not exactly the best thing to use for a roof, but these people do the best they can. Old, discarded, couches and armchairs are scattered around along with rusty, broken down, cars.

Not all of the pieced-together shacks have doors. Instead, a ragged piece of cloth hangs where a door should be. Not only does that fail to provide safety-if there's any safety to be had-it doesn't keep out water, bugs or anything else in the area.

These "houses" have no running water and no plumbing. The people gather water from a communal well or the small stream that flows down the mountain. People and animals use the outdoors for bathrooms; outhouses with pits are rare. Without a planned septic system-however crude-garbage and human filth and waste wash down the ravine when the rains start. This makes life even more miserable, and unsafe, for those living at the bottom. I try not to imagine the flooding there and what those people live in. Disease must be rampant but there's very little medical care and no way to get to a doctor even if they needed to.

Women in ragged dresses and men in shorts and torn t-shirts sit in front of their huts or stand around with nothing to do but wait. But wait for what? There are no jobs and no money to buy even the most basic things. Babies wearing nothing but dirty diapers squat in the dirt and scribble with a stick or try to stack small rocks they have found. Children play the universal games children play anywhere: Tag, Hide 'n Seek and clapping games said to rhymes. Hacky Sack is popular but they are most often made from a plastic bag filled with rocks. There are few teenagers; most have gone into the city to try to make a better life.

There's absolutely no reason for tourists to be here. Even Dominicans are afraid to go down there. Guys that we meet later in prison talk about being afraid of the neighborhoods in that area. The cops are afraid to go down there. In the lower tiers, people have put up barricades to keep the cops out. It's not unusual to have Molotov cocktails thrown at the police.

Diego says, "The worst neighborhood is down there. You do not want to be there. You do not want to go there. The worst place in all of the DR is down there underneath this bridge. Whatever you do, do not ever go down to that neighborhood." Even so, it seems like the neighborhood we just left was located somewhere under the bridge.

The traffic on the bridge is horrendous with more stopping than going in each direction. We finally get past the mid point and start down the other side. We're approaching a huge traffic circle at the end of the bridge, but before we can get off the bridge to safety, all hell breaks loose.

Two guys on a moped cut through traffic and stop in front of the car. Traffic is already crawling along and now Diego can't move. People start honking their horns but there isn't anything he can do about it. The men jump off the moped. They look like ordinary men wearing regular clothes. They pull out guns. "Moped Guy Number One" moves toward the driver's door while "Moped Guy Number Two" stands in front of the car with his gun pointing at all of us inside.

Diego begins to curse. The girl becomes hysterical and is crying and screaming. Jeff is ghost white.

I size up the situation quickly and decide it's probably a carjacking. We just have to give these guys some money and we'll be on our way. I need to walk away from this with my life, Jeff's life and, to a certain extent, the girl's, number one, and with as many possessions as possible, number two.

I'm trying to take in as much of the situation as possible because, God forbid, if we're left here, I have to figure out a way out of this location. If they take everything, if we have no money, we have nothing. How are we going to get back to our hotel? How am I going to figure my way out of this shit? Now I begin to create different plans in my head.

I begin to split up and redistribute my cash into the many pockets of my baggy board shorts. That way, when it's time to pay out, I can give them some of it, not all of it.

Moped Guy Number One yells something in Spanish and pulls Diego out of the car. He's being fairly aggressive. He puts handcuffs on Diego. This doesn't make sense to me. Why would a carjacker have handcuffs? Then he motions to the rest of us to get out of the car, which we do.

Moped Guy Number Two doesn't move, but I can tell by his facial expression and body language that he doesn't want to be a part of it when he realizes there are Americans involved.

It appears that Diego and Moped Guy Number One know each other and not in a good way. There's bad blood there. He gets pretty physical with Diego and Diego's in his face, screaming. I have no idea what they're saying, but it looks like Diego could get shot if he doesn't shut his mouth.

Finally, Moped Guy Number One takes the cuffs off Diego and shoves him back in the car and everyone else gets back in.

"Corey, you got any money?" Diego says.

"Yeah, I got money."

"We're going to have to pay these assholes. These fuckers want money."

As Diego and I prepare to pay them off, this simple carjacking turns into a nightmare. Things are in place for everything to go completely wrong. It's a perfect storm.

Over the next few weeks, Jeff and I hear over and over again, "How did that happen? That's impossible. You shouldn't have been arrested... gone to court... been sentenced... ended up in prison... There's no way. How is that even possible?"

But the impossible keeps happening and we have no control over the situation. We don't speak Spanish so we don't really know what's going on. All we know is what Diego tells us.

I'm so mad at myself. How could I get close to someone like that? How could someone like that get close to me? Today, especially in our culture, we want to blame someone for the things that happen. At the end of all of this, it comes back to me in the mirror.

While all of this is happening, I notice uniformed police officers, in two marked police cars, on the other side of the bridge watching us. They see Diego, the girl, Jeff and me standing outside of the car and the actions of Moped Guy Number One. They see what appears to be Americans with Moped Guy Number Two holding a gun on them. Something isn't right, so they park their cars right where they are, in the middle of traffic, get out and start making their way across eight lanes, including the median dividing the bridge.

When they get there, they recognize Diego's vehicle. These are the same police that Diego introduced us to the day before in his neighborhood, the police Diego pays taxes to for protection from situations like this.

When the moped guys see the cops coming toward them, they reach in their back pockets and pull out baseball caps with the word "*Policia*" across the front. They put their guns back in their holsters. Since Diego obviously knew the guy that pulled him out of the car, he must have known they were cops, but until then, we had no idea.

It appears to me that these two rogue drug cops—which is what I figure they are according to what happens later—planned to pull a tax job on Diego not knowing he has tourists in the car. Once they realize this, they've gone too far, and now that the uniformed police are involved, these guys are in some deep shit. They have a couple of problems:

They are on the wrong side of the bridge. This is not their jurisdiction; they are pulling this tax job in someone else's district. And, they are robbing tourists. This is a serious problem. The DR government and police department are very clear about carjacking; they are even clearer about carjacking Americans. Tourism is their major source of revenue and this kind of activity gives the country a bad reputation. It's bad for the economy.

There are hundreds of cars on the bridge and a lot of them have more than one person in them. This is what's so amazing. It shows how fearless the cops are. They don't have a problem committing a crime in broad daylight where hundreds of people can watch it happen.

Later on, when we go to court, the cops fabricate the case saying they have us on videotape, and they have witnesses saying they saw us purchase narcotics in a known drug house. They say all of that even though all of those people on the bridge–and the uniformed cops–see the whole arrest. They say they arrested us back in that bad neighborhood underneath the bridge.

But you know what? No one ever produces a videotape, a recording, a photograph, a witness, or a testimony–nothing. There's no evidence because their whole case is made up.

The rest of the conversation is in Spanish, of course, but by watching body language, paying close attention to how things proceed, and from conversations I have with Diego later, here's what happened:

Diego claims he had a run in with Drug Cop Number One about paying a tax to him. Knowing Diego, when they had the previous run in, he not only said, "No," he probably let that guy know what he thought about him. I'm almost confident that that initial conflict did happen because of the way that guy went after Diego. The verbal exchange and the physical contact that was going on between those two was intense compared to the situation being what it was.

I thought it was going to go from an armed robbery to a violent robbery. Diego is spitting and cursing. He's yelling in this guy's face, back and forth, and having it out. Diego's escalating the situation. It's like gasoline being thrown on this thing. Diego's reaction is way over the top for the situation. It's not an appropriate response.

Four uniformed cops walk up to the car. They have a verbal exchange with the drug cops and whatever the drug cops are saying doesn't seem to be making much of an impression on the other cops. Here are these two so-called cops in street clothes who never identify themselves, or show a badge or anything. I'm guessing they might be undercover narcotics officers but that's my guess. One of the uniformed cops orders everyone out of the car.

While the cops are talking, Drug/Moped Cop Number One leans into the car, comes back out and says, "I found drugs in the car." He never shows anyone the drugs he says he found. We find out later that the drug cop says he found them on the floorboard of the car behind the driver's side. That would have been right in front of my feet and there was nothing there.

Initially, four cops head over to us but it doesn't take long before there are more police cars and a dozen officers surrounding Diego's car. Everyone is standing around, dumbfounded. Nothing makes sense.

Because I don't speak Spanish, I have to rely on what Diego tells me people are saying and what is happening. I don't trust Diego. I think Diego is telling me what he thinks I want to hear. I have to remind Jeff constantly that we can't rely on what Diego says. The only thing we know for sure is what we actually see.

The uniformed officers are asking the drug cops what they're going to do. If they found drugs, they need to arrest someone. However, these drug cops are not in their district, they are in the uniformed cops' district. Eventually the uniformed cops agree to bring everyone in for questioning.

The uniformed cops separate us from Diego and the girl. They put us in the back seat of a four-door pickup truck that has "Policia" on the side. We're sitting against the doors with a cop between us. Apparently, no one has ever opened the door and jumped out. There are two cops in front.

To get off the bridge, we go around the traffic circle, through traffic, back underneath the bridge and eventually pop out in the neighborhood where Diego's father-in-law lives. His neighborhood is not under the bridge so there was no reason to take us and the girl there. We end up in the substation where we were the day before.

Everyone gets out of the truck and walks into the building. They separate us. They're asking me questions and even though I understand a few of them like, "What is your name?" I don't answer. I don't speak much Spanish and I'm not going to help these guys out. Jeff knows even less Spanish so the cops don't get any useful information out of either one of us.

Two cops go through my wallet, pat me down, find some cash, take some for themselves, and hand the rest back. I put it into one of the pockets in my shorts. The next cop comes along, pats me down, takes some money and the rest goes back in a pocket. None of them are seriously searching me. They're taxing me, but they're losing track of what they're doing, and I'm able to hold on to my phone.

Jeff has his wallet and phone, too, and is getting taxed like I am. They give us back our wallets, minus the tax money. Now that the cops have their money, I'm hoping they will let us go.

They put us in a holding area outside in the yard. It's a 40' x 40' concrete box with a roof. It's pitch black with no windows and a little open gate that anyone can walk up to. When our eyes adjust, we see two younger guys in there with us.

Very few people know that we're in the Dominican Republic. I didn't tell my parents I was going to the DR. I'm 33 years old and I didn't think it was necessary to keep them informed about my vacation plans. Now I need to let my friends know what's going on.

I take out my phone and type in a text message: "Hey man. We're in jail." and send it to Lucas, Connor and Mike. These are the only guys who know we're in the DR. I've been texting them all day.

One of the guys with us in the box sees the phone and asks if he can use it. I hand him the phone. He makes a call. We hear someone coming so he turns it off and hands it back to me. It turns out to be a woman, not a guard, and she starts talking with one of the guys.

I use my best Spanglish/Spanish and ask one of them what's going on. The guy says,

"They hold you here until you pay up. You have to come up with enough money–500 pesos, 1,000 pesos–then they let you go. If you have 1,000 pesos, you guys can leave."

I can manage the payout but I'm doubtful. Nothing has been that easy all day. For now, we're hanging around, waiting. I haven't received a response from my last text but people are busy, doing whatever they're doing in the course of the day. If they got the text message, who knows if or when they're going to read it?

Finally, I get a text back from Lucas.

Lucas writes, "You're joking, right?"

I open my phone and it glows in the dark room. I'm trying to respond as a guard walks up to the gate.

The guard motions to us to come out and sees the phone in my hand. He reaches for it. I stretch my left arm out and away from the guard as far as I can and manage to type N–O. The guard grabs my arm and starts pulling it towards him. As he takes the phone out of my hand, I hit "send."

Now there are people on the outside who know our situation.

A guard brings us out of the holding area, and around the corner, where we see Diego in the bed of a small police pickup truck with three or four other guys. Everyone is handcuffed together and crammed in. The girl is sitting in a car parked next to the truck.

By now the word is out. The whole neighborhood is standing around the police station asking Diego what's going on and he's telling them what happened.

The guards handcuff me and Jeff together and put us in the back of the pickup facing the tailgate. It's already packed with too many people and with Jeff at 6' 2", and my huge shoulders, it's unbearable.

This is a different truck than the one that brought us to the substation, and these are different police officers. They're wearing drug enforcement uniforms complete with bulletproof vests. I shake my head. Things are way out of hand. Diego tells us they're transporting us to another jail. I give up my last hope and accept that I'm not going back to the hotel tonight.

It looks like the officers who brought us to the substation are telling the drug enforcement officers that they don't want to deal with this. The drug enforcement officers started this mess and they're going to have to finish it. I'm wondering why Diego pays them for protection when they won't do anything to protect him.

Before we leave, two more cops climb onto the bed of the truck. They sit on the two corners of the tailgate holding the infamous pistol grip pump shotguns and stare directly at us. This is fun time. This is the most fun they'll ever have in their lives. This is the day they get to drive around while holding guns on two Americanos. Plus, they have Diego who has been screwing them out of money for years.

We're going for a ride around town so the cops can show people what they've caught. Everyone in the truck, but more specifically me and Jeff, are on display. For the next hour and a half, they ride around town in rush hour traffic. It's hot and humid. The smell of exhaust from hundreds of cars, buses, mopeds and whatever else people are driving is overpowering. It's enough to make our heads ache and turn our stomachs queasy. It's loud. Most vehicles don't have mufflers. There are horns honking, people shouting and the ever–present sound of music blaring from boom boxes.

We're packed into this pickup with no opportunity to shift position. Being handcuffed together means that when one person uses that hand, the other person's hand has to come along. There's no chance to use the restroom but, then again, there's no water available, either. We're stiff and sore. There's no way to stretch our legs or move even a little to get more comfortable.

I'm concerned, but Jeff is terrified. He's never been arrested, never gone to court, and certainly has never been treated the way he has since the moped cops pulled in front of Diego's car on the bridge and drew their guns on us.

And it's only going to get worse from here.

We're sitting there, and this cop is pointing a gun in my face, and laughing and pointing it at my groin area, like that. These guns are unsafe, unpredictable. The smallest wrong move can make them fire. They have their finger on the trigger. We're hitting bumps in the road. The gun's banging against the side of the truck. They're very loose with it. I don't know if there's a round in there or not, but they're having a blast.

This is what they've been waiting for their entire lives. They're looking at me. At this point, my switch goes off. I have the Stare of Death going on. My shaggy hair is in my face. Whoever looks at me, I look right back at them. I'm seeing right through his eyes to his soul.

One cop is trying to be funny and be my friend. The other guy is trying to be a tough guy. Neither one of them are making any progress. Eventually, the whole show comes to an end. They don't want to put on their show like they did when they got us because they realize whatever effect they were going for wasn't going to happen. I checked out.

Jeff's sitting there staring at the bed of the truck and I look right through whoever's in front of me like they're not even there. They're playing around with the gun, they get their camera phones, take pictures of us, they have their arm around us with the gun, and they take pictures, and they're calling up their buddies. We go on a parade around town until it gets completely dark which means it's after 9:00.

It's hot. We're sucking in the exhaust from the road. We're driving around town in traffic, families and kids are sitting in cars looking at us, and buses pull up. They have a bunch of guys handcuffed together, other guys with shotguns and the people who see us are like, "What the hell? Did I see some Americans?"

Everything's running through my head. I'm thinking about grabbing that gun, tackling the guy right off the back of the pickup into the street and start squeezing rounds off until they shoot me dead because I ain't going to go out like this. There are a lot of ways I plan on dying and leaving this world, but it's not going to be like this.

Diego is still talking nonstop. He's talking to the other prisoners, talking to us, talking to the cops. He's telling us what other people are saying and what he's saying. He never stops making noise.

He says, "Hey, man. Why don't you stop and get me something to drink? Hey, I need a cigarette back here. What the hell you got me arrested for anyways?" He's a classic criminal who never stops talking. I've seen these guys before. The other guys that are arrested start feeling bad for us.

They say stuff like, "Why are you messing with the fucking Americans for? What the hell?"

One of the cops says, "You shut up. You ain't shit."

By now, it's very late and pitch black. Jeff and I haven't slept in more than 36 hours. We're hot, sweaty and thirsty. We're hungry, too, but still avoiding food knowing that after that first meal we'll be sick.

The truck pulls to a stop outside a fenced area with a park and playground. There's a guy in the park with a megaphone yelling at us. I recognize the words, "Jesus Cristo" and assume the guy is telling us to repent of our sins before we go inside the fence to whatever we will face there. The truck pulls through the gate and into the parking lot of what looks like an office complex.

There's a large building in front of us that doesn't look like a jail. There are regular cars parked here and people are walking around. They're hanging out in front of what looks like apartments. It's really late but it's still so hot; I'm guessing they can't sleep.

They take all of us out of the truck. The girl is in the backseat of a police car. The guards leave me and Jeff handcuffed together and they put Diego and the girl together. They would never handcuff a man and a woman together in the States.

The cops take us to a small, clean, well-maintained waiting area. The waiting room is air-conditioned and someone is nice enough to bring each of us a small bottle of water. It's the first thing we've had to drink since lunch at the Hard Rock Café twelve hours earlier. Although not enough, the water is a welcomed relief after hours of riding around in the sun. We move around as much as we can to stretch our legs and back without drawing the attention of the guards.

Someone asks each person his name and where he's from. Diego kicks into his translator role and answers the questions for us.

37

It gets a little tricky when they come to, "Where do you live?"

Of course, no one's ever heard of this country in the Caribbean where we live. I'm beginning to doubt that they've even heard the word "Caribbean." Even so, I decide to stay with it instead of giving the man an address in the States, since it's the truth. If anyone ever tried to verify our information, our place of residence would come back as that country in the Caribbean.

The guy asking the questions says, "Americans? What the hell are you guys doing here?" in Spanish. We have no answer since we still don't know why we have been detained.

When everyone in the truck is checked in, two of the cops walk the group across the parking lot to another building. Along the way, Diego is saying,

"Hey, man. Let these guys go. They have nothing to do with any of this that's going on. They don't belong here."

One of the cops says, "We should let them go. We shouldn't take them in, let's let them go."

The debate goes back and forth until the other one says, "I don't know, man. We'll go ahead and take them inside, see what the police chief says." This is as close as we come to getting away from this nightmare but we miss the opportunity. We would need money to pay them off and the guards took everything earlier.

Everyone goes to a holding area inside this white building. All of the men that rode around in the back of the pickup are still cuffed together in pairs and standing in the hallway. We wait and wait.

There's a lot of waiting and wondering what's going on and it's getting to me. I have a serious case of ADHD–Attention Deficit Hyperactivity Disorder–that I manage fairly well with exercise, music and beer. Except for Caribbean music, which I hate, I have not been able to access my coping mechanisms for almost two days. I force myself to focus on what is going on around me.

Finally, a guy peaks his head out, comes out and he's holding my phone in his hand.

He asks in Spanish, "Is this your phone?"

I say, in English, "Yes, that's my phone." Diego translates.

He nods his head and goes back inside.

Supposedly, the police chief gets out of bed and comes in to deal with this. The two guys in the back of the pickup truck with the shotguns are acting like statues on the wall now. They're not tough guys anymore. They're not waving their guns around; they're just standing there. The contrast is so funny.

The head guy shows up, and he barks some orders at the cops and they scatter. He comes out, he looks at us, goes back inside, comes out, talks to us, looks at some papers and he's like, "What to do? What to do?"

It's gone up the ladder. It's blown up really big. Now they're saying, "OK. What do we do? This other district knows that we arrested these people. So, what are we going to do now?" And it's getting bigger, and bigger, and bigger.

So then, this asshole guy comes out that speaks a little bit of English. I'm not sure if he is the police chief or one of the head sergeant dudes. Everyone looks really young. He comes out, talks to us in a little bit of English and asks us if we're from America.

We say, "Yeah," and then tell him what we do for a living.

Now the guy wants to have some fun. So, he's asking us our names and we're telling him. He can't understand us. He's trying to say our names back. It's comical but I don't let myself laugh.

Diego tries again, "Let these guys go. They don't have nothing to do with this. Whatever issue there is, it has nothing to do with these guys, let them go." He's trying to convince the cops.

The guy says, "Don't worry. We'll deport them back to the States."

Jeff says, "Oh, that's great." He's getting a little excited.

I don't see that happening. No one gets deported, especially out of this crap hole country.

We stand around for what feels like hours. Finally, a few guards take everyone down the hall to an area that appears to be a narcotics central booking station or holding area. The people we walk past look like they can't believe their eyes, "Are those Americans?"

The guards put the other guys in cells, two to a cell. One of the guards says, "We're going to put you guys in a holding cell until you get transferred to court tomorrow." Then they take my belt, shoelaces and socks. They let me keep my shoes.

The three of us are getting preferential treatment. Instead of being put in a cell immediately, we hang out with the guards and watch baseball on a little TV.

Diego says to one of the police officers, "Can you get us some chicken and some drinks? We're thirsty."

He says, "Sure. No problem."

This is when I begin to realize that we can get anything we want as long as we have enough money. Even though the guards took all of our money, Diego still has some that he stashed. Diego gives the guy some money, and he brings back chicken, French fries and drinks for us.

We don't eat any of it. We're trying to hold off as long as we can, knowing we will get dysentery once we do. Staying hydrated is critical so we drink the bottled water.

After hours of waiting, a guard takes us to a narrow cell, about four feet wide and eight feet long, with a set of bunk beds. It's a cell designed for two but we need Diego to translate so we'll have to make do. By now, it has to be past midnight.

There are no windows so the only light in the cell is what filters through from the hallway. The cell is dirty. Former inhabitants have scratched graffiti and Spanish words on the grey walls. Cobwebs cling to the ceiling. There are dirt and rat droppings on the floor. There's a filthy, thin mat on each bunk.

"Dude," Jeff says, "I wouldn't let my dog sleep on that!"

At the end opposite the bars is a raised cement platform with a hole in the middle and a trough leading to the hole.

Jeff looks at it and says, "Do they really expect me to shit down that hole?"

I don't bother to respond. What can I say? We're facing more serious issues than where Jeff should use the toilet.

Jeff is going to provide some comic relief, but I'm also very concerned. Jeff has never been in jail before, has never even been to court. He has a nice wife and two children. I'm worried that whatever lies ahead will change Jeff from the happy, fun-loving husband and father to... I stop myself there. I try not to think too far into the future.

I realize it will be up to me to help Jeff get through this without it ruining his life. The burden of being in jail in the DR has doubled to include taking care of another person. Jeff wants to believe anyone who tells us that it's all a big mistake and we shouldn't be here. The people around him reassure him that we'll be free very, very soon.

"Americans?" they say. "You don't belong here. Don't worry, you'll be back on the street, *en la calle*, very soon."

I would like to believe that. I know we did nothing wrong and there's no reason for us to be locked up, but I'm street-smart enough to know that just because it shouldn't happen doesn't mean it won't.

Jail is not a new experience for me. I went through a wild, self-destructive, time in my life when spending the night in jail was not unheard of. But I've worked hard to change my life and walk away from the anger and negativity that got me into trouble.

I've lived peacefully for almost two years, and going back to jail is a harsh slap in the face. Now I'm trying to get rid of Corey, the person enjoying his great life and bring back someone that hasn't been around for a long, long time.

I've been so far removed from that self–destructive behavior. I told myself I would never be in that environment again. I'd rather die than go into that environment again. I made the deal. Changed my life. What the hell? I'm not supposed to be here.

The three of us settle in for the night. Jeff takes the top bunk so his feet can hang out over the edge and Diego and I share the bottom bunk. I'm not a large man but I'm larger than Diego. I stay as far away from Diego as I can, but there's not much room. I'm punching him and elbowing him all night because he's kicking me and he's snoring.

We spend the night in there. It isn't the best sleep, but I haven't slept for 36 hours. The overwhelming stench from that open pit is enough to keep me awake. If I hadn't been tired, I wouldn't have been able to sleep in that situation at all.

Thursday, June 18

The sun comes up and there's traffic back and forth out in the hallway. They're not the kind of people I expect to see in a jail. They aren't wearing uniforms or anything like that. I see people dressed in normal casual clothes, men and women of various ages. It appears to be more like an office. People walk back and forth in front of our cell constantly, looking in. Everyone's discussing things in Spanish and I understand very little. Jeff's not able to grasp anything. We're not saying much. No one knows anything. We're waiting in there for hours.

Jeff is saying random stuff and asking questions that there are no answers to. That's the way he is, he says whatever's on his mind. This becomes a problem later on. He's married, so he talks about everything like he's talking to his wife. They talk about everything; that's the way he processes things.

He says things like, "God, I hope they don't plan on making me go to the bathroom on this concrete slab." and "I wonder what kind of food they have in here." He's really odd. He says whatever's on his mind, observing.

I don't respond. My mind is going around and around like a hamster in a wheel. The tension is building inside me and it isn't like I can go run five miles to get some relief. I'm shaking my head trying to ignore him for the most part.

A guard comes to the cell about noon and takes us to a hallway with a bunch of doors. As we walk there, I see a whole row of cells. He ushers us–without Diego–into one of the offices. There are two office desks with a man sitting at each one. Several others have men and women in front of computers doing some kind of data entry.

They ask us questions but, without Diego, we don't understand. I try talking to the officials but they don't understand, either. Finally, they get the U.S. Embassy on the phone. This is the first time we speak to someone in English–other than Diego–since being arrested. The man from the Embassy is named Chandler.

He starts with "Hello" and asks us our names and where we're from. We give him our information with our current addresses in the Caribbean.

"Do you guys know what you're charged with?" Chandler asks.

I say, "No, we don't. We don't know why we were arrested."

"Well, it sounds like something to do with being in a vehicle where there were drugs. Do you guys know anything about this?"

"Not much," I say. "We were in a vehicle, we got arrested, and we don't know anything about any drugs. The driver's name is Diego. He's our tour guide. He was taking us back to our hotel when all this happened. That's what we know. Basically, we don't know much and no one here talks to us in English."

Chandler asks us more questions to get a better idea of the events. Then he says, "This doesn't sound right. It doesn't make sense." We agree with him.

Chandler switches gears and says, "OK. Who do you want us to notify?"

We give him our family's names and how to contact them.

"What would you like them to know about you?"

I say, "Well obviously, my current situation, what's going on. The same thing I told you." Jeff agrees with this.

Whenever we talk with somebody at the Embassy, they ask us the same two questions right up front:

"Has anyone physically harmed you, abused you or threatened you?" and

"Has anyone attempted to extort you in any way?"

Americans are under the mistaken impression that if they get into legal trouble in a foreign country, they can call the American Embassy and there are people there to help them.

Not so–even if they are innocent. This is a myth perpetuated by movies and television programs. If someone loses their passport or needs help getting home in an emergency, the Embassy is the place to go. If an American is in legal trouble, the only time the Embassy can step in and help is if that person has been threatened, injured, or is subject to extortion. This is a shocking revelation for us.

I say, "No. No one has physically harmed us or anything like that. It's a difficult situation. We don't know what's going on. We feel we've been falsely accused."

Chandler says, "Are you sure this is what happened? Explain it again."

I explain what went down again. Chandler can't answer our questions because he doesn't have any information.

We're on our own.

I consider our options based on previous experiences in my life. Eventually someone will come along and say, "OK. Let's get these guys out of here."

If they let us out, we have no money. How the hell are we going to get back to our hotel? How are we going to get money? All of that's running through my mind. Is this a game to see how much money they can get out of us before they let us go? I've been down that road before.

Everyone is fascinated because this is our first time in the DR.

"Well how long have you been here?"

"Less than 24 hours." This becomes a reoccurring theme. Everyone asks how it was possible to be arrested in less than 24 hours of being in the country.

We hang up with the Embassy. The two guys in the office try to get our side of the story again. The language barrier makes it too difficult. We get a sense that there's something's wrong with our case. We don't fit the description of drug traffickers and we should never have made it to jail to begin with.

While we're talking to the Embassy, I notice a few people stop working and take a lot of interest in our conversation. I'm thinking, one of these sons of bitches speaks English in here, and can understand exactly what I'm saying. He's going to play stupid during the whole situation. Here we go. We're playing cards. This is a freaking poker game.

Some tourists from the U.S. and other countries go down to the DR to do drugs. That's why they go there. Usually, it's a minimal amount. If there's a situation, they pay whoever the arresting officer is and go on their way. That's common everywhere you go in Mexico and most of the Caribbean.

We find out later that if we were Dominicans it would be even more difficult to make a case against us. The Dominican Republic is a drug trafficking hub, so they go after people moving kilos, huge volumes of narcotics. The amount changes every time we go to court, but it's always less than three grams every time. Three grams is .10 of an ounce.

One of the cops says, "What the hell are they doing arresting tourists?"

Arresting tourists is bad because me and Jeff will go back and tell everyone we know to never go to the DR–ever–because of this situation. It's bad for tourism and the economy. That's what they thrive on. If someone isn't involved in drug trafficking, then the only other source of income is tourism. There's no other industry here.

There's something bad going on if they're taking it this far. We get a sense that there's confusion on the part of the people processing us. They don't understand. The few questions that we can answer don't clear anything up. They ask us if we knew Diego before we came to the DR. We say we didn't.

"How did you meet him?"

"He's the guy that drove us around. He's supposed to be our tour guide. This is the hotel we're staying in. Here are our receipts."

They check it out and we're staying there. Everything is covered. Our identification makes sense. We are who we say we are. We have a significant amount of credit cards.

If someone is involved in drug trafficking and narcotics, he wouldn't have the documents in his wallet that we have. He wouldn't have four different credit cards and all this travel information.

I'm hoping that someone will show up and release us. I hope it's a matter of how much money it's going to take to make bail or pay off the right person. But I'm thinking in terms of how the legal system works in the States and we soon find out that even though the Dominican Republish is a democracy and they have adopted many U.S. laws, the DR legal system has very little in common with ours.

As we're being processed, people come in and out of the office. Diego is asking anyone he can what's going on. "We're here to process people, that's all we know, that's all we do. We really can't tell you much more about it," they say.

We're transferred to a different office. I start tuning into body language. You can understand a lot by studying body language.

There are two ladies sitting at desks facing each other. One of them tries to look like she's working but I can see she's more interested in us. She seems to be empathetic toward us. I have a stuffy nose and ask her, in Spanish, if I can have some tissues. One of cops doesn't want her to give me any, but she does anyway.

People ask questions but it's all in Spanish. We tell them our names but they have no idea how to spell them.

I try some Spanish, *"papeles de lápiz, escribes palabras"* or "let me write the words out for you." Someone gives me a piece of paper and a pen and I write out our names. Sometimes people are very proud and don't want me to write it down. They don't know English and it's embarrassing to admit they don't understand.

Then we get back to that question that's even more confusing: "Where are you from?"

I consider giving them my parent's address in the States. It would be so much easier, but in the end, if someone checked, it needed to be correct. The DR is a very under-educated country and the people doing the processing have a limited worldview.

The vast majority of Dominicans can't afford to travel. For many, their island of Hispaniola–which includes Haiti–is the only place in the world. Others have heard of Puerto Rico but that's about it for the Caribbean. For people who can afford a television and cable, their world expands to include New York, Texas and California. If you are an *Americano*, you live in New York, Texas or California. Period. They have no concept of 50 states and the size of the country.

I make the assumption that people have some form of education, that they know how to read a map, that they've seen a map. This is an error in judgment, assuming someone knows where things are on a map. They don't even know what's next to their country. They know that Haiti is on the other side of the river. They've never been outside their country; they've never traveled.

They're trying to write our street addresses down. Again, some people are pretty bright and hand us a piece of paper. Others want to do it verbally and it's a train wreck. They don't understand; they've never heard of it; they think we're making up a place where we live.

I thought about saying we're from a state that they would recognize. But, at the same time, I need it to make sense in case they check our information. Our airline tickets say we came from this country in the Caribbean. All my credit card information says that. That's where my employer is. It's going to check out, if it comes to that.

Next, we go to a room where we're fingerprinted, photographed and our height and weight are recorded. The thing that takes me by surprise is how young the employees look. Part of it is that they look young as a culture, but these guys look like they're 18 or 19 years old.

They talk about how cute I am. My hair is shoulder length, I'm out in the sun all day and I have a good tan. I look like something they've seen in the movies. There's a guy, I assume he's gay, that was taking fingerprints and he tells his friend how cute he thought I was. Me and Jeff start cracking up. There are all kinds of bits of humor within this horrible tragedy.

During all of this processing, Diego is still talking non–stop. He's trying to get whatever information he can. Where are we going? Who do you know? Where do you live? Maybe he knows one of their uncles or cousins. It's constant. That's the upside of having Diego with us. If there's any information out there, he'll find it.

I push myself to learn Spanish as quickly as I can. The more Spanish I understand, the less I have to rely on Diego. I'm bright and I catch on to things quickly. I may have flunked Spanish in high school (twice), but I worked construction at one point and what I once knew is coming back to me. I concentrate on the Spanish being spoken around me. I'm trying to pick up on words. If I heard them before, where did I hear them? In what context? What do they mean?

I try to read body language and put the words in context. My mind is slowly filling in the vocabulary. This is what my life becomes. It's mentally exhausting because while I'm doing that, I'm thinking about everything else that's going on. What's going on back home? Are we going to die here? What is the last thing we did?

We find out later that they have a horrible record keeping practice. It's possible that they record people's information for the fun of it. The software that they use was probably from the 1980s. It had the drop down boxes where you have to highlight one and check it. It reminded me of when I first started working. We had this software program called Peach Tree. It was something like that.

People are asking us our profession. I explain what I do. They ask about education and I tell them I have several college degrees. As the word spreads, people file in and out of the office trying to look like they're working but they're really trying to get a look at the Americanos.

My appearance is drawing a lot of attention, as well. I work out every day at the gym. My shoulders and arms are huge from bench pressing. I hear people say, "*Fuertes Americano, mucho fuertes*," which means "very strong American."

Finally, they have all of the information they want and they take us back to our cell. Someone tells us that we have to go in front of the judge. At the same time, we're told that it's not a big deal, we'll pay a little fine and then we'll be free to go. Everyone repeats this: police officers, guards, people we meet that day and in the days to come, and everyone we meet in jail. Absolutely everyone says it's just business. We pay a fine, they get their money and they'll let us go.

Jeff's saying things like, "Well, they have to let us go. They can't hold us here. Someone's going to show up, and let them know that we shouldn't be here and they'll let us go. We'll be out of here. There's no way a judge can hold us for this bullshit." He's using American logic. Diego agrees with him.

I, on the other hand, am in thinking mode. I go up to the top bunk and lie down. I'm trying to think, trying to get the brain going. What can happen next? Worst case scenarios, best case scenarios running through my head. Worst case, they throw us in a hellhole and that's the end of our lives.

Best case, they walk up here any second now, open the gates, and say, "You guys are free to go. Here's your identification." We go back to the hotel and meet up with Victor and Lucas later.

Usually, I'm making decisions on behalf of some company or operation. I'm not the operation. Now I try not to see myself as me. I try to see myself as an entity in a scenario. A piece on a chessboard. Here's all the possible scenarios I could go into. What's the best way to handle each one?

At the same time, I'm thinking, "How the hell did I end up in a fucking DR jail? How did I get here? I'm smarter than this. I should never have gotten so close." I'm pissed at myself more than anything else for letting it get this far. I'm thinking, "Maybe it's a tax job and it will be over soon. Man, I'd love to beat the shit out of Diego right now, just pound his head into the wall."

While I'm thinking things through, Jeff and Diego are pacing back and forth along the seven feet or so from the bars back to the concrete toilet. They're talking, talking, talking. I wish I could tell them both to shut up but I don't. I try to put myself in a mental state where I don't hear the noise.

This is the longest period of time that I've been sober in the last five years. My life has times of sobriety like when I'm at work. So, there's usually an eight to ten hour period in my day when I don't have alcohol around me or in me.

I've been drinking for three to four years straight, nonstop. Every free moment I have, that's what I do. There's always a beer in my hand. Part of it is the culture. That's what I'm used to doing.

When I'm at work, I can focus on projects, knock out some work, do some project planning and go to meetings. On my own time, I keep my brain numbed down with beer. Now I go through this huge stressor and I haven't had a drink for days. I don't have work in front of me and I don't have alcohol to take me away. I'm not trying to mindlessly entertain myself on vacation, either.

I'm hitting this wall. There's no escape. My brain is taking off. Usually the hamster in the wheel is chugging along, not going too fast. All of a sudden, the wheel is picking up speed. If the hamster gets going fast, if the wheel starts spinning too much, I slow him down with alcohol and exercise. Now, the hamster in the wheel is spinning faster than it has in a long time and it's going faster, and faster and faster. It's the ADHD thing; it kicks in.

Usually, my mind runs between 0-65. I'm already at 85. There's no way to slow it down. It's gone. My mind's racing, racing, racing. The ADHD thing gets started. I don't have anything to focus on. I don't have a task at hand or a way to check out.

I don't have my music. That's even worse. My music is what saves me. It takes me away. My music is gone now. Normally, I listen to music all night while I sleep; my MP3 player, my iPod, they never stop playing because I can take my mind somewhere else when I listen to it. That's gone. My work stuff is gone. Work stuff doesn't mean anything anymore. Everything I have ever accomplished in my life and in my career is gone. Oh, shit.

I don't have these crutches. I don't want to say crutches, but possibly, maybe, they are the crutches that help me be functional and normal. That's gone, and that's gone and that's gone. I'm running down the list.

Now the hamster in the wheel is spinning so fast that he's not even in the wheel anymore. Now it's a sphere. It's like a glowing orange-red ball. It's spinning out of control inside my brain but everything's coming through. Boom, boom, boom, from when I was a little kid to what happened earlier in the day.

Everything is flash, flash, image, idea, idea, like that. I try to focus on something. Pick up the Spanish of the people walking by, jumping in and out. I can hear everything that Jeff and Diego are talking about. I'm listening to everything I can in Spanish. I'm running option A, option B, option C through my mind. What am I going to do here? What is the last thing I did before I died if I died right now? Am I cool with it?

All of these things move through my brain and it's taking off like a rocket. At the same time, it's very hard to let my brain do that and keep it from having a physical effect as well. It's not like I can lie on this bunk while my brain goes and my body doesn't do anything. I become tense, anxious. I don't have the release that exercise gives me. I can't go run five miles right now.

So, I'm lying on this concrete bunk in some kind of a lockup in the DR and I'm going down the white-knuckle ride because all of my control mechanisms are gone. And right there in the middle of all of this, guess who shows up? Five-year-old Corey. He's waiting at the end of the line and I see him because everything else gets stripped away. Five-year-old Corey and 33-year-old Corey are at the same place in life. He has no control over anything around him. He's at the mercy of other people, too, and both of us just want to get the fuck out of there.

There he is, five-year-old Corey getting in trouble at church again. There I am, tears in my eyes, my mom yelling at me. I can even tell you what I'm wearing; he's right in my face. Five-year-old Corey is sitting there with his shaggy mullet haircut, wearing this little red and blue striped shirt and blue jeans. He wears track shoes from Kmart. They have Velcro straps on them.

I need five-year-old Corey because where I'm going next, or whatever's going to happen next, I'm going to need that attitude. And I know he's there. He's always been there. He's just been in a little file cabinet way back in my mind. Now he shows up. The switch is turned on while I'm lying on the top bunk.

Corey and living with ADHD

Having Attention Deficit Hyperactivity Disorder (ADHD) is like jumping off a skyscraper. You're falling–fast–and you keep going and going and going. Have you ever had that sensation when you're dreaming that you're falling, and you jerk and then you wake up and the feeling is gone? It's like that, but it doesn't stop. You don't get the wake up. You're white knuckling it and you're screaming and falling the entire time. That's what it feels like my brain is doing. It's gone.

Someone out there is going to understand what I'm saying and what this feels like. You get to a point where you want to hit the bottom because you're so tired of falling. When I say, "hit the bottom," I'm talking about making my brain stop permanently. I want to go smack! on the bottom.

As you're free falling, there are people talking to you about this and that. Everything is still going on around you, but your mind is doing this free fall thing kind of like the movie, the *Matrix,* where Neo is doing the fall. At the same time, Jeff's right there, Diego's right there, the building is right there, but it's a different image right in front of my face and I'm screaming down the wall.

This becomes a hell of a ride later on, but this is the beginning. It almost sounds like I'm a drug addict, but I'm not a drug addict at all. My coping mechanisms are gone and I have some Obsessive–Compulsive Disorder (OCD) stuff mixed in with the ADHD. I always told myself that I didn't have a weakness because of these things.

People keep telling me, "Oh, it's just like any other condition that people have, that people suffer from."

I don't think so. Most people I know who have similar problems end up falling into a world of heavy drug use. The mechanisms people with drug addictions develop to cope with it fit ADHD, too. I've always convinced myself I wasn't that bad. I didn't behave like that because I didn't want to be like my friends who ended up going down the drug route. Drug use makes it so much worse even though it seems like you're making an escape for yourself when you make a choice to go down that route.

But, friend after friend, I've seen it. There's no turning back once you cross that line. It's like adding more gasoline, more fuel, to the spinning ball in your head. You think you're checking out, but all you're doing is making it harder later.

I convinced myself that ADHD isn't what everyone told me it was. I convinced myself of the opposite because if I acknowledge it, then I'm powerless against it. I can will it. I can will whatever outcome I want. Whatever's necessary, I'll do it and I'm not going to let this thing be what everyone tells me it is and what I need to do for it.

I'm thinking I can white knuckle through it. I do not have to be like every other ADHD person. It's a battle day in and day out, but I'd rather use alcohol to work my way through it in a controlled manner. In my mind, I'd rather die my way than die because of drugs. It's a conscious decision.

Instead of medication, this is how I'm going to deal with it: I'll go to the gym; I'll run; I'll use music to help me un-wind my mind; I'll focus on a difficult job. I have all these things and they're the underpinnings that keep me going.

If I go this route, I'm going to live a very lonely life. When I say lonely it's not in the normal sense. I say this often, and I think people immediately get the wrong impression. It's not so much about having a relationship with another person, like the husband and wife thing. When I say a "lonely life" I mean I can have a lot of people in my life and still feel very lonely knowing that I have to be out there on my own with this. No one's really going to be able to understand it. I'm not going to do well around other people, which I still don't. Things that other people find fun, I'm not going to get any enjoyment from. I'm going to have to go and find my own solitude and enjoyment.

This is what I found out at age 33. This is what I learned during my time in the DR. I didn't know this while I was going along the process. I didn't know it until now. I have an extreme amount of clarity in my life because of this experience in the DR.

Once I went through it... I don't know if there are words for it. But, I use descriptions, things like roller coasters. When the roller coaster was screaming as fast as it did around the corner in the white-knuckle horror, it wasn't a new experience. I go through this week after week, day after day, after day.

All of a sudden I thought, "You know something? I'm going to let go for a little bit here, take my hands off the bar."

It's still fast-as-hell scary. I have no control. I'm riding along in it. But I'm going to try not to white knuckle it as much and put my hands down. That's kind of how it is. That's how the ride is now, right now after the DR. I went through all of that because I not only rode the mental part of it, but the emotional thing as well. That's what's really, really hard because while you're on that roller coaster, all it takes is one little emotional blip and BOOM.

I refuse to go to any ADHD education classes. I refuse to get involved with any of those studies, I refuse to go to those self–help classes. They told me I could do the "students with disabilities" class in college. I said, "No. 'F' that." You want to know why? Because when I go get a job, my boss isn't going to give me an extra two and a half hours to get the work done.

Now, you give these kids all these special things to study with instead of telling them to grind and focus like everyone else is and eat it. Instead, you're giving them all these special arrangements. What the hell are they going to do when they get in the real world? They're never going to hold down a job. It's impossible.

You're better off saying, "This is everything that's wrong with you. Accept it. Deal with it. There's a kid over here that's paraplegic, there's a guy over there that's blind. He has to deal with it, too. Guess what? You have this mental stuff that you have to deal with and you have a hell of a time controlling your emotions.

You're going to fly off the handle left and right. No one's going to give you some kind of special medication you think is going to make it go away, because it doesn't. You move from pill, to pill, to pill and they always have some crazy side effect. You lose one thing, you get another one. That's how it works. This is what they don't tell you when you start taking those pills,

"Oh, by the way, we'll take care of this problem. But, guess what's going to show up over here?" It's not a cure. You trade one off for the other.

I think people need to refocus on what they think they know about this. I hate saying disease, or condition, or whatever it is because they really need to be honest about it. This is what it is. It's right here in front of you.

Now, there's a job in this world, a life in this world that's perfect for this person. But it's so hard to find. And exactly the way you are, with the short–fuse temper, and your hyper–focus, or your fascinating ability to do creative artwork, or whatever, but you also have your inability to handle the pressure of social situations. There's a perfect job out there in the world for you where people will pay you an immense amount of money and you can have everything you want. But, it's very rare, and it's very hard to find because the rest of the world isn't like that.

When I was younger, growing up was hell for me. School was hell for me. I hated it. I didn't belong there and no one knew what to do about it. That was during the 80's. It was all new.

"He acts this way because he's not paying attention."

"Well, make him pay attention."

"How do we do that?"

"I don't know. Let's hit him." So, they beat this kid until he pays attention. I don't know. My parents didn't know what to do. There were no self-help books.

"Oh, and by the way, I have other kids I have to worry about. He's not doing what he's told. I don't know. I'll keep hitting him."

"Hitting him doesn't work anymore. What do we do now?"

"I don't know. Good luck."

Here was my parent's philosophy, "Well, when he turns 18, we'll have him join the military. Then, he'll be their problem."

That was my mom's solution. Seriously, that was my parent's solution with me because they lost control of me—I don't mean lost control of me—they couldn't get me to do anything I didn't want to. There's no amount of punishment that was going to change me.

At the same time, my mom hated it so much because she'd see glimpses of brilliance. Everyone will say this about someone who has a kid like this. You'll see a glimpse of brilliance and then you'll see the wheels come falling off, and it crashes and burns.

And parents are saying, "What the hell? How did you go from this to acting like a three-year-old having a temper tantrum?"

I can't tell them why I'm acting this way because when it happens, I'm in The Box and I can't get out. When the ADHD feelings become too much to cope with, I feel like I'm surrounded by a box with sides and a top. I end up in this box when I feel out of control, overwhelmed and frustrated. The box is crushing in on me and I don't know how to communicate to someone outside about what's going on.

Everything I've heard and understood about how professionals deal with a kid with ADHD is that they try to do whatever medication, whatever psychotherapy, or whatever educational system to keep the kid out of the Box. I disagree. I think if the Box in his mind is a natural place for him to go to when he's overwhelmed, you need to try to get the kid comfortable in that box and not be scared of going in it.

That Box is like a nightmare. It's like a monster. It's going to come get me when I go to sleep. Let's get him to not be afraid to go in that Box. Let's get him comfortable in his Box and not tell him it's wrong to be in there and see if he can start there and learn how to work his way out because that's the only thing that's going to save him.

This is what I explain to people when they ask me how I got to where the disability doesn't rule my life. I don't know my multiplication facts to this day. I don't know what seven times six is. I don't. I can't tell you. I could shuffle the memory cards in my head and find the answer but that's a lot of work when I have a calculator in front of me.

When I took a test, I couldn't get the whole test right, never could. But, I can get enough to get by and get the "C" and that's all I really need because I need to get through this. Most people will tell you 90% of the time you don't need to know what seven times six is, do you? It's useless information. But, the stuff I do know how to do is really, really useful to the rest of the world. I need to get out of this world the DR put me in and go to the one where I can use the skills I have to help people.

Thursday, June 18, cont.

As I'm lying on the bunk, thinking about all that stuff, I see a cockroach walking up the wall.

I say to Jeff, "I heard roaches are high in protein. Is that true, Jeff?"

Jeff says, "What are you talking about?"

"I heard they're high in protein, pretty nutritional is what I hear."

It's crawling along and I'm looking up at it. "Yeah, I think I'll eat that."

"What? Are you crazy?"

"Yeah, I think I'm going to eat that roach." I tried to catch it but it ran away.

"Corey lost it. He's talking about eating a roach. He sees it go up the wall and he wanted to eat it," Jeff says.

Finally, one of the guards comes to the cell door and says we're going to go see the judge now. They handcuff us together, and Diego and the girl together. The four of us walk outside and join the line with the other prisoners we came in with the night before.

In front of us is a small pickup truck with a cage on the back. It looks like a chain-link fence type of dog cage you can get at a pet store with a gate on one end.

The top has a solid, metal, roof. There's a bench on each side and a metal bar near the roof going from the front to the back. The benches are narrow and small. A cop with a pistol grip pump shot gun sits on a stool that sticks out on the back.

The four of us go into the cage first and sit on one of the benches. More prisoners come in and fill up the rest of the benches. Then they let the other prisoners in. They push as many people as possible inside this cage, like cattle in a stockyard. These guys are the bottom feeders. If you are somebody, you get to sit on the bench. If you are nobody, you have to stand the entire trip holding onto the bar at the top for stability. These guys look like crap.

It's packed in the cage and the girl is the only female in the group. Even though Diego is handcuffed to the girl, some of the guys try to grab her. She's sitting in the corner crying. This is a bad situation for a woman to be in.

Diego yells at these guys, "Get the fuck back," in Spanish, "You know who I am. I live here. I can get you taken care of. You know better. You're nothing. You don't even know who you're talking to."

He's playing the Joe Pesci role again. I'm picking up some of it even though it's in Spanish. My Spanish is getting better and better by the minute.

There's an older, short guy smaller than Diego who's talking the most shit. He's running his mouth. He and Diego are going back and forth.

He looks at me with my long hair and says, "Pretty girl. You are going to be my girlfriend with your nice hair, American." I look through him like he's not even there, like he's a ghost, like he's a walking dead man.

I have turned off everything that made me a quality human being and I'm now in prison-survival mode. They don't know that I understand some Spanish and this is a valuable tool later on. Jeff is sitting there, completely dejected. He looks like Play-Doh waiting to be played with.

The other thing these guys see are my shoes. If you have the coolest shoes, you are the coolest guy. There's nothing special about these shoes to me, but it's clear that they'd like to take them off of me. I come up with a plan in case anything starts to happen.

I have no problem fighting someone if there's no other way to handle a situation. I trained as a boxer and I know what I'm doing. However, avoiding a physical altercation is more valuable than getting into a fight. My shoulders are huge-I'm wearing a large white tank top and it barely covers me-so these guys don't know for sure what would happen if they get into a brawl with me. That uncertainty keeps people from approaching me.

Part of why I don't want to have a physical altercation is because I have no way of knowing what's going to happen. This would be a very bad time for me to break a knuckle on my hand. If I do get cut, whatever kind of infection I could get I could die from. I have to make it really count if I'm going to fight, and I have to make sure I walk away in one piece because who knows, the guy sitting there across from me might be carrying AIDS. But still, I have a plan.

I say to Jeff, "If something happens, both of us jump up there, grab a hold of that bar and we're going to kick these mother fuckers from here to the other side of the cage. We jump up and grab a hold of the bar. You can't throw a punch because you only have one free hand. Those guys are all lined up together. We grab a hold and use both feet to smash them out the other side of this thing and we're going to keep on kicking them until there's meat coming out the other side."

I have a free left; I'd rather have my right. I tell Jeff, "If it goes off, you hold with this hand and punch with the other hand. They're going to be disorganized because not all those guys over there on that bench want to fight and once they see us stand up, they're going to realize we're like three times their size."

Jeff says, "I'll hit my head if I stand up."

"It doesn't matter. All you have to do is get up there, and get your hands on the bar and you're going to kick those fuckers all the way through the other side of that cage."

I have it all planned out in my head, which one I'll grab first, how I'll do it. I'll grab this guy with my free hand–he has loose cuffs on–and stab him with his own loose cuff, gouge it right underneath his chin and see if it can come up right underneath his ear and hook him. That should make him bleed pretty good. If we start putting the beat on, if we do end up fighting, who knows what's going to happen.

The guys sitting on the other side of the truck can see what's going on. They're seeing the look in my eyes and they're telling the guys who are standing up to knock it off because if it goes down there's no place for them to go to get out of the way.

We're riding in the cage to hell with the bottom feeders. We're cruising through town, on display like animals in the zoo. When we come to stoplights, people are yelling at us, honking their horns. They're yelling at the guys in the cage, trying to get their attention, trying to talk to some of them.

It's a horrible, miserable experience. Welcome to hell. It's sweltering hot. My clothes are soaking wet with sweat. We haven't had a shower in two days and we stink. We're hungry, but mostly we're thirsty. I know we're dehydrated but there isn't anything we can do about it. We're surrounded by filth. It's right in our face.

It takes 25 minutes to make our way through *Santo Domingo* traffic to *La Casa de Justicia*. It's the big high rise next to the house that Diego grew up in where he told us it was his job to keep us away from. It has a big, open–air patio in the middle of the ground level with benches, trees, flowers and a fountain. An atrium soars up three flights. There are large windows on each floor with a view of the atrium below.

When we pull up to the courthouse, there's a crowd waiting. Friends and family of the guys in the cage who figure they've been arrested because they haven't seen them for a while. They don't know for sure that they are here, but sooner or later, everyone turns up at the courthouse. When the guys in the cage see their families, they start yelling to them for help. It's sheer pandemonium.

We know that we have to go see the judge when we get to the courthouse. There's a real sense of panic right now, especially for me, because of everything that's going on.

I'm thinking, "Dude, what are we going to do? We don't know anyone. We've disappeared for more than 24 hours now. No one knows where we are. No one can find us."

The truck stops and all these people surround it and guys yell out back and forth. They open the back of the cage. Getting people in and out of this cage is a mess because they're handcuffed in line. The opening is so small, they can only get one person out at a time and that person falls. There's no step off the back of this thing. Guys get water and food from their family while talking to them.

Diego's trying to find someone he knows and he happens to see Marco walking down the sidewalk. This is important but, later, it's also a double-edged sword. Diego yells his name.

He says, "I know that guy. He's a lawyer."

I'm thinking, "No way. Maybe there's a God after all in all this nonsense."

Diego yells to Marco as we're dragged inside the courthouse.

We have no money, no food, nothing, and we're trying to figure out a way around this. Diego says, "We need to figure out a way to get some money. We have to get some money. We need some money. That's what's going to get us out of this." I know this is true.

We need to start hustling. I'm in work mode. We have to come up with something, and fast.

I say, "Dude, if I have to put the beat down on one of these guys for money, I don't know how I'm going to do it, but I'll figure out a way. We have to come up with a way to get some funds rolling."

Marco makes his way to us and hands Diego his card. He and a woman lawyer follow us up three flights of stairs spiraling around and around. The woman lawyer wants to take our case but quickly understands the Marco has a prior relationship with Diego and disappears.

I get the impression that lawyers camp out on the street in front of the courthouse and wait for this truck to show up. They're ambulance chasers. They know there's no way you can have any contact with legal representation between processing and the courthouse. The DR justice system is to bring you in front of the judge without a lawyer and, in our case, without knowing what you're being charged with.

As we walk up the stairs, there's a landing filled with people on each floor that we have to move through. We reach the third floor and the area is crowded with the guys we came in with, guards and other people. The guards wear uniforms and in addition to a gun, they carry pieces of wood of varying sizes—like a 2" w 4". Everyone is just standing around. There's a desk next to the large window looking out at the atrium.

After waiting awhile, some of the guys start to sit down on the floor. One of them sits on a guard's foot and the guard starts beating him with his stick. Whack! Whack! Whack! He's one of the guys talking smack in the cage and eyeing my shoes.

A guy sitting at the desk with a clipboard needs to take our names and information. It would be so easy to disappear between getting off the bus and the third floor. No one would ever know. It's very low security there. This is where we should've saved some money, paid someone off, and got out of there. No one even knows we exist yet.

"Two Americans? I didn't see them. What are you talking about?"

They don't know our names. They don't have our passports or anything like that. This is the best opportunity to disappear. We just didn't know it at the time.

This lobby area is packed. They're remodeling this floor. An inmate–called a "trustee"–is painting the walls a light yellow and a light blue color. I'm never quite sure about the set up. He's an inmate, but he works here. He does all the work for the guards. Other people are doing tile work on the floor.

I'm thinking, "What the hell? Do they put people to work while they're in here? What's going on?"

The guy with the clipboard starts calling out people's names. We know when he gets to us because he can't pronounce our names. As he calls out names, they take guys away. Me, Jeff, Diego and the girl are at the back of the pack. We walk around the corner into the prisoner's area and a guard takes off our cuffs.

We watch as a guard with some five-gallon buckets—some with stale bread and some with water—moves through the crowd and places them on the floor next to a wall. The guys we came in with race over to the buckets and start scarfing down this bread and trying to drink water out of the buckets. It has been more that 24 hours since all of us were arrested. We've had some bottled water and Diego's eaten. These guys haven't and, obviously, they've been in here before.

The trustee starts yelling and getting these guys out of the food and water he's supposed to give to everyone. They go diving in after this dirty water and nasty bread like it was nothing.

Jeff says, "Did you see the way they dove for that? These guys start fighting each other to eat that nasty ass bread and drink that dirty water."

"Oh, God," I say.

A guard comes over, grabs me, Jeff and Diego and walks us down the hall. He brings us to a cell door and it's completely black. The smell of raw sewage is overwhelming. When our eyes adjust to the darkness, we see a cage with what used to be human beings. Guys are standing there stark naked. There's no toilet or running water. No bedding or bunks. Just a cage with a concrete floor.

The guys inside the cage see us at the cell door and start going crazy like a bunch of wild animals. I would say they've become animals except we treat animals a lot more humanely. They stick their hands out, begging for money, and the guard goes over and starts swinging his stick at them.

The guard says, "Here you go." He starts talking to Diego in Spanish. "You guys want to go in here? Is this where you want to stay?"

Diego says, "What the hell, man? You can't put us in here. You can't put the Americans in here." This is the worst cell we see in jail. This is where the guards put all the guys they don't like.

When Diego protests, the guard says, "We can work something out." This is when the taxation begins, when jail becomes very costly. Even though we don't have money, the guards know we can get it.

A guard takes us down a long hallway. It appears that they're remodeling the area. They're putting in little offices and painting, and stuff like that. There's a lot of traffic coming in and out of our area all the time.

He brings us to a horseshoe–shaped room. Everything is made out of concrete. The room is large enough to hold a couple of dozen men but they built it with a limited sleeping area and a lot of open space in the center. There are concrete slabs on three sides of the room but no one's there. There are two levels on each concrete slab with three bunks on each level. Theoretically, six guys could sleep on each concrete slab. There are three small foam mats on the bottom level and each person actually has a pillow. We find out later that all of the cells have a similar layout.

The bottom level is far enough from the top level that I can sit up straight, but Jeff hits his head so he spends the time either hunched over or lying down. There's nothing up on top. Underneath the bunks is an empty space that goes back. It's a little shaded. Later on, we stash stuff under there to hide it because every time we buy something or have something, we have to pay the guards the tax, and inmates know we have stuff and they want some of it, too. We have to constantly share everything.

There's a fan circulating the air. At some point, this oscillating fan was mounted to the wall. When it broke off, they used bungee cords and wire to mount it to an office chair. Now we have a high-powered fan on wheels that can be moved around. Under any other circumstances, you'd throw this thing away because it looks like an electrical hazard, but it's the most important thing in the room. There's no air moving in the room at all. It's over one hundred degrees and we're sweating. This fan blows cool air around the room to make it bearable. It doesn't have the front piece, the wire cover, anymore and the blades keep hitting people. It gets me twice and Diego once.

This is our home for the next five days.

This room is the break area for the guards. They go back there, hang out, watch TV, and do whatever they want. A guard is sitting on one of the bunks watching TV. Other guards are lying around, relaxing. Then we come along.

Diego negotiates the deal. He tells the guy in charge, "We'll pay you some pesos if you'll let us stay here." The guard is good with that.

He walks over to the other guards, grabs them and kicks them off the bed. He has no problem doing that because he's not going to make money off his own guards. We're the golden ticket.

"Sit down, please," he says, and takes the fan, points it directly at us and tells us it's ours.

Diego is trying to set up something so the guards will let us see Marco. Not only is Marco our only contact on the outside, he's our only hope of getting some money. Without money, we can't continue to stay in the horseshoe room. Early on, I understood that Diego is our only way out. Without Diego, we can't get to Marco. As much as I would like to wring Diego's neck, he's our only, and best hope of getting out of the mess we're in.

There may come a time when we walk through the gates and he doesn't. Or, I kiss him on the cheek and hand him over to someone else to take care of. Or, I take care of him myself if I know I'm never getting out of here. All that's running through my head but we need him now. I understand it. I can listen to Diego's conversations. He doesn't know what I'm picking up and what I'm not picking up when he's having a conversation with the guards. That's another valuable tool throughout this time.

I start picking up on the culture. I make it a point to introduce myself to everyone who comes in the room. I'm always friendly to everyone no matter what the circumstances. I call everyone *jefe*, "boss," as a sign of respect. When guards come in, I introduce everyone.

"They just want you to notice their existence. Don't act like they're not there. Who knows? We may get kicked out of here and have to go back there, in hell."

Jeff is terrified and that's all he talks about. "God, I never want to go over there. That is the worst place I've ever seen in my life. Did you see those guys? They're covered in filth. It's nasty."

Our stress level rises as we wait and wait and wait. Are we going to see the judge now? What's going to happen next? Are the guards going to come get us? Is someone from the U.S. Embassy going to stop by?

We have disappeared from the face of the earth for more than 24 hours. I find out later that the text I sent out to my friends gets them talking, trying to figure out what's going on. When Connor asked me if I was joking, the text that I managed to send back saying "No" is critical. People know we're in trouble but that's all they know.

Connor tells me later that his first reaction was to call Jeff's cell phone and say, "Hey, man, I think Corey is in jail somewhere. You might want to try to find him." It never occurs to him that Jeff could be in jail, too.

Victor and Lucas are supposed to leave for the DR after work today but Jeff made the hotel reservations so they have no idea where to go. They debate both sides of the problem, "Should we go? Should we not go? What are we going to do when we get there? We don't even know where to find Corey and Jeff."

Every second we're afraid we're going to get pulled out and thrown into the cage with the animals. My main fear, though, is that we get separated from Diego. We need Diego to translate, but also, he knows the system and how to get things done. Later, a search of the records shows no criminal record for Diego. It doesn't make sense, though. He knows too much and he has too many connections inside for this to be his first time in jail. Maybe someone can buy a clean criminal record. I don't know, but there's a great story there somewhere.

Marco shows up and lets me use his phone. I leave a message on my parent's old–fashioned tape answering machine but the message is garbled. My mom and dad are not able to figure out what's going on. All they understand from my message is, "Hi, it's Corey. I need you to wire two thousand dollars to my lawyer." The rest of the message is not understandable.

As far as my parents know, I'm still in the country where I've worked for the past two years. They assume my work there is going to continue until the end of the month, but the company chose the 15th as the last day for all contract labor from stateside support. I don't call my parents and tell them when I'm going on vacation. They would have no way to know that I'm in the Dominican Republic.

I can't call out and talk for a long time. That costs Marco money. Other people can call us, though, for free. I call Connor. He rarely answers his phone during work hours but, thankfully, he picks it up.

I say, "Hey, man. This is what's going on. We're in jail in the DR and we don't have a whole lot of time to talk. We need to get some money so we can get out of here. We don't have a phone and we can't call out too much on this one. So, you can't call me back right now but we need to get some money together. Can you Western Union $2,000 of your money to this guy? Here's his information. Here's his phone number. Here's his e-mail. I'll give him your number also. When you get a chance, go by my house. The key is underneath the pot. Go ahead and go inside. There should be a white box there. Write yourself a check for however much money you need."

Connor is cool, calm and collected. He writes everything down. He says, "Dude, what are they charging you with?"

I give him a real short version, "We were riding in a cab, cops pulled us over, they said there were drugs in the car and our driver says they're charging us with drug trafficking but we haven't heard anything from a court official."

"Oh, shit, man, I've been there before." Connor does a lot of traveling. "Alright. I'll get on it." He didn't ask any questions other than that.

Connor stops everything he's doing at work and starts hustling. He figures things out with Western Union and gets the money to Marco right away.

I don't like asking people for things. I like to do things on my own. I helped Connor out with a lot of stuff. I helped him move and do various things, throw parties and stuff like that. And I've never asked him for anything. That's not my thing. I don't feel comfortable asking people to help me do things.

"Tell everyone I know that this is what's going on. Jeff's with me," I say.

We have money coming; that's our first concern. Diego's trying to reach his family because we need someone on the street to make moves for us. All of our belongings are still back at the hotel. We haven't been back for more than 24 hours. Our passports are there which is our number one issue now.

After I get off the phone with Connor, Jeff makes a phone call. He gets hold of his mom and wife. This is bad. Jeff is beyond emotional. When he tells them he's in jail, he starts crying. I can tell they're asking him questions he can't answer. I can imagine the confusion this causes with his family.

I notice that all of the inmates we came in with are locked up in cells but the three of us are allowed to walk around freely. We can go in the back where we sleep or walk up to the front where the guards are.

While we're hanging around, other inmates and guards are asking, "Why are you here?"

I tell them what happened and the inmates are saying things like, "You guys are going to be gone. They can't keep you for that. Really? Why didn't you guys pay them off so you could go?"

"Dude, we tried it. It all got messed up. We couldn't do it," Diego says.

"You guys are going to leave. You go in front of the judge and he'll let you out. You'll be out by the weekend." We receive this reassurance over and over again from guards, lawyers and inmates–anyone we talk to.

Diego comes around the corner with takeout: Cokes, and chicken and rice.

"Hey, you guys hungry," he asks.

We're trying to hold off from eating as long as we can. We know that the first bite we take that's not in a sanitary bottle, like water, we're going to get sick. My stress level is keeping me from being hungry.

"Where did you get all that stuff," I ask.

"Marco and some guys went out and got us some food," Diego answers. We haven't paid Marco yet, but he's willing to take a chance because he wants the job and he knows that the rest of the lawyers are lurking in the shadows waiting to pounce.

We're trying to find out what we're supposed to do. Marco says the lawyer for the court is going to present what they're charging us with, then we're going to tell the judge what happened.

At the same time, there's constant action going on between Diego and the girl. He's trying to make sure she isn't planning to make any other moves or say something that isn't true, or whatever people are trying to put into her head. Diego is afraid the police are going to offer her a release if she will turn on the three of us. Her whole family shows up, a lot of people from the neighborhood are there; it's getting bigger and bigger.

When the guards are not transferring prisoners, people can come up to the third floor. The guards let them come up. They can sit out in the lobby area where there are chairs, and visit with their jailed family member. They can talk for hours, until the guards say they have to go. Their family can bring them food, clothes, whatever they want.

Diego is in hustler mode. I'm seeing a whole different side to this guy. Diego's in his element because he, like everyone else, wants to be somebody and wants everyone to know who he is.

The same people we met when we went to Diego's neighborhood come by. We become like a family later, and that becomes a very important key to everything that's going on. As far as me and Jeff go, our concern is that all of our stuff's back at the hotel.

Diego is able to reach the people at the hotel and explain the situation. He also calls his father–in–law, who we met previously. He's been to the States before and speaks a little bit of broken English. He's a pretty large–sized black guy, a very nice man. Every time he sees us, he hugs us and smiles. You get a feeling from him that he's kind of like a big goof. Really, the nicest guy in the world. He's not too bright, but he's really, really nice. He'll do whatever you ask him to.

Diego's father–in–law goes to the hotel and is able to get all of our possessions from the hotel room and get them out of the hotel. Our passports are in our bags, along with all of our clothes and everything, and now they're at Diego's father–in–law's house, the same place that we stopped by and visited the day before. So, that's good. They are going to hold on to all of our stuff.

We're talking about our options. Diego's family is asking, "Should we bring all the stuff to you guys when you go to court tomorrow morning, so when you get out of court, you have all your stuff, and you can go do whatever you want?"

We're sitting around talking about that when all of a sudden a guard comes up and grabs me and Jeff and drags us over to the other side of the room. Diego isn't around. Diego is out doing something and we're like, "What the hell?" We're looking at this guard and acting like we don't speak Spanish-which we don't. Someone says something and Diego comes running back over.

He says, "No, no, no."

It's the shift change. The new guards are coming on duty and this one wants his tax money. There are four different shifts. We're finding this out each time, but we're in this jail for so long that it's like a family by the time we leave.

One day a guard comes over and sits down next to me and Jeff. As the guard talks to us, he takes his gun out of its holster, lays it on the bench and says, "Watch my gun for me." Then he goes to use the bathroom, comes back out, and he's looking around. He can't find his gun. I moved it to see what he'd do.

I say, "Here you go, man," and hand his gun back over.

The guard says, *"Sí, gracias."*

What the hell? I'm just shaking my head.

But now we're sitting around nervously waiting to go to court. We've been told that the court functions 24 hours a day. They have to keep pushing people through because it's an economic system, not a justice system. They've got limited space in the jails, so they have to keep pushing people through. It's the cycle of life in the DR penal system. Because of this, there's a constant turnover of people coming and going.

During the shift change, we have to do a roll call. The three of us have to come out of our area in the back and stand there while the guards bring everyone else out.

The guards pull all of the guys living in hell out of there. They walk out of their dark cage and squint in the light. They stink so bad that everyone takes a few steps away from them until they're standing in a group by themselves. It's obvious they aren't getting enough to eat. They have skin hanging off their bones. They don't even look human anymore. They're naked and I can see the caked on human filth on their skin and in their hair.

These are the guys that the guards don't like or they don't have money to give to the guards so they can live in a better situation. I assume they also don't have anyone on the outside that cares enough about them to bring them clothes or food. The jail gives them one bowl of gruel a day. I don't know how much water they get each day. They might not get any. There's no way out for these guys. They will spend the rest of their days there. Even if they have served their time, they can't show up in court naked and filthy to be released.

After the roll call, I ask Diego about the girl. There's a door near the area where we're living that goes to the women's section. There are only four or five women in there. Diego can go to the door and talk to her. Diego is monitoring everything, what's going on, what the guards are doing. The biggest thing that Diego is worried about as far as the girl is concerned is the police cornering her and getting her to roll on us.

The police could get her to say, "I saw these guys buy the drugs," so she can get out.

She's kind of like Jeff, except she cries a little bit more. Diego is constantly encouraging her. He's having food sent to her also, making sure she gets it.

After Jeff sees the food and drinks Diego brings in, he says, "What else can we get?"

"Anything you want," Diego says.

"I need some cigarettes." Jeff smokes non-stop. Someone brings him cigarettes.

We can get whiskey if we want it. Beer was the one thing that was the hardest to get. Beer is the only thing I drink but it's way too hard to smuggle it in. And I don't want one beer. That's enough to make me mad. I need more like eight.

We're back there and we're on edge because they said we are going to go to court any minute and all this other stuff is going on. Marco's guys are bringing stuff in. They come back to our area and see us, ask about things. Supposedly, they're starting on our case.

No official has ever told us what we're charged with. Diego translates what people are saying, but there's no way that either me or Jeff can know for sure if he's telling the truth. This is an ongoing issue. We don't trust Diego, but he's the only person doing the translating. Is Diego telling the police what we want him to say? We have no way of knowing.

The pressure is really getting to Jeff and he loses it. He's mad at Diego. He starts yelling at him. They argue back and forth. Jeff's still in shock or whatever you want to freaking call it. Maybe denial.

He keeps saying, "What's going on? What's going on?" asking stupid question after stupid question.

• • •

We're sitting back there in our mini horseshoe area with three foam mats for sleeping and it's hot. The fan is blowing, but it doesn't help much. When the fan isn't blowing, it's real, real bad. It's like being in a sauna. There's no window to look out of. You look up at the ceiling and it has a hole in it with this concrete lid on top of it. Light comes in, though. All these wires are running in and out of it.

There's no ventilation, so when Jeff lights up a cigarette, the whole place is full of smoke. It sits there. You can see it when you walk out and walk back in. The guards tell him to go smoke in the bathroom.

We're all sitting like that with a little concrete space in the middle. A little bit more closed in. The three of us are sitting there. Some of the guards come in.

They come and go all day and all night long, especially during the day. There's a lot more traffic.

The animals down the hall are yelling. Guys are screaming. It's messed up. This place is locked-down-hell misery.

I'm getting even madder at myself. How did I let this guy get this close? Why did I relax my guard so much? I was way too comfortable. We've been in here since about noon and I'm getting more and more frustrated.

We're going over game plans, figuring out what we're going to do if we get thrown in with the animals in hell because it could happen at any second.

I say, "If you get over there, Jeff, the first person who puts his hands on you in a way you don't like, you start swinging and don't stop until someone pulls you off of him." That's what I tell him. He doesn't like that at all. He says he's no good at fighting.

I say, "If you ever want to see your kids again, you better get good at it in a hurry."

Diego's says, "They might have some knives over there, some weapons." Although, with them all being naked, it would be pretty difficult to hide anything.

The three of us go over all the plans because it could happen at any minute, any second. It's us three against everyone else now. That's the real situation. We keep running through scenarios and talking about them.

From what people have been saying over and over the last 24 hours, we believe we'll pay a fine and leave. We each pay Marco $2,000 which should be more than enough. That money is supposed to cover his fees plus whatever fine, bond or bail we're going to have to pay. If we post bail, we should be able to walk out the door. If we can't post bail right away, we might have to spend 24 hours in this holding area before we get out.

Diego gets his hands on some money from Marco and starts making his moves with the guards. Diego always lets us know when someone important is there. When the head guards come in, we introduce ourselves, tell them our names, we shake their hands, acknowledge who they are and thank them for letting us stay there.

"No, no, no," the guard says. "You are a guest in my house. Anything you need, you let me know."

This has to be the strangest thing I've ever heard. We're locked up in jail, but the guard tells us we're his guests and to let him know what we need. None of this makes sense. I want to say, "How about we go for a walk outside and we disappear. You take the money and buy yourself a new scooter."

Diego says, "Yeah, we're staying here tonight. We'll go to court tomorrow."

Jeff pulls himself together and calls Victor, "Yeah, we should be out of here tomorrow morning. We're going to court tomorrow morning. You guys should still come over. We still have all our hotel reservations. We should make it to *Puerta Plata* by Saturday morning at the latest. Friday night, we'll be outta here."

The guards leave their clothes on the other side of the room when they go shower off. They leave their uniforms and their guns lying around. I wonder how hard it would be to put on their uniforms, take their guns and walk out of there.

The only bathroom at this end of the jail is around the corner off our room. We go back there to check it out. There's a little sink and a toilet, but no toilet paper.

"We got to get some toilet paper," Jeff says.

"Well, we have some newspaper. That's a start," I say.

There's a pipe coming out of the wall where a shower might be. We never know when we'll have water so, whenever it flows, we collect it in a 55–gallon drum. Next to it is a 30–gallon bucket and a smaller bucket. The small bucket is used to scoop water out of the drum and dump it into the 30–gallon bucket. We have a smaller container for water to dump down the toilet to make it work. Usually the water flows early in the morning when they have water pressure.

There's a couple of five—gallon buckets back there where the guards take showers. The way it works is you fill up the five—gallon buckets. Then you dump one on your head, lather up and use the others to rinse off. It's such a rush because it's so hot in there and the water is so cold.

The guards go in there and take three showers a day. They strip down, go back there, and rinse off. We start to figure out this concept. There's no shower curtain, which is common in Mexico and third—world countries, so there's water all over, all the time. It's on the walls, the sink and the toilet. It's impossible to keep toilet paper completely dry. The water goes down a drain in the floor.

Every night we have a different guest and they have a different story. This is when my Broadway musical idea comes in. The set stays the same with the horseshoe. The characters change. Diego is constantly being Diego. The way he acts and walks, and he talks to everyone. It's constant. Then, there's me and Jeff and everything that happens throughout the course of the day. There's humor in it but it's mostly miserable.

On our first night, there's this kid sitting in our area. He's white, looks American, but he's Dominican. He tells us how he takes models and beautiful girls around the city on his moped to these parties. He works for different advertising agencies. He knows a little bit of English. He has the nice American look about him. It's the "plastic classic" scripted out of a Hollywood movie.

Our fan is a huge benefit. We have the only form of cool air anywhere in this place. We invite the kid to come over and sleep on our side of the cell with us. He put his bed right down on the floor so he can get some of the air from the fan.

Throughout the course of the day, me and Jeff sit there in our own world talking back and forth about God knows what, telling stories about our lives. We sit in silence for hours upon hours, which men like to do.

Then, one of us says something and the other one says, "Yeah, I was thinking the same thing. I was wondering if you could do that. You know something? That would be a real good idea."

It's getting dark by now and we understand we're going to be spending the night. It's been 48 hours wearing the same clothes and not eating. No shower, no nothing. But, we still smell the best compared to everyone else because we had a shower at one point in time during the week. My hair is getting nastier and nastier. Because it's so long, it's oily. I'm sitting in a sauna all day. I'm sweating constantly.

We spend a miserable night there. This is the beginning of hell with Diego. Diego snores all night long, horribly bad. I can't stand it. I remember lying there and his feet kept getting near my head so I was hitting them. This is the whole night; it's a light sleep.

It gets real quiet at night. It's not like a county jail in the States where guys scream and make noise all night long. We can turn our own lights off. We have the switches right there on the wall.

One of the guards comes in and says, "All right, guys. You might want to lock up for the night in case someone gets out or something goes on." We're prisoners but we lock ourselves in at night in case something happens. Diego goes over and latches the door.

This is when I discover that Jeff can sleep for 12 hours at a time. He lies there all day. He gets up every now and then.

I say, "Hey, man. What's going on?"

I don't sleep very much and there he is. People ask me all the time,

"What's that?"

"Oh, that's a bear. He's hibernating."

Me and Diego make up stories about Jeff while he's sleeping,

"Oh, he's dead. We killed him last night."

They come over and touch him. He wakes up and moves. This scares the person who touched him. Stuff like that.

Jeff grumbles, "I'm trying to sleep. Leave me alone. Tell Diego to shut up."

So, we go to bed that night.

I sleep a little bit off and on. I don't need a lot of sleep and I can't sleep unless my body is physically tired. For the past 48 hours, I haven't had an opportunity to lift weights, run or go to a gym. I'm not physically tired.

We wake up in the morning as soon as the sun comes up. We slept in the clothes we've had on for two days. I had to be so filthy by then.

Friday, June 19

I'm not doing well Friday morning. I'm running through all of the scenarios. No matter what anyone says, you never know what's going to happen when you stand in front of a judge. You never know. Everyone thinks they know what's going to happen or the probability of such-and-such happening, but no one ever really knows. All of the possibilities of what could happen when we go to court run through my head.

I'm trying to stay sharp, trying to think, "Corey, you're smart. Think it through."

But, I can't. I'm white knuckling it. When I can't think my way out, one of the first things that comes to me is I want to hit the bottom. I'm tired of white knuckling and falling. I don't want to do this because I don't have my outs. I don't have exercise, beer, work or music. I want to go. I'm shutting down. Get me out of here.

This ride is going to last a long time but I don't know it yet. Eventually, I'm more comfortable in it. But, I lose my life along the way, too. I get comfortable in the chaos; that's the trade off. I don't want to be a good person anymore and that's scary. I'm in a bad environment. This is where bad people go.

• • •

My dad said something to me when I was about five years old. He said it on more than one occasion. He wanted me to have a real good understanding of it. My dad grabs a hold of me, looks me straight in the eyes and says, "People like you end up in prison or dead."

That stuck in me and it's never gone away. My mind was way advanced for my age. I could read through people. He was serious about that. So, I figured I better be ready for when I go to prison or die. He wanted me to have a clear understanding of who I was.

I know what living through the events in my life did to me. It changed me permanently, almost to the point where now I have no interest in letting people into my life. It's just another opportunity for more pain.

My mom doesn't understand me, never has understood me and really doesn't want to. It's too much. And again, I don't knock her for it. She has other kids. My mom dislikes me. She never really liked me.

My parents had no problem letting us kids know that every negative situation existed because of us.

"Mom, I want to go do this."

"Well, we don't have the money to do that because we have more kids than just you and you guys cost money."

My parents had no problem saying those things to us as a kid. So, you get a sense that you're a burden. My parents were struggling with who they were so they got involved in church. This is what I understood growing up.

My dad was very unhappy with his life. He wanted to be someone else. My parents would yell and scream at us to go to church so we'd go to church. My parents became different people at church. As a little kid, around five, with ADHD I was pretty much out of control. I would be bad again, running around the church after the service, playing with my friends and being loud. We'd get home and I'd spend all my time hiding from my dad. I was the only outlet for his anger. A lot of things he had to deal with were taken out on me.

When I was young, the biggest thing I was angry about, was that I was born and I didn't want to be born. I didn't ask to be born. Why the hell can someone make me be here when I don't want to be? That's how miserable my life was as a kid. I was so mad about that. That was my approach to life as a kid. I had this conversation at a very young age, in a very adult fashion. I was a four-year-old.

Me and God still have this out all the time in my head. Why the hell do I have to stick around here if I didn't ask to be here? That's the bare essence of me. You strip me all the way down to the bone, that's the one that I struggle with day to day.

I'm thinking about this when I'm five and six. I'm there already because I got this religion stuff shoved in my head and I'm struggling with it. Then I find my favorite verse in the Bible ever. Paul writes it. I always get it confused–again, ADHD. It's Thessalonians or Corinthians, but he says the greatest line ever. He says, "I despise this world." No, he says basically, "I'm longing to die because I want to go be with God in Heaven." So, here's how far advanced Corey is at a young age and why confusion reigns throughout the rest of his life. If the apostle Paul wanted to die so he could be with God, what was wrong with me wanting the same thing?

• • •

We're sitting around waiting for the call to go to court. We have no idea when that's going to happen. The day shift guards come on duty and do their roll call.

The guy that stayed the night with us gets ready to leave. He gives us a hug and tells us good luck and he will see us on the street. That's a common phrase, *en la calle.* That's what everyone says all the time. *La calle* means "the street." It means anywhere outside the court. *"La calle, mi amigo."* He means he's done his time and he's back on the street.

Our cell is the last place a guy stays before he goes out *en la calle.* Everyone who comes into our cell has a positive outlook on everything because they're getting out. At the same time, they're surprised to see Americans there. They want to talk to us about all kinds of things.

There's coffee waiting for us that morning. A guy is offering us little shot glasses with coffee or espresso. We're wondering what's going on. This is where we start to understand the economic system of a jail in the DR. People have little businesses because the people running the jail don't provide the inmates with decent, edible food. People from the outside bring food in and sell it to the guys that are incarcerated there.

Some guy comes around and a guard actually hands a little shot glass of coffee to me.

I say, "Oh, *gracias,* thank you. *Café?"*

"Sí, café."

On top of no shower, we still haven't eaten anything. Sooner or later, we're going to have to eat. Diego has some rice and Johnnycakes, which are similar to pancakes in size and shape, but are made from corn meal instead of flour for breakfast.

Someone offers us food but we're so nervous about seeing the judge that we're not hungry. We want to get together with Marco and go over everything again, but he's not around. We sit there and wait all morning.

The night guards leave and the day shift guards arrive. Diego has to pay them, too. He's negotiating with each shift. There's a head guy for each shift, a boss. Diego doesn't want to pay the guys below him; he wants to pay the head guy. The guys below the boss don't really count.

The guys below him will ask for some of our soda if we get some Cokes or ask to have a piece of our chicken, something like that. These guys are bottom-feeders. They're always hanging around. They're beggars.

Our relationship with Diego is delicate. We're family now. We have to stick together no matter what. The girl may turn, but we have to stick together. Jeff is furious with Diego for putting us in this situation. As for me, it's already happened. There's nothing we can do about it. We have to work from where we are now.

I'm trying to get Jeff in that mindset, but he's upset about so many things that have happened. Of course, his mom doesn't help the situation. She's still stuck in, "How could this happen?" When Jeff talks to his mom, she's upset and angry, and it keeps Jeff that way, too.

He says stuff like,

"I want to go home. Now. I have a wife and two children. I can't stay here."

"How did this happen? How did we end up in a fucking DR jail?"

"I want to kill Diego. It's all his fault. How do we get rid of him?"

"I can't take this. This is the worst thing I've ever seen. I can't believe how bad it is here."

I don't have answers for him. I tell him, "You don't know how bad things can get or what you'll be willing or not willing to do."

He says, "Man, I can't take a crap on that toilet back there."

"Bro, you should be happy there is a toilet back there and that it has a seat on it," I say.

Or he says, "God, that water is so gross."

"You should be happy that we have water, you know what I'm saying?"

"It can't get any worse than this," he says.

I tell him, "Jeff it can always get worse." He has a real hard time understanding this concept. Even the day-to-day. For him, this is the worst there is. It's the worst thing he's ever seen.

He repeats himself, "It can't get any worse than this, can it?"

I say, "Yeah, it can get worse if we don't get out."

"Well, we have to get out. They already told us we're getting out. You heard the lawyer, right, he said we're getting out," Jeff says.

"Jeff, you can't believe anything anyone says unless it's the judge doing the talking."

Finally, around noon, guards come to take us down to the first level where the courthouse is. They handcuff me and Jeff together, and Diego and the girl, and take us down the stairs. There's a significant crowd of people out there. Mainly, it's the family members of the guys that were arrested with us, but a large number of them are from the girl's neighborhood. She's a really nice girl. Everyone knows her. Her family's there and people in her neighborhood are there, and they are trying to figure out how she ended up in this.

We start seeing a lot of dislike toward Diego for putting the girl in this situation. When they see us, they're like, "What are you guys doing here?" Diego starts getting this shadow cast over him. People are saying, "What are these Americans doing here?"

Someone else tries to explain it, "They were with this driver, and this driver got stopped." The explanation doesn't make sense, though.

"But what was he doing? Where were they? What were they doing on that bridge?"

That comes up again. It's starting to become more and more obvious to everyone who looks at it, that we don't fit the description of criminals. You also see this girl here and there's a lot of concern for her, and then you have Diego. He's the one that looks at fault. There are a lot of angry looks toward Diego as we go down the stairs and into court.

The other inmates try to talk to each other even though they're in handcuffs, so we stop a lot. Their families try to talk to them and there are various lawyers there, I guess. The lawyers are dressed like used car salesmen. They wear suits, but the pants don't match the jacket. They look like low-level ambulance chasers. Marco doesn't look much better. Marco is waiting for us down in the courtyard when we get to the ground floor.

We see the guys we rode with in the dog cage to the courthouse. We all come down to court together and they're like, "Dude, where did these guys hang out?"

They start to understand that we aren't back in the cell area where they are. We have our own area. They've seen us walk around a couple of times. Now everyone wants to be our friends. *"Americano, Americano. Qué pasa?"*

It sets in how important it is to be somebody, whatever that level is. The same guys in the dog cage—that wanted to take my shoes off against my will—now want to be my friend. They use whatever English they know to talk to me. So I say something back in Spanish, *"Bueno, bueno. Sí, sí."* I give them a fist pound and they feel really good about themselves.

They look at their friends and say, "Hey, see? I know the American. He's cool with me. I'm not like the rest of you guys." It's a constant status thing.

Their lot in life is never going to change but they can say they know someone who has a different lot in life. Like I said, the closest thing I can think of is the caste system in India, where you're born into it, and that's who you are, and that's where you stay. It's kind of like that except with a capitalistic flair and American television influencing how they view the world.

We walk across the atrium lobby to a desk where a clerk sits. The court has a Spanish-style tile floor and there are old wooden doors with metal latches you have to play with to get them to open. You come inside and there are old wooden pews on each side with an aisle going down the middle. In front, you have the judge. He sits at this pulpit thing or whatever it's called. There's not a whole lot to it; it's pretty simple.

You're allowed to bring one family member into the court with you. They have to be related to you legally. In the hallway are tons of people who have an interest in the people inside. Diego's father-in-law shows up with more of his family. It's packed outside the courtroom.

The lawyers for the state sit in the front on the left side. The defense lawyers sit in the pews on the right. Family members sit on the left and the guys waiting to see the judge sit on the right. We sit in the back row on the right. The guards all sit in the back. They're there to keep the peace and order.

They bring all of us in, take our handcuffs off, and we sit down on the benches. Diego, the girl, Jeff and me sit together because we're all charged together. This is what's really strange. We never see any other females the entire time in the court process; it's always guys. It really doesn't make sense that she got arrested along with us and that goes back to how messed up the original tax job was.

They never say they found narcotics on any one individual. They say they found them in the vehicle. Not once, in the entire time we go through this, does anyone ever produce any evidence of drugs. They never have a container or plastic bag of any kind with cocaine or any other substance in it. One day Marco shows us a picture of a plastic bag lying on a table with some white stuff in it. There could have been anything in there; it could have been anybody's or someone could have fixed up something to take a photo of.

People say things like, "Well, why did they even arrest you guys? It's not your car; you're a passenger. It's a taxi. Who knows whose it could've been?"

There are no legs for this case to stand on. The police can charge the driver with it but then it's such a low-level crime, he'd bond out and go. They don't understand why the girl is charged and why we're there. There's nothing to be gained by this. This is why the case draws a huge amount of attention. I'd be surprised if the entire city didn't know this case was going on. There are news reporters around all the time.

People stop and stare at me, mainly because of my long hair, I look like a semi-celebrity, Hollywood, type and at Jeff who is huge compared to the average Dominican and obviously an American. And then there's this girl with us and this guy, this older guy, who they say is the driver. Everyone asks about our case

While we sit there, two guys from the U.S. Embassy walk over. One of them is white and the other guy, Chandler, the guy we talked to on the phone, is dark.

"You guys the Americans?"

"Yes, we are."

We have a short meeting with them. They say, "We heard about your case. As representatives of the U.S. Embassy, and you guys being U.S. citizens, we're here to advise you."

I say, "This is what we know that's happened. Everything else is what our driver over there is telling us. We don't know enough Spanish. No one's telling us anything."

He says, "Have they brought anyone to talk to you in English?"

We say, "No, they haven't."

"According to their law, they're supposed to notify you of what you're being charged with in English within forty-eight hours. When did you guys get arrested?"

We tell them it was Wednesday afternoon. We spent Wednesday night, Thursday and Thursday night in custody, so the forty-eight hours expires while we're at court this afternoon. The Embassy tells us they know the charges because they looked it up, but them telling us doesn't count, either.

Chandler says, "They are charging you with drug trafficking." He brought a breakdown of the possible sentences. The sentence for what we're being charged with is one to three years. We look at it, and we're like,

"You have got to be kidding me!" We're in shock.

One to three years is what they have on the paper. It's all based on the amount of drugs the cops say they found. For some reason, during all of the court appearances, the cocaine volume changes; it never stays the same. One person, not four people in a car, has to have above 2.9 grams on them to be charged with trafficking. The first time we hear the amount, it's below 2.9 grams even though they don't show any evidence of it.

Chandler asks us again, "No one's talked to you?"

"No one's talked to us," we tell them over and over again. "We haven't talked to anyone because no one can speak English."

Jeff is still of a different mind-set. He says, "You guys are going to do something, right? Hey, man, we're Americans. No one here speaks English; we don't know what's going on. This guy drove us; he got us into some shit. You guys are going to get us out of this, right?"

He's still thinking U.S. style, like someone's going to come in here and fix this and we're going to get out of here. We're Americans, we didn't do anything wrong. Jeff's really adamant.

I see all this; I inventory all the information. I do very little talking and let Jeff go on and on because I can't stop him. I'm exhausted from trying to explain to him what's going on and that this is not the U.S.

Jeff refuses to accept what the Embassy people tell him, which is essentially, "We can't do anything for you other than observe. If something bad happens to you, or someone tries to extort money from you, you can notify us. Here are our names and numbers. You guys got a phone yet?"

"No, we don't have a phone. We haven't been able to call anyone. You're the only people we've talked to."

Both guys go talk to Marco. They come back and say, "Your lawyer should be getting you guys a cell phone soon so you can let people know what's going on."

Jeff wants to talk to them about anything and everything, but the Embassy guys say they can't do anything else. Jeff isn't getting it. Before they leave, they hand me a sheet of paper with a list of lawyers on it.

In movies and TV shows, the U.S. Embassy steps in when an American is in trouble and negotiates a deal or figures out a way to smuggle the person out of the country. It's all theatrics. In reality, if an American is in trouble with the law in a foreign country all they can do is make sure you aren't being physically abused or extorted for money.

Jeff acts like he doesn't understand this, but really, he simply refuses to believe it. He has his mindset of what he's seen in the movies and, for him, that's reality.

It's too emotionally exhausting for me to manage Jeff and try to get him to understand what's going on. We go back to the same issues again and again. He's never been arrested in his entire life; he's never gone to court in the States, let alone a foreign country. Now he's trying to grasp how another country works.

I have enough experience, and heard enough stories, to understand how it's going to work in other countries. I've been in this kind of situation before. It's not the same system as the U.S. and I know it's money-based.

I'm waiting for the point when someone says, "This is how much it costs for you to get out." We'll pay it and go. I'm waiting for that and I'm getting really annoyed that it's taking so long.

I lean over the girl to talk to Diego and say, "What the fuck's going on? Find out how much we have to pay. Get that dumb-ass lawyer over here, find out who we have to pay and let's give them the money. I want to walk down these stairs, right out the courthouse door, and get the fuck outta here. I got shit to do."

Diego says, "I know, I'm trying to work on it. I don't know what's going on."

I know I have to run the show for the group over the next few days. I need Diego to do Diego stuff. I need Jeff to stay in Jeff's area, and I need to be in control of the group in some way, shape, or form.

I know I'm the smartest one among us; I know I have thought out the best options. I have to figure a way out of this. Right now I need to make sure the girl has her own lawyer. Our lawyer has to give her lawyer some money so he keeps us together. If we split up, there's no chance in hell anyone's getting out. We need a coordinated defense. Marco is supposed to be working on all of that. This is all on the fly. I don't have time to plan anything out; I'm thinking on my feet.

A court official bangs a gavel and calls the court to order. The judge comes out in his robes and stops where he stands when he sees us. Even in the back pew, me and Jeff stick out. He does a double-take. I'm reading body language again. He's a younger guy maybe thirties, forties, light-skin complexion, and he has a look on his face that reads,

"I want to get this thing out of here. I don't want to deal with this."

He sees the commotion it's going to cause and the headache that he's looking at. He briefly makes eye contact with me. He sits down and looks at all this paperwork. Then he goes out, comes back in, goes out, comes back in. There are a large number of lawyers in the courtroom. It's obvious that all of them aren't here for the other guys who showed up for court today. There's obviously something going on.

The people that work as assistants to the judge are younger, college age probably, and one of them comes up and talks to us.

"Are you Americans?"

"Yeah."

He says, "I went to such-and-such college in the States."

"Oh yeah, I've heard of that."

"I'd very much like to go back and finish my education."

I don't want to be impolite, but I say, "We need to get out. What do we do? What do we say?"

"Don't worry, we're going to take care of it," he says. "You guys talk about what you do for a living and what you're doing here as tourists and then you guys should walk right on out."

We should be able to pay and be out by tomorrow morning at the latest. That's my mind-set going in.

I know they're going to call us first and sure enough, they do. We go down to the front, and the four of us sit in the front row.

The guards have to move all these guys out and put them back where we were sitting because there's not enough space in one row for all these lawyers; they take up two rows. It seems like there are two lawyers for every person sitting up here.

The way it goes at this hearing is the District Attorney tells their side of the story; then the people being charged tell their side of the story; and then the lawyers can say whatever they want to about the changes being brought against their clients.

The judge makes eye contact with us. The Embassy guys are sitting in the back of the room. The DA stands up and says we're charged with drug trafficking because they found 2.95 grams of cocaine in the car.

That's the first time it's been over 2.9 grams. The personal level is 2.9. Now that they've decided to raise it to 2.95 grams-five hundredths of a gram-we're in the drug trafficking category. And now, the DA says there was also marijuana in the car. This is the first time we're hearing this. They're making stuff up as they go along.

Everything's in Spanish. Diego gets up first and starts talking. He's a crowd pleaser, so the first thing he says is, "Your Honor, this girl has nothing to do with anything that's happening here today."

Then he starts with his story about how the police officers arrested us when we came across the bridge, and the DA says, "No, they were arrested in this ghetto, 'hood area."

"No, they arrested us on the bridge," Diego says.

Of course, we don't know any of this until after because right now, everything's going on in Spanish.

Diego says, "I had a run-in with these police before. They were trying to extort money from us. I travel around with tourists, showing them the city. This girl needed a ride back to her neighborhood. This is where she lives. No one up here has a criminal record. We're not involved with anything of this nature."

Diego is using the girl as the reason why we were on the bridge. He says she lives in that bad neighborhood where he left us in the car. This is an outright lie. He told us she saw us when we visited his father-in-law's neighborhood. Diego lives a couple of blocks away from his father-in-law. Her neighborhood isn't anywhere near that bad one. No one calls him on it.

The judge is like, okay, nodding his head. Then it gets to the girl.

She says her piece and it kind of reaffirms Diego's story about what happened across the bridge. They pulled us out of the car and then they put us back in. They said they found drugs. We never saw any drugs; we don't even know what they're talking about.

The cop that said he found drugs in the car isn't in the courtroom. He never shows up to give any evidence.

The judge says, "Okay, okay."

Then he gets to us, we're supposed to tell our side but, oops, we don't know any Spanish. Diego starts translating for Jeff because he has to tell the judge what he's saying.

The judge says, "Hold it. You guys don't know any Spanish at all?"

And Diego says, "No."

The judge says, "We can't even do the court proceeding then. They need a certified translator to tell them what's going on in these court proceedings."

When Diego tells us that, we turn around and look at our great lawyer. "How the hell did you screw this up?"

It turns out that Marco doesn't know anything. We find out later that what it takes to be a lawyer in this country is pathetic. It's less than an associate's degree in a local community college in the States.

The Embassy guys can't translate for us. It has to be a court-appointed certified translator. The judge says, "We're going to postpone your case until Monday morning."

We're like, "Damn it!"

We look at Marco and we're pissed. "How did you mess this up?"

Diego's pissed at Marco; he's letting him have it.

Then this huge commotion erupts between all the lawyers, and the family members are upset and all these other people in the courtroom. Now the judge has chaos on his hands.

People are upset, "Why is this happening? This is a bullshit case. Why are these people even being charged to begin with?"

The judge is trying to continue with this proceeding, and he can't talk over all the commotion that's going on. The guards can't do anything except to ask the crowd to be quiet. *"Por favor, Shhh."* That isn't working. People keep on talking. Finally, the judge excuses us because he still has to hear all of these other cases.

We get out in the hallway and there's a huge, loud commotion there, too. By now, they can't even hear inside the courtroom because of all this noise going on. There are even more people out here than when we went into the courtroom. They are yelling, too. We go back and forth with Marco and everyone's family.

"What the hell's going on?" the families keep saying.

Someone says, "Why are these Americans still here?" They listen to Diego and Marco to hear what happened, but it doesn't make sense—even to the locals.

If you're a local on your way to a club, cocaine use is as common as alcohol. It's there. They don't view it as necessarily a bad thing. With that amount it's obvious the person doesn't want to sell it or distribute it.

The cop who said he found cocaine in the car, but never showed it to anyone, said it was 2.9 grams. Along with this mysterious cocaine he says he found but no one ever sees, he must have had a mysterious scale, too, to weigh it.

Then, according to Dominican Republic law, when you find drugs in a group, like at a party or in a car, you have to divide that amount by the number of people there. When you do that, there isn't enough to charge anyone with anything. The people in the court who hear the number of grams are confused. Every time we go to court the amount of the drug changes, but it never goes above 2.95 grams.

Jeff and I never saw any drugs of any kind in the car. There was no cocaine in front of my feet. Jeff and I don't use drugs. We drink beer but we don't do any kind of drugs—not even pot.

If there was any cocaine in the car, Diego is the only one who could have had it. If he picked up cocaine at some point in the day, we didn't know about it, and if that's the case, he should've been handling it himself. The girl and Jeff and me, have nothing to do with it. And it's not even a misdemeanor offense; Diego would pay and go.

This isn't drug trafficking. They know what drug trafficking is. They see it every day, guys with kilos in their trunk. I'm pissed at Diego, I'm telling him what to do and what to say to Marco, and Diego's all over him. I don't get emotional in a crisis, but people know when I'm not happy with what's going on. I speak very directly, very specifically.

I tell Diego, "Let him know that I don't expect this kind of screw up from him. What are we paying him for? If he doesn't think he can handle this, he needs to let us know right now so we can go find someone who can handle this. Bring him over here. Let's have this discussion right now."

I talk in a low voice, it's very direct, it's without emotion and there's a cold-heartedness about it. This is a serious matter, so we're going to handle it as such. I don't raise my voice or yell or scream or anything like that. I'm not getting hysterical like everyone around me is.

Diego gets all fired up when he talks. When I talk, they can read my body language and the tone I use. Then Diego regurgitates my words, and it has a huge effect because they can tell I'm saying something very important.

I pick up on body language; pick up the looks on people's faces. Everyone involved is confused. When the first District Attorney read the charges, she didn't read them with the kind of confidence we hear later when a different District Attorney reads them. She didn't go into detail.

The opportunity for victory was in front of us, I believe, at that point in time. If we had had the translator there, we would have walked. There wasn't a whole lot in the case that had been embellished at that point in time.

Now we're standing there, trying to absorb the fact that we will be locked up over the weekend.

Jeff says, "What if we don't get off on Monday? Then what?" He's crying.

Some of the guards say, "No, no, no. You guys are going to get out. No problem. Monday you guys are walking out of here."

Other guards are shaking their heads. There's so much confusion and it's so loud that they take us back upstairs. They tell the guards that stayed upstairs to watch the other prisoners what happened.

We're on the platform on the third floor. They take our handcuffs off. It seems like the whole neighborhood wants to get up here and talk to us and I'm thinking, uh-oh, we're making extra work for the guards. The guards try to let the lawyers through and the few people they think are family.

I get a phone and try to reach my parents again. My mom happens to be home and she answers the phone. I'm very straight forward, very calm and matter of fact.

I start out with, "Mom, this is Corey. I need you to write some stuff down." I'm thinking my mom knows the basics of what's happened. Because Thursday's message on their old tape answering machine was undecipherable, my mom is hearing that I'm in the DR for the first time and she's upset and confused.

She says, "What do you mean? You're where?"

I tell her three or four times, "I'm in the Dominican Republic."

"Why are you there?"

"That's not important right now," I say. "I need you to write down this information." My mom is in a panic. I've been in trouble before but nothing like this. We're not making much progress with her writing down the phone numbers. It's too much for her. I try to give her the lawyer's phone number.

"Here's the lawyer's number," I say, again. "Write it down."

I also try to give her Connor's number because he's getting me some money. It's too much for her and we have a limited time that we can talk. While I'm on the phone, the guards tell us we can't stay there because the other guys are coming back from court. The guards are upset because of the chaos. I tell my mom I have to go and repeat the phone number for them to call me. I hang up not knowing if she got everything–or anything–right.

I talk to my dad that afternoon and say, "We have to get off Monday morning when we go to court or it's going to be really bad. We also need to keep a low profile. No media. Don't get any political stuff involved. Americans are seen as walking ATM's. The more attention we get for our case, the more of a payout people will expect."

I also tell my dad we have to get some networking on the street. We need someone to make moves for us. I tell him this repeatedly throughout this ordeal but it never happens. I don't know if I'm not explaining it clearly enough or if he can't grasp the concept. My dad's a really smart guy but for some reason this goes nowhere.

I say, "We need a better attorney here than we've got, but getting someone from the U.S. involved is not going to help. Diego's family has all of our stuff including our passports. I'll have to figure out a way to get it all back."

My dad says he called the U.S. Embassy and talked to Chandler. Later on, when my dad and Jeff's mom try to get a recommendation for a lawyer, there's an important message Chandler tries to give them that they don't catch. He says he can't give them a recommendation, but they maintain a list of lawyers. The hidden message is, "The lawyer you have now is not on our list. We can't recommend a lawyer to you, but listen! You should get one that is on our list." Neither of them catches that at the time. Chandler gave me the same list but I didn't catch it right away either.

We are supposed to be out by now. We were going to be hitting the street. Everyone was full of confidence about that, but it didn't happen. Now we have to wait for this court-appointed translator. We're going to be here all weekend.

I'm taking it all in. There's a song I heard once. There's a line in there... the guy says, "I finally shut my mouth so I could hear myself think."

I don't know why I remember that line. It sticks with me. So what I do when this type of situation is going on is I say very little. Mainly because I'm a calculated thinker to begin with, and now everything I say is very, very important. I'd better be very careful what I say and how I say it. Unlike Jeff, I trust no one in the situation. I haven't up to this point and I still don't.

There's a naïve-ness about Jeff. He trusts Marco and what people say to him. He's an open audience and this becomes a reoccurring problem later. He wants to hear what people have to say and he wants to believe that and not question it. I am the complete opposite. I size up everyone now. I had a little bit of expectation that this was going to be resolved, but I had already considered the other side.

It's frustrating but this is what I come to accept, what I come to understand. I watch people's behavior, see what they do, listen to what everyone has to say. This goes back to what I do for a living. When something goes wrong at work I ask myself, "What is the worst thing that can happen and the best thing that can happen?"

The worst thing that can happen is that they work the girl over during the weekend and get her to roll on us and corroborate the District Attorney's story so she can get out. Or, maybe, Diego rolls on us. He can say it was the Americans and we might be stuck here. Diego could walk out of here this weekend leaving us behind. Are we going to get extorted by the guards? What is this lawyer going to do? Is he going to take our money and run?

All of these possibilities run through my head. Now, I have to start playing chess and I'm so far behind in the game it's not even funny.

While we're standing on the platform, I switch over. I stop the emotions I'm feeling. I can't have an emotional reaction to everything going on. I have to think. I have to figure a way out of this. I'm thinking, thinking, thinking trying to get my brain to go as fast as it can.

Now I'll use a skill I have that no one else has as far as I know. I haven't had to do this in a long time, and I've never done it when my life depended on it. I figured this out when I was younger and trying to find a way to live with ADHD. I learned how to file pieces of information in the back of my brain and then pull out exactly what I need when I need it. I'm going to out think everyone. I have to get to a point where I know what everyone is going to say before they say it.

Now I'm taking inventory and storing it in that file. Here's the way this thing works:

I study the guards. Which guard does what? This guard takes the handcuffs on and off, that guard acts like he's not sure about what he's doing. Is he new? Could he be bribed? When Diego gets excited, Jeff gets excited, too, and not always in a good way. Diego is bragging to the guards but that guard looks like he thinks Diego's a piece of shit. If something goes down with Diego, he might be a resource. The handcuff guard can't get enough of whatever Diego is dishing out. Marco is talking to another lawyer and he's smiling. What does he have to smile about? I want to wipe that smile off his face with my fist. I save that for another time. I don't like the bald black inmate because he's trying to be friends with Diego. I study his body language to get a feel for what he's trying to get. I need to test this theory I have about the best way to get a guard to do what I want him to do, to see if I am right about this.

This goes on and on and this file is getting bigger and bigger. The critical thing is that I can retrieve the information when I need it.

I look over at Jeff and see him clinging to every word that everyone is saying. Jeff never really ever gets it.

He asks Marco, "How do you feel about our case?"

Jeff wants him to say, "Yeah, I think you guys are great and I'll get you out of here."

That's useless information, but he needs to hear it for reassurance. He needs to hear it from his mother and his wife. He needs that constantly. I'm not giving it to him because I'm thinking worst–case scenario already.

He gets upset with me, he gets mad at me, and he says, "Why do you have to be so negative all the time about everything?"

That's his response because he's still living off of emotions. He lives in an emotional world. He communicates with his wife. They talk about everything. They talk about how they feel. I don't live in an emotional world and I can get where I need to go a lot quicker. He's lagging way behind. It's a concern for me but at the same time I can't do much about it.

I try to do the tough love thing. I try to be a jerk to him and see how far that goes. But, at the same time, there are situations where I appreciate that he can keep a positive attitude because I can't. He has what I don't–I could never be that person no matter how much I tried.

He can become what I am. It takes a bunch of bad things happening to you. He can become me, but I can never be him. In my mind, I don't want him to become like me, I want him to be a zombie if he can. I want him to say nothing and do nothing and just stand there. It's not fair to say this, but I'm trying to figure out a way to frame him up in a box. How do I get him to not say too much?

At the same time, we're in this together, and that's the bottom line. What's funny, Jeff and I didn't really know each other that well before this. We worked with each other, but I can't say anything negative about him as a person. The situation is very, very difficult and very hard to handle. It's something very new for him.

He did a good job of handling this situation for someone who has never been down that road before. He comes from a close family, and in the world that he knows, this is as foreign to him as the moon. The biggest thing he has the entire time we are in the DR is an extensive communication with his side of the family. He's always on the phone and he needs that.

I'm not making too many phone calls. I'm not getting on the phone unless I have information that I know is true, not what I think I know. I can repeat what Diego says to me but I'm only going to act on whatever I absolutely know is true and what I think is really going to happen.

I don't think my family's too worried for the most part. They're worried they may never see me again. This is their biggest concern. I don't think they're too concerned about whether or not I'll be able to handle the situation.

My death at a very young age was a real possibility that my family had to deal with for a very long time. I've usually been able to keep my life in order and do the risk taking simultaneously. The thing that I tried to do over time is to make sure that my self–destructive behavior was only going to affect me and not everyone else around me. Because of this experience in the Dominican Republic, I have a huge amount of guilt about how unfair it was for me to put my family through this. It's very selfish of me to continue putting my family through stuff like this.

They care about me more than I care about myself and that's the story of my life. Throughout this experience, my personal situation was never my concern, ever. My greatest concern was how upset I was making my family. I felt so bad. Here we go again. I wasn't supposed to do this to my family anymore.

So the idea was that no one will be caught up in this situation; everything will be okay and I'll be able to handle it. I was thinking we would get out in a day or two and by the time everyone finds out about it, they can call me up and I can tell them what happened. That is what I was hoping. Now it has gone too far. Now everyone knows about it. They know I'm not safe and I'm still in a bad spot.

We realize that we're going to be stuck in this place. There is nothing we can do between now and Monday. So we're trying to make the best of it. Connor sent the money, so we have funds available for now. Diego is in his element. He has money. He's making moves on our behalf. He's somebody.

He says, "Anything we need we can get. You name it. I got all the guards taken care of. We've paid everyone."

People are coming back to visit us. The whole building complex knows that these American guys are there and all of the different guards working in the different areas of the complex want to come and meet us. At the same time, Diego is telling Marco to get him a phone.

We come back to our cell after our court date and there's a white kid sitting in our area. I'm thinking, "What the hell is this white kid doing here?" He looks like a stateside kid and he's looking at us and we're looking at him and he says,

"*Americano*?"

I say, "American? Yes, and you?"

He shakes his head. "Dominican."

Jeff says, "How are you?" in Spanish. He's picking up words here and there.

"How are you?"

"I am good."

This kid looks totally American, a younger guy like 21– or 22–years–old. This is our guest for the night. I can tell that he wants to talk to us so I start doing some things with him. He comes over and sits with us. He just got done doing 30 days. He got busted with a bunch of cocaine and Ecstasy on him. He was loaded up on cocaine and riding his moped around and the police stopped him. He was high and out of control.

I can tell by looking at him that he's pretty sharp. He's whiter than me. He's working on his English plus he's caught up on American customs... you get this from the younger crowd. They have TV and stuff like that. This is where we start to understand that people who live in the DR are every color and skin tone that you can imagine.

He's the one who first says I look like Nicolas Cage from the movie *"Con Air."* He says, "I like him. Very good actor."

The guy speaks pretty good English in certain areas and we're talking. He's about my height or so, a little bit smaller, and he's like everyone else, the first thing they notice is how strong I am and he wants to know,

"How many pushups can you do?"

People are constantly asking me this. They ask me how much I weigh, how much can I lift? And I have to figure it out in kilos. I have to convert pounds to kilos, back and forth, and stuff like that, but I have plenty of time.

That evening, one of the inmates says I look like Nicolas Cage and it gets back to the other side of the jail where the animals are. Someone says, "Oh, he's... I told you I know him!" And so it goes, on and on, and eventually I'm going to fly a plane to Vegas because I look like Nicholas Cage.

We're using Spanish, talking back and forth, and Diego starts to fill in the gaps. He's trying to be Mr. Translator. What I find out is that the guys I talk to would rather try to do their best in English while I try to do my best in Spanish instead of using Diego to translate. That helps both of us. We start to understand each other and we can kind of communicate through words that we both know and using body language.

Me and this kid spend a lot of time together and we start making jokes about Jeff because he's funny and the stuff that he says. People ask me,

"Why is he that way? What's wrong with him?"

They're asking because he's not doing anything. He's just lying there. He's sleeping. Or he's asking me to ask the kid questions about whatever.

I say, "Damn, Jeff, I'm trying. Like what do you want me to ask him? What do you want me to do, man? Help me out."

Jeff asks me to ask really vague questions that I can't even do in Spanish because they are so open-ended, like, "What do you think about..." and even when I ask this kid, he's confused.

There's not much we can do but wait and try to make the best of it. We're stuck here for three days. Diego is starting to hustle and do whatever he can.

A long time ago I figured out the key to life. The key to life is to not get too happy during happy times, or too sad during sad times. Try to stay in the middle. If you're too happy during happy times, if one little thing goes wrong you can't handle it. If you get too sad in sad times it means the end of the world.

I'm trying to get on an even keel with the emotional stuff. I have it bottled up, but the anxiety is still rolling around, high–low, high–low. Now I'm here and now I'm not. I'm okay with the highs and lows but this is still a bad situation. Who knows how long we're going to be here?

Jeff needs to talk to his wife and family. He's on an emotional roller coaster. It's like being in here with a girl. I call him that later on. He's all emotional. Everything flusters him. He becomes a burden from that side of it, and he and Diego are constantly going at each other.

Jeff says, "I don't understand why this is happening."

I reply, "Because it is. We're in a different country, you know?"

We start to think. We can get anything we want around here because we have money. And we got the guards all lubed up so we can walk around anywhere we want in the entire area. Free reign anytime we want to walk out there and see the guards up front, talk to other people if we want to. People are coming and going. We walk back where the animals are kept and everyone wants to be our friend because we have money and we're somebody.

Diego loves this. He's finally going to be somebody. "Yeah, I'm with the Americans and the Americans are with me. I represent them."

The whole time I'm giving him plenty of tasks to do so he'll leave me alone. I get a control mechanism in place where he has to be respectful when he addresses me. The other thing I do is keep him away from Jeff.

I don't want any emotion. I want to be able to think. I'm running things through my head, random stuff that me and Jeff talk about.

I tell him, "All right, Diego, you can't go to Jeff with anything. You come to me first. If I don't want to handle it. I'll go back to Jeff."

Now that we know we're going to be here all weekend, it's time to eat something. We're hungry and this is the first time that we're going to eat in more than 48 hours. Our last meal was lunch at the Hard Rock café on Wednesday.

Diego says, "Corey, may I have a moment of your time?"

"Okay, what do you want to talk about?"

"We can get these guys to go get us something to eat. What would you like us to get?"

"Well, I really don't want to eat rice and beans. How much are they going charge us for it?"

Diego says, "I don't know."

"Well, go see and come back. Get two guards and bid them against each other and figure out who will get us drinks and food cheaper, because if we keep using one, it doesn't give the other one an opportunity."

"I like the way you think. That's what I'm saying. Corey, I like you man. When this is over, man, we're going to be friends for a long time."

I say, "Yeah, man, we will." Inside, I'm thinking, "No way in hell."

The first thing I want is more bottled water. We need that and we need sugar for our blood. I know we're going to be dehydrated from the amount of time we're going to spend in the bathroom. It's just a matter of time before we get sick in this environment. We won't stay well much longer. I know we'll be sick right after we eat that first meal.

We get water, Coke, Gatorade, anything in a bottle, to drink. We ration it out as we go because guys are constantly coming to us and begging for water and food. I'm pissed with Jeff about this because he smokes a cigarette and then complains that he's thirsty.

"Well, yeah, you smoked a cigarette and now you're thirsty, Jeff. What the hell?

"Well I wasn't thirsty before!"

Sometimes I shake my head and walk away. There's no use trying to get him to understand anything.

They bring us really, really, good fried chicken. The best I think I've ever had. I don't know how they make it but it's great. We also have rice and beans and some drinks. Everything has to come in a bottle for us–none of the bad water. 'Water' means bad water over there.

The guys who work for Marco, the go–fers, can only get us stuff until 10 or 11 at night. After that, the guards have to go get us stuff.

Jeff constantly says, "Cigarettes, cigarettes. Have you got any cigarettes?" Jeff turns into "Puff the Magic Dragon." He smokes nonstop once he gets cigarettes. He's constantly puffing away.

Diego has that "I'm somebody" attitude around the guards and inmates, but I make sure he knows who he's talking to every time he talks to me. I make sure that I keep him in check and make sure he respects me.

"All right, man, stop right now," I say. "If you are going to talk to me, this is how you're going to talk to me." Then I explain the ground rules.

"I am so sorry. Corey, may I have a moment of your time?" Diego says, very formally.

"Yes, okay, what do you want to talk about?"

"Corey, you are absolutely correct. I am so sorry. That is what I like about you, man. If it was you and me, man, we'd be running this whole place. Jeff isn't like you. I can't deal with him."

I say, "Jeff is Jeff."

"You are right. I am sorry."

I'm constantly doing that with Diego.

While we eat I say to him, "I made a decision. Either you talk to me or you eat, but you can't do both because I'm tired of your food landing on me."

"Diego says, "Well, excuuussse me!"

I say, "You are excused. Now go sit over there."

Diego is such a drama queen. "Oh! So it's really that bad!"

"Yeah, it's exactly that bad. You can eat or you can talk to me. We're not doing both. You understand? You decide right now if you want to talk or eat."

When it comes to talking, Jeff does this thing, too. He says what's on his mind without thinking about what he's saying. I look at him like, "What the fu–? Why are you even saying that to me, man?"

It's Friday night, and we're trying to figure out how to keep ourselves entertained. The kid sitting with us says, "Cards, Hearts."

I tell Diego to go get us cards and some pen and paper and stuff like that so we can write stuff down. He's working on getting us a phone.

We want to play cards with the kid so we try to think of a game that we can all play together despite the language barrier. We play three of a kind and two of a kind; we're just trying to pass time. This kid is super friendly. He likes hanging out with us. We have food and drinks coming in and he gets to hang out with some Americans.

We start to get a sense that people want to be around us. Guys are constantly coming into our area and begging for stuff. If we get some food and don't want all of it, we don't throw it away, we send it down to the animals on the other end. These guys, the animals, want to get to know us. They want to be our friends.

"Hey, can you ask the Americans to come see us? The strong American."

Now that they know we have money and stuff, they want to have a pushup contest to see how strong I am.

They say, "Oh, no, the American, he's *fuertes*–strong, stronger than any of us."

Diego is going around making up stories about us.

They say, "What's up with those two guys?"

"The guy with the long hair–the strong guy. His hands are registered. He can't hit you. He's a registered killer," Diego says, feeding them all this stuff.

"Yeah, man he looks like it," they say.

"You're lucky he didn't come in with you guys because if he did I couldn't help you."

"You mean?"

"Yeah, I'm protecting you from him."

In this way, Diego serves a great purpose. They ask him about Jeff and he says, "Oh, that guy. He lives in the woods and eats bushes and wild animals. We call him *"el oso."* (Spanish for bear.)

"That's why he looks like that?"

"Yeah, he sleeps all the time, man. Like a bear. He lives in the woods in the wild. He lives with bears.

"Really?"

"Yeah. He's a crazy mountain guy," Diego says. "He'll eat meat without even cooking it, you know, chew it right off the dead animal."

"Nooo..." they say.

"Really, yeah, he's crazy. What are they doing here? You don't even want to know about these guys. You'd better stay away."

"Why are you with them?"

"I'm here to work for them, man. That's all I do."

This is what Diego is doing the whole time and the guards are loving it because Diego is getting these guys to calm down. The animals are screaming one night and we're trying to sleep, so Diego yells for the syndicate dude, the trustee, and says, "You go down there and tell them to stop screaming."

The syndicate guy goes back there and tells them that. He says, "Hey, man, whoever is in here screaming, you need to be quiet because you're pissing off the Americans and they're already offering 100 pesos to anyone who makes you shut up."

The one who's screaming shuts up. Then he points at another guy and says, "Hey! You tell the Americans I'll cut him right now. I have a knife. How much money for that?" This is happening because those inmates have nothing. They'll do anything to get some money. He'll cut someone who isn't even screaming just for the money.

We talk a little before we go to bed Friday night. We're trying to make the best of it. I'm not feeling a lot of anxiety right now, because I know that we're not going to court for another two days.

SUSAN L STEWART

Saturday, June 20

Saturday morning Jeff and I are hanging out having a little breakfast but our stomachs hurt all ready. I talk to Jeff about this. I say, "Dude, here it comes. We can't avoid it. We have to keep eating no matter how painful it gets. We're going to get sick. This is the way it works." So we deal with it, accept it.

From my medical training I know we have to keep drinking sugar as much as we can and keep drinking bottled water. The sugar is for the electrolytes. As you get dehydrated, you're losing them. You need the sugars because your body can sustain itself off of sugars. Simple sugars are basically carbohydrates. That's all that Gatorade and soda are. You need that sugar to keep pumping through you. I explain that to Jeff.

Marco shows up that morning and now we have a phone. I talk to my dad. I give him all of my account information. I don't have a problem remembering it because I have a couple of phrases that I use for everything. If, and when, we get out, and we get our possessions back, I can make moves quicker if I still have my ID's and everything activated. Now my dad can monitor my accounts to see if any activity pops up. If that happens, I'll shut everything down and start over. If we get out on Monday, I need a way to get money to get out of the country.

Jeff and I start running through every possibility we can think of to get out of here. Jeff has a pilot's license so if we can steal a small plane he can fly us out. We could charter a boat; Jeff takes boats out all of the time. Jeff's father had some really high-powered boats. He's convinced if we can get outside this building, we can get to Puerto Rico, no problem. Once we get to Puerto Rico we're good. All we have to do is get out.

Once we get out, we get a boat and BAM! When we get close to Puerto Rico, we can stop by U.S. Customs, show our passports–or even if we don't have our passports–show them who we are. When they figure out we're Americans and we get to Puerto Rico, we're safe. We're out of the game. Coming up with exit strategies keeps our minds occupied. It puts Jeff in the right state of mind.

When the U.S. Embassy met with us on Friday, they handed us a piece of paper. It has a list of lawyers on it and the first one on the list, in real bold letters, is the lawyer that we end up going with later. Right now, it's a touchy, delicate, situation that I'm trying to manage. Can we get away from Marco? How are we going to get out of this? We're stuck with Diego and we have to ride that out.

After what happened in court on Friday we have our first sense that Marco can't handle this. Marco stopped by Friday night on his way out to a club and he's wearing a tight black shirt that has skulls on it that are flaming and some jeans and some glittery cowboy boots.

I'm looking at him. He's a young person. It's a cultural thing but it doesn't instill confidence. The hearing is scheduled for Monday. Now comes the chess game that I have to start playing. We have the information in front of us about what we're charged with and the Embassy is quietly recommending that we not do what we're doing right now which is using Marco as our lawyer.

I talk to Jeff. I'm trying to get Jeff to go through his mother to contact an alternative lawyer. I'm trying to figure out how we can get this ball started without jeopardizing what we have right now, because right now we're in the best situation we've been in the entire time. Food. Drink. Everything we want. How do we improve what we have without jeopardizing what we have already?

I have this business philosophy. I talk about it with people a lot and it applies to life as well.

In life you have what I call your guaranteed money and when I say guaranteed money, I mean you have a steady income, that's your guaranteed money. But everybody wants to get more money in life, right? I tell people all the time that the worst thing you can do is to risk your guaranteed money going after more money and then lose it all. You need to separate those two things if you're going to pursue them.

I have a different way of applying this in life. In my mind, we have our guarantee, Marco, right now. Now let's start pursuing other options. Diego is working every connection he has. We have a lot of people interested in our case right now. We're developing relationships with them daily, networking with other lawyers through Diego.

I tell him I don't want to be in a position where we only have alternative A. I want to have A, B, C and D and this is how we're going to go. I'm thinking this way like I do at work. I'm talking to Diego about this. I'm giving him little assignments and he's eating it up. He's enjoying that. While Diego is off doing stuff, I have a conversation with Jeff.

"How in the hell are we going to get out of this problem with Diego?" Jeff asks.

"When it comes down to it we'll figure it out. Yeah, I know he screwed us over and he got us in this bad spot. I hate him as much as you do, bro, but you have to keep your enemies close."

Jeff is listening to this but it's not really sinking in. Later on he understands this really, really well, but I'm there already and I'm trying to get him there but he's still having a difficult time with it.

He says, "I don't like talking about this. I'm going to lie down."

Diego's ex-wife comes to meets us, and introduces us to other people in the family. All of our stuff is at her house. She assures us that there is nothing to worry about. Now that she has it, no one is going to get it from the hotel room.

She has our passports there, too. This is very huge and we make a real nice family bond here. They are going to make sure that nothing happens to any of our stuff. If our passports had been on us when we got arrested, we never could have gotten out of the country. Our passports are all that we need to get out via the legal system or the non-legal system.

They ask us what we want them to bring. "What do you want out of your bags? We'll bring anything you like."

I don't remember how I have my bag set up, so I say bring me my razor and some clothes. They're going to bring stuff to us from Jeff's bag and stuff for Diego, too. So they go off and do that.

After the family leaves, I talk to Diego and say, "Let's work a deal here with these guards. Who knows that we're really here? They don't have our passports. If there is a way to walk out of here, we grab those passports and we're gone. Who are they going to look for? They don't know who to look for. They're not going to stop us." Unfortunately, this plan goes nowhere.

The head guard comes up to me and says, "You guys need to take a shower. You really need to." It's been four days and we stink. When the family comes back with our clean clothes, me and Jeff take showers and get cleaned up. It feels good to get the grime off my body.

Marco has four grand. He has the two thousand dollars that my buddy, Connor, gets to him and Jeff's family sends him two thousand dollars. Four grand is huge money down there—more than enough to make sure we get anything we want, anytime we want it, to get us out of here, and cover our bail if we need bail. He'll still walk away with a nice bit of change.

At this point, the image of jail really isn't jail anymore. Now that we've lubricated the wheels with all the guards and everyone has their money, we have free reign. Marco's guys are bringing us lunch and drinks. They are good at bringing in food and whatever else we need. Toilet paper, pen and paper, cards, whatever we want.

Marco's goal is to keep us happy and he understands that. Diego will let him know if I get upset. He's is constantly talking all of the time–blah, blah, blah. Diego is very smart on his end, too. He builds me up into something bigger than himself. I don't say much and I don't do much, but when I want something done, I'll say it to him in front of other people. I'll say it to him in a very cold–hearted, no emotions way.

"Make sure I don't see this guy back in my cell ever again." Whoever it is, the guard or trustee, that annoyed me and pissed me off. "You let him know. I don't want to see him ever back here in my presence. You tell him right now, Diego."

He tells this guy, "Do you understand? Look at him. Does he look happy to you?" and then this guy's boss's boss would say, "Hey! You get the hell out of here."

They would yell at him, kick him, whatever it was. I never went around being abusive. If someone really pissed me off and wouldn't leave me alone after I told him to, I tell his boss, in the best Spanish I can, "If I see this guy again, that's it man. Is there another place we can stay in here? Maybe we need to go to another jail."

"No, no, no, no, we don't want you to leave!"

We're the cash machine and entertainment. People say, "Look what we have. The Americans." Everyone wants to come up and visit us and the guards get this prestige about them.

"Can we see the Americans?"

"I don't know. Let me go see."

"My friend wants to meet you. I would like to introduce you."

I say, "Okay, let's go ahead," and I'll shake his hand.

I say, "Hello. How are you?"

"Hello, nice to meet you. This is my wife. She worked in the States before," he says.

She speaks a little bit of English and his kids are there and they know a little English that they've learned from watching TV and music and stuff like that. I'm very friendly and acknowledge them. They appreciate that and that goes a thousand miles.

Throughout our time in jail, we get more and more stuff until we have a stockpile of it in our little living area. Everyone sees it and they want it, so now it's like the stash game and we have to hide our drinks underneath our little bedding area and put the food underneath the bottom where it's dark and no one can see it.

People want to use the cell phone chargers and they want to use our phone. We don't want to be total jerks and not let them use it at all, but we want to stay in control of it, too. I'm discussing with Diego how to manage that appropriately. Diego and Jeff are constantly at war over the phone, which is common in a regular jail. I tell my dad to give the phone number to anyone who wants to call me.

Most people know me enough to know what to expect if they do call me. I'm not going to get a whole lot of phone calls during the course of the day, but if I do, you better get off because for someone to call me it's fairly important. They understand the importance because of my family involvement. I don't think any of my friends call that day because my Dad hasn't given out my phone number a lot.

I talk to Connor and give him an update of what's going on. Connor is a real cool customer. The people I select to contact me are those who will know how to handle the situation. They know how I am. Many of these people have known me for a long period of time and have had experiences with me. They know what is useful to do and what is useless. I never really cared how I felt and I don't want other people to care how I feel.

I say, "This is what's going on. If you can help me out with a few things, I'd appreciate it."

We hang out there all day Saturday and it's miserably boring. We're becoming more and more popular. Inmates and guards come to see us. We get more comfortable walking around. Other prisoners get to walk around, too, but not in our area. We start talking to them. This is where we meet Geraldo.

Geraldo is this short fat guy. I'd say he's about my height, 5' 10" or so, and probably weighs about 270. I don't even know how he walks and moves around. He's always smiling and saying, "How are you, my friend?" "My friend" is the English that he knows. I'm talking to him in the hallway. They're painting it and I'm working on my Spanish.

I say, *"Azul y amarillo, sí?"*

"Sí, sí, pero esta..."

They are painting it blue and yellow, but then he gives me the specific color names in Spanish. It's light baby blue and a different kind of yellow. I don't know enough Spanish to understand that so I don't say anything. The less I say, the more powerful it is when I do say something in Spanish.

Geraldo's wife and family are there. His wife speaks a little bit of English and they say hello. The roommate we had last night leaves on Saturday and Geraldo moves in.

Geraldo's story is that he's going back to La Victoria prison where he used to work, but now he's going to be a prisoner, not a guard. La Victoria is supposed to be a lot worse than Najayo, the prison we end up in. He tells us that drugs in the prison are readily available and a bunch of kids were hopped up on pills. They were fighting and it got out of control and Geraldo shot and killed one of the kids. This is what he said.

Who knows what exactly happened? From my experience in Najayo, the guards don't carry guns. There is only one place where you see guns and that's on the perimeter fence. Those guys carry firearms but you usually don't see them there much, either. They're not in a hurry to shoot at all, period.

My guess is that his story isn't exactly true. My guess is that he probably took money to kill someone because later, when we go to prison, the guards say for 3,000 pesos I can have anyone taken care of. Anyone that gives us problems.

Geraldo's studying English and his whole thing is he hates the Dominican Republic. It's corrupt and the police are corrupt. He really despises the country. He's hoping to go to Puerto Rico to get a job there and that's why he's trying to learn English. He doesn't want his family to be in the DR. The schools are bad and there are no opportunities, there are no jobs and he wants a regular job. So that's Geraldo.

I call him Buddha. He looks like the Buddha. He's a big guy, fat belly, and he's always laughing, "Hee, hee, hee."

He says, "My friend, my friend, ha–ha–ha–ha." He laughs like that.

"Oh, mi amigo!" and whatever he says to me in English, I say back to him in Spanish and he loves that.

We walk around together and he introduces me to some of the guys that are locked up and some of the animals. They see me with Diego all the time. Now I'm with Geraldo so the inmates are like,

"Whoa man, this American guy, he's connected."

Whatever English they can say, they say to me and I acknowledge it and say it back to them in Spanish. Acknowledgement is what they really want out of it and, of course, everyone asks for money all the time. Food. Whatever. It's the culture.

During the day all of these guards are coming in and out of our area. The funniest thing is seeing these guards that look like young kids, maybe fourteen or fifteen years old. They're probably older than that. They come in and sit down next to us, propping their pump shotguns against our beds with the barrel pointing down and talk and hang out. Any minute someone could pick it up and start blasting. The guards come in to use the shower. They take off all of their stuff, including their guns, and their clothes. We could put on a uniform and walk out the gate.

We talk to Diego about trying to escape and he says,

"There's nowhere to hide here, man. Everyone knows who you are. There is no place to hide. We walk outside and it'll take a matter of seconds before someone sees the Americans. They know where we are and they are going to come back and arrest us for something else. There is no escape. Even if we go to Haiti they are going to find us because they know there's something going on."

He's constantly saying that. We need a straight shot from wherever we are to a boat, or a plane or something to get out of the country. We can't hang around because we could easily walk into another taxing job. Somebody is going to figure out a way to arrest us again. Especially once they figure out who we are. By now I think not only everyone in the building knows we're here and who we are; I think everyone within a five mile radius of the prison knows who we are because we've been here for so long.

Geraldo hangs out all day with us. We play cards to pass the time and talk about various things. A guard comes in and tells us that some guys want to have a pushup contest. Everyone wants to see how strong I am. So it becomes a big event. All of these guys, including the animals back in the cages, want to see this.

I do pushups regularly, by myself, to occupy time. I do pushups and sit-ups and the guards watch me doing them. Some of the guys try to do a little workout with me. One time, I was doing handstand pushups where you put your feet up on the wall and our current resident tried and fell over. It was hilarious.

The guards come in when I'm back there working out. I come up with different ways to do workouts. I'm used to going to the gym every day, sometimes twice a day, and running. I don't want to sit around and let myself go. So far, the dysentery isn't bad enough to affect my strength and the muscles I've worked so hard to achieve. I plan to keep working out.

When I was in the county jail in the States there was a guy in there nicknamed Diablo. He was a big black dude that kind of befriended me and we hung out. He had this whole jailhouse work out that he came up with without using any weights or anything that. You take your sheet and put a bunch of books in it and you do curls, bar dips and leg workouts. I was the only white guy working out with the 'hood.

The guards start talking about me working out and Diego says, "That guy over there ain't no joke."

"Who is he? Who is that guy?"

Diego loves this because he gets to make up stories like the Nicolas Cage one.

"Yeah, man, that guy, he's in movies, man."

"Oh really? Yeah, I think I've seen him too, man."

"He does all the fighting and martial arts, you know. His hands are registered. If he hit you, man, that's a violation."

"No way!"

They are very uneducated people and when Diego says, "Yeah, he's from California," they believe him.

"Oh yeah, California?"

"Yeah, that's where Hollywood is, man. I told you." The guys are going off about that.

Throughout Saturday afternoon, Marco, some of Diego's family and the girl's family show up. The girl's family wants to speak to us. We're still trying to keep her as close as possible. The girl tells her family, "No, the Americans are really nice guys and didn't do anything. They bought me lunch and we hung out together."

"They weren't like...?"

"No, I didn't have sex with them."

That's usually what girls do in that scenario and she says, "No, they weren't like that at all. They were very kind."

A friend of theirs, who speaks a little bit of English, is with the girl's family. I do a little Spanglish. It's a work in progress. Basically, I'm trying to become Dominican is what's going on.

Saturday night gets here and the guards tell us the guys want to have the pushup contest now. Diego is going back and forth and he's running the show. The guards like it because they can't get these guys to do anything. Diego can because we're somebody and we have money.

Diego goes up to the animals' cage and says, "Hey! You need to settle down over there. Shut up! You're screaming too much." The next thing you know, it's dead quiet.

Diego says, "If this guy mouths off, I'll buy whoever makes him shut up a chicken dinner." Eight guys volunteer.

We go down to the cell next to the animals' cage. They're watching the whole thing. The guys who want to do the pushups do them inside their cell.

This guy says, "I can do fifty. Can you do fifty?"

I say, "I don't think I can do fifty, man." Actually, that's nothing for me.

I'm in the hallway and he says again, "Yeah, man, I can do fifty for sure."

I don't say hardly anything. Again, you never know when the tables might turn, so I don't say anything unless I have to. Everyone is doing the talking for me and I don't understand anything they are saying.

All of a sudden, everyone is talking. Diego pulls me aside and says, "Well how many can you do?"

"I can probably do at least a hundred."

Diego says, "You sure?"

"Yeah, if I have to. I might not be able to do pushups tomorrow but if I have to right now I can get a hundred." So they go back and forth, and the guards are in on it now, too

Diego says, "Who is your strongest guy? Who thinks he can do more than the American?"

They're looking at me and no one knows but, finally, this guy says, "I can do fifty." He looks like he's probably the strongest guy there. He's an older guy, too.

"Do you think you can beat the American?"

He says, "How many can you do, American?"

And I say, "I can do fifty. I can probably do more."

"More? Ah, no, no, no, no."

Here comes the gambling process.

"How much do you want to bet?"

Diego says, "I'll bet you on the American." He's loving it.

Jeff watches all of this. He's standing outside of our area. It's kind of dangerous bringing Jeff out because he still looks like Play–Doh and if he isn't crying, he has this goofy looking grin on his face. I keep telling him, "Jeff, stop smiling," but he continues, so it's dangerous for him to be out here.

I say to Diego, "Tell them this. Tell them that if I can do more pushups than they can, then they can't ask us for anything ever again." They are constantly asking us for food, cigarettes and everything like that. Now they're all looking at each other.

"I don't know about that one."

They ask again, "How many can you do?"

I say, "I can do twice as many as whoever here can do the most."

I'm still feeling pretty good, physically. I'm dehydrated a little bit so I'm starting to lose weight. I know I can't keep it on in this situation, but I still have all my strength.

Everyone has their bets and now the guards say, "No way. He can't do a hundred, man." Diego is taking action all over the place. All the other guards are going against each other.

"Who you got?"

I tell the guard, "All right man, if I can do a hundred then you have to bring me a cup of ice every time you bring me a drink from now on. I want ice in all my drinks. I don't want to have to wait for it, you know. Whenever you bring me drinks."

They say, "Okay. Okay. *Sí, sí.*" Now everyone's got their bets and we start doing the pushups, boom, boom, boom...

The guys in the cell count for their guy and the guards count out in the hallway for me. We start going and counting. When we get close to fifty, they are counting him down and his count is getting slower. I'm still going when he stops.

"Corey, you killed 'em." I'm on 70 or something like that and Diego says, "You got 'em, you got 'em. You killed 'em."

I keep going and I'm wondering if I can do a hundred. I start going and all of these guys start counting...

They're yelling out loud and I hit a hundred, and they're yelling, and I keep going, and the guards are like, "No. No. No more. No more." I get to 110 maybe 115 and my arms are done. I drop down.

"Americano! Americano!" They're yelling it, *"Americano! Fuertes Americano! Americano!"*

I did the most and everyone is cheering and this guy who did 50, he felt bad. I go over and shake his hand and congratulate him.

He says, *"Amigo, mi amigo, sí. Mañana otra vez."* We'll do it again another time.

I let everyone know that I still think he's a strong guy. He's huge.

The guards are going back and telling these guys up front how many I did and it goes through the whole building. Later on Saturday night, everyone is coming to see the strong American guy. "He's the one."

The next day, the guards that were off are coming to see me. "You're not going to believe it. He did like 120 pushups or something like that."

Geraldo stays the night with us on Saturday and he has a sweat gland problem or something like that. He sweats all the time. He's a horrible sleeper and it's so hot in here at night in our little area. I let Geraldo stay down where I sleep. He puts plastic down and I ask him why he's putting plastic down.

He says something in Spanish that sounds like sweat in English.

I'm up in the top bunk this time. I'm sleeping up here because I'm feeling kind of cold. I think I'm getting sick or something. Geraldo and Diego are down there with Jeff and during the night Geraldo is snoring. I could barely sleep and Jeff is farting all night and Geraldo is sweating and snoring and he's loud, and annoying Diego. Diego's head is right next to Geraldo and Jeff makes sure that his ass is pointed in Diego's direction while he farts.

Humorous stuff does happen while we're there. We laugh and find humor in these things. In the middle of the night, Geraldo ends up sleeping on the floor because he's so hot and the concrete is cool. He's sleeping on the floor almost completely naked. I'm up on top and the fan's going.

Sunday, June 21

Sunday morning, the guy in the syndicate, the trustee, wants to come in. We lock our door at night so he can't. We get to sleep in. We don't have to get up like everyone else because we have that privilege. Our fan is going all night.

The trustee is a beggar. He's always asking us for cigarettes and everything else. What he does, though, is get it from us and turns around and tries to sell it to the other guys. This kid is annoying me, right?

He annoyed me the night before and I said,

"Diego, you tell that guy that from now on he stands at the door and if he wants to come in here, he has to knock before he talks to us. If we're busy, he stays out there. You tell him he's not allowed in here unless he has permission. He stands at the door and knocks."

The trustee has a key to the lock and he comes in Sunday morning after we had it out with him Saturday night. He comes in to get a trash bag and decides to walk over in front of us and open up this trash bag to wake us up because he wants to ask us for something. Who knows?

He didn't get it the night before. This is how dumb these people are. There are dumb, dumb people in the DR, especially in jail. I mean, you go to any jail in the States and they're not too bright, either.

He goes over, shakes out the bag, gets it caught in the fan because it doesn't have that wire cover over the front, and breaks it.

He looks up and I start yelling at him. Everyone wakes up, and he's standing there. This punk kid broke our fan. Not only is the fan for us, but it's for all the guards and everyone who comes back here to cool off.

When the guards come in to shower, they turn the fan toward them and use it to dry off and cool down. There are no towels and it's hot and we share it. If a bunch of people are sitting on the opposite side from us, we turn the fan and point it toward them and we sit over here and do whatever we're doing.

Now the fan stops spinning. He got the plastic caught up in it and there's like this huge Bang! Pop! from the black trash bag. We're already miserable being there, period. Now the whole thing went from bad to worse. Now we don't have a fan.

The one thing that we had that was good isn't working any more.

"Ah, shit."

We didn't have to do anything to this guy. He goes running out and the guards come in to see what happened. They ask us, "What's up with the fan?"

We tell them, "The syndicate kid broke it this morning."

And the guards are pissed at this trustee who is already standing on the edge of everybody's nerves.

I tell Diego, "I don't want to ever see him again."

"I'll take care of it, boss."

He goes to the guards and says, "You know, that guy has been screwing up for a long time."

"You're right man."

"He's taken too much liberty with everything he's doing."

So the guards throw him in one of the cages. He's got to spend some time in there.

He used to have some privileges but he's been working these guys all over and now he messed up in front of everyone. Now the guys in the cage have him.

Diego goes down and tells these inmates in the cage, "The trustee is causing us problems. Do you guys want to straighten him out for us?"

A guy says, "Hey man, I'll cut him. I'll take care of him for you. How much?"

Another inmate says, "I'll cut him for like 50 pesos." That's less than $2.

Diego comes back to me and says, "All these guys are waiting. They want to beat him up. They have him right now down in the other cage because they know he made us mad and that we're not happy about what he did. We can give 'em 100 pesos and they'll beat the shit out of him."

But I say, "No, no, no. We're not going to do that. No. We have to let people know that we handle our own dirt. We don't pay other people to do it for us."

I'm in prison mode already.

Diego says, "No, you're right. You're a hood, man. I love you, man. That's what I love about this guy."

Diego goes back to the cage and repeats what I told him, "No, man, we take care of our own business. Let him out. Let him out."

When he steps out, Diego pounds him right on the chest.

Diego yells at him, "Go grab your mop and clean up the floor!"

The guards and the other guys from the syndicate are happy that we did that. "Yeah, man he had it coming. Put him back to work. That'll make him work harder now."

The inmates say, "I told you, man. That guy ain't no joke, man. He's *tigre*. That's *tigre Americano*."

"Tigre" is the word for tiger. I'm not exactly sure what it means in a Dominican Republic jail situation. A sign of respect, I guess.

The trustee that got beat down had to clean up. The inmates keep asking Diego, "How come you don't let us do that man. We'll take care of him for you."

Diego says, "No, no man, we take care of our own mess. We don't pay people to do it, so you know."

They say, "Oh, man, they're gangsta. You know what I'm saying?"

Diego is constantly learning from me. I don't want to say I put him on a leash, but that's kind of how it goes. I use him when I need certain things done.

At the same time, he'll say, "You're right, you're right man. That's what I love about you man. That's much better." It happens in nearly every situation because he wants to do it the Dominican way and I say, "No, we want to do it like this."

People are asking us for change and stuff like that, and always asking us for money, especially this one inmate.

I say, "Diego, this is what you do. I'm tired of this guy coming in and asking me for something every five minutes. Let's make him a deal right now. We'll give him the 100 pesos he's asking for right now but he can never ask us for anything ever again. So how important is it that he gets 100 pesos?"

"He says that's all he needs to get out."

I say, "If that's true, he'll take the deal. He'll say, 'Okay, I'll take 100 pesos and that's my bond and I'll have enough money to get out of here.' If it's not true, he won't take the deal and he doesn't need 100 pesos to get out. So after that, then we're going to make him work before we give him anything."

"Yeah, yeah, I like your idea."

The guy doesn't take the deal.

I'm trying to get in the mindset and use natural business sense and intelligence in each scenario. How best to do whatever. A lot of it is to occupy my time and at the same time, it kind of makes us more than the traditional guys there. I'm constantly doing the same thing with the guards.

Everyone is so impressed with my shoes. That's all everyone wants to talk about, the guards, everyone. *Zapatos.*

"When you leave can I have them?" That's all everyone wants.

"Can you get me some like that, too?"

They aren't that special to me. We were going to walk around a lot, so I put on my running shoes. My Nike Air Max shocks that I got from Taiwan really cheap. Anyway, that's a whole other thing. I look like a hood to them. I have the wife beater tank top on, baggy shorts and the nice Nike shoes. I look like a hood.

Now I'm establishing the necessary image. It goes back to my time in county jail in the States. The image, perception, is more important than anything else when dealing with the criminal element.

I take a different approach when I'm dealing with the lawyers and the justice system. You have to be able to play one role at one time and play the other role at the other time. It's constant–they intermingle throughout the day.

Sunday is a big day. Very stressful for us.

By now, me and Jeff have dysentery and we have bad stomach pain. I think, "God, here's the beginning of it."

One of us says, "Oh, I have to go to the bathroom," and bodily functions become our normal topic of conversation.

One time Jeff says, "Did you smell that one?

I say, "Oh my God! How can you make that smell and not die?"

You have to understand how bad the odors are. There's the raw sewage smell in the jail all the time, but the smell that comes out of his body is worse than that. Guys that live in the jail all the time would get up and leave our cell, that's how bad he stunk!

Both of us are stinking and he says, "Yeah, man, my farts stink all the time."

I ask his wife about it and she says, "Yeah, he stinks all the time." It's hard to offend a Dominican Republic inmate, but he manages to do that.

Sunday starts and the go–fers come by with food. Diego's ex–wife brings us clothes and toiletries and we shower and change. I wore the same white tank top for four days without a shower. I take it off and I can't believe it. The part against my skin is black. I'm blown away by how dirty it is. It's so gross.

We get a lot more people coming into our cell. Enrique is this construction engineer, a business guy. He's probably in his 40s, 50s. He has his Blackberry and his headphones and he's reading books. I talk to him for a little bit. Then we see this guy come in that looks like he got beat down like Rodney King. He comes staggering in and mentally he's not all there and we're not sure what's going on.

He's staggering around. His arm is in a sling. His face is stitched all the way around. We don't know who this guy is but he hangs out in our cell. He's talking to everyone and we're like, "What's going on here?"

A guard comes over and says, "Hold up, the warden is here to inspect the construction work. All you guys have to leave and go in this other cell." We hurry up and hide all of our stuff underneath the beds. The guards help us.

We go back to the cell where we had the pushup contest. It's worse than ours. They're sizing us up when we come in but we still don't know how this is going to work. I'm trying to figure out who runs the cell but I'm not sure.

I'm in work mode. Jeff's got tears in his eyes and he's still got the big goofy look on his face. He sits down and Diego starts running his mouth talking to everybody, and everyone is looking at me.

I'm thinking, "What should I do?" So I start going around and saying, "What's up?" to everyone. I start doing my fist pounds to each person there.

"Qué pasa? Qué pasa? Bueno. Bueno. Eres mi amigo. Amigo, sí."

I'm doing this to everyone so there's not that awkward pause or size–up possibility. I break the tension and put people at ease.

We're asking each other's names. I'm talking to the guys a little bit. Who knows how long we'll be in here. All this time these guys know we live on the other side, but we need to show them respect. This is their "house."

Who knows what's going to go down? We're outnumbered. Any way you look at it. No matter how good you are, the biggest guy in the world, when you're outnumbered, you're outnumbered. You're not going to win.

So, someone's boss was in the area and wanted to take a tour. We're not supposed to be back in that area; that's supposed to be a break room for the guards. This has happened before. We get pretty good at stashing all of our stuff like our sodas and food every time we have to change rooms, because if we don't, people take it and we come back and we don't have anything. We get real good at hiding our stuff in our little cubbyhole. We work with it in the situation.

After the trustee breaks our fan and we have it out with him, we're getting a lot of phone calls. My phone number is out. The phone is ringing all day long. Diego is trying to work his angle. He says, "Where's our lawyer at? He should be here. We're going to court tomorrow."

I tell Diego, "I want to know everything that's going to happen. I want to know that we're walking in there and we're walking right the fuck out. We go in and then we keep on walking. I want everything taken care of. I don't want any surprises when we get to court."

I'm all over him, "Make sure this gets done. Find Marco and have him do this. Tell him to get down here. You need to work on every connection we have."

Diego is constantly on the phone. He's able, somehow, to get the head District Attorney for the narcotics division to come down and meet with us on a Sunday. When she shows up, whoa, that's someone very, very important. She comes to visit us on a Sunday? Everyone says, "These guys must be really important." The guards and everyone else are amazed.

She's mainly talking with Diego. He's friends with her husband. He helped her husband out of a jam a long time ago. She comes down to be sure we've exhausted every avenue and every possibility to find someone to help us out in our situation.

All of the guards say, "Yeah, the DA did show up."

Me and Jeff didn't get to talk to her, but later Diego tells Jeff that the DA said the charges will be dropped on Monday at the hearing. That it's all a misunderstanding. So that's what Jeff tells his mother and she relays that to my dad. My dad calls me later that night and repeats what he's been told.

I say, "That's what Diego says that she said. Whatever. That's what he claims, but as far as the real conversation, who knows?"

Like all the conversations Diego has on our behalf, the language barrier is a big problem. That's ongoing for me. I don't have enough energy to keep telling Jeff not to repeat what Diego tells him. I tell him to shut up, that's not what Diego said. He doesn't know how to distinguish the difference between what Diego says and what he has personally seen and heard. He has diarrhea of the mouth and he repeats what Diego says and he thinks that it's real.

I have this conversation with Jeff because he doesn't understand it. He says the first thing that pops into his head and he thinks there's nothing wrong with that. That's not what you should be doing because everything you say has consequences. You need to make sure you know what you're saying and how it's going to be received.

We give Marco's number out to everyone, including the families, with the objective to apply a bunch of pressure on him to let him know the severity of the situation. We talk about it on Sunday while we're sitting around. That guy's phone has to be getting blown up because Diego is calling all day and he's getting calls from everyone's family and all of these other people. He's under a wave of interest he's not accustomed to.

After we boot the syndicate trustee out, a new trustee comes in. We have some money on us so we send one of the guys down the street to come back with some cleaning supplies to clean our cell up real nice.

I tell Diego, "Hey man, this might be our last day here. If it is, let's let the new trustee clean it out and show some respect toward these guys." We have the trustee clean the whole cell area because we don't want the guards to think we don't respect them. So he cleans up and sweeps the whole floor and mops it up. When he's finished, we pay him.

By now we've met Julio, the guy with the stitches all around his head, and Enrique, the construction engineer. They're inmates, also, but they are on our level. Julio is incredibly famous. He's legendary. Enrique stays farther down the hall. He's been there awhile. I think that's where our TV went. He was arrested for stealing millions from a government construction project and all of this other stuff. I mean everyone's a thief in that country.

Throughout the course of the day, especially on Saturday and Sunday, Jeff randomly starts singing 80's songs that crack me up, like Bon Jovi's, "Living on a Prayer." Then we start singing Johnny Cash, "Folsom Prison Blues." That becomes our song. We talk about random stuff.

Out of the clear blue silence, Jeff says, "You know, if we get back to the States, I'm going to buy a gun."

I say, "Dude, I'm thinking the exact same thing."

"I'm going to get a gun and anyone who comes near my property, I'm going to shoot them." This all stems from being so helpless in this situation.

Also on Sunday night, this famous skinny singer shows up. I've forgotten his name. He sings classical music and stuff like that. He can sing and play the guitar. He sang in America. He speaks perfect English. He just got done doing a couple of years in Najayo. He tells us funny stories about that.

He's on his way out. He's telling us stories about how the drug cartel guys run the front end of it. He and Diego are having a ball. They're up all night long snorting coke and making a bunch of noise. All. Night. Long.

So... Diego does cocaine. This gives me a lot to think about.

At that point in time, me and Jeff are thinking what a crazy story this is going to be when we get back. The night before we left for the Dominican Republic, me, Jeff and Victor had dinner after work. I told them the story of what happened when I got arrested in Mexico. It kind of scared them.

I told them, "It was just a shakedown. They wanted money. I totally deserved everything that happened there. We were a bunch of kids down in Tijuana having too much fun and it got out of control."

Jeff keeps going back to that story, saying, "What a coincidence. You tell us that story the day before we left and how these things can happen, and then it turns out we go through this."

There is so much noise, men screaming and music blaring, back in the cell area that it's hard to get away from it. I go out to the platform to have a short discussion with Diego's father-in-law about our stuff. It's so quiet out here that after he leaves I stay for a little bit with an older guard–a very, very nice man. Some of the guards are fairly insignificant but he had some privileges like a little portable radio. It's just me and him.

He has soft music on and turns it down while I'm talking. I finish my conversation, Diego's father-in-law leaves, and I ask him, *"Por favor. Más música?"*

He says, *"Sí. Sí. Sí."* He turns it up and he sits at the desk to eat his little dinner his wife brought him and I'm sitting right there at the edge of the desk looking out the window to the courtyard below.

This is the first time I hear music I like in more than a week. I don't know what she's singing, but it's mellow music. It's relaxing and quiet and I think about where I am and where I'm going and what I have to do. Part of me thinks we'll get out tomorrow, but a bigger part of me thinks we won't. I always try to prepare for the worst-case scenario. I say a couple of prayers that I've said most of my life.

The first one I say is: "God, please watch over my sisters and don't let anything bad happen to them. If something bad has to happen, let it happen to me."

The second one is about Solomon in the Bible. God offered him anything he wanted and he asked for wisdom. I keep praying, "God give me wisdom. Give me wisdom." Especially in this situation.

The thing I like about wisdom is you know it when it's there. I always feel a connection with Solomon because he struggled so much to understand God. The way he struggled with God is kind of how I feel when I struggle with Him, too, asking Him to "make it make sense to me."

The last one I say goes back to "you get what you pray for." I used to say it all the time, "God help me to be humble." I struggle with being humble, but when you ask God to make you humble, you're going to find yourself in a lot of humbling experiences. Right now I'm sitting there, praying, "God I think you've humbled me enough for now. If this is the humbling you think I need, so be it. But damn did it have to come to this?"

I have to be honest about who I was before this. It was life in the fast lane. "I'll get back to you when I can. Gotta go."

I didn't think there was anything wrong with that. It was on my time and I thought that was all that mattered. I always told myself no one cared because that made it really easy to live my life the way I wanted to.

But now, going through this situation, I see how many friends and family are really concerned for me. The fact that these people come back into my life in this bad situation, and have no problem doing it, changed my outlook on life. They made me take a look at what I value and what I really care about. There are a whole bunch of people out there who care about me. Maybe I'm very selfish living my life the way I have been. This is something to think about.

Monday, June 22

Monday comes around and, of course, there is a sense of urgency and excitement. This should be it. We should go in front of the judge and finally be done. There's a lot of confidence that this is going to come to an end today. We're getting out and from there we say things like, "Yeah, as soon as we get out, we're going to grab two *Presidente* beers and drink them."

Our plan is to go in there and tell the judge our story. We tell him who we are and he will decide that they've held us long enough. Then he'll say, "We're sorry for the confusion. Have a nice day," because they don't want a bad reputation for American tourism.

We're supposed to go to court at 9:00 a.m. and it's delayed. We're sitting around waiting for them to call us. It's hot and miserable back in our area. One of the guards, I think, messed with the fan and got it going again. The syndicate guy, the first trustee, was never allowed back in our area again. He had to stay at the other end of the jail and only tend to the prisoners down there.

The new trustee takes good care of us. He's a lot better than the first one. If we tell him to go get us something, we let him keep the change, or we let him have a cigarette or give him some of our food or drink and he loves it. It's like the best gig. He says "Please" and "Thank you" for everything and I talk to him a little bit in Spanish.

By now, my Spanish is getting sharper and sharper. I'm forcing it on myself, picking up what people are saying and trying to understand. Jeff sees that I can understand what people are saying.

He asks me all the time, "What are they talking about?"

"The guards are asking Diego why we're here and he's telling them the story and what the cops said."

Jeff says, "What did the guards say?"

"Well, the guards don't understand why we're here either."

Jeff is doing this constantly.

Marco comes to see us and he's not looking good. The same attitude isn't there. I pick up on it and Diego does, too.

Diego says, "I'm not feeling good about this. There's something up."

We ask Marco, "Has everything been taken care of?"

Meaning was there plenty of money? Did everyone get their money? We don't want any surprises. We make it clear what our expectations are.

Marco's response is not strong. He's kind of stuttering, "I think things should go well." It isn't the reaffirming, "Yeah, you'll be outta here by noon tomorrow," like we're expecting. There is a whole lot of interest now in what Marco is doing.

I think Marco realizes that he's in way over his head on this one. He's beginning to understand the severity of the situation and what's at stake. He doesn't have the connections that he needs and we expect. We find this out after we go to court because Marco doesn't say a word during the court proceedings, this other lawyer does. We've never seen him before and don't know who he is. Whatever their strategy is, they have a Plan A and that's it. They don't have a plan B, C or D.

We're starting to understand from the paperwork we get, that if we're not with a named lawyer–a lawyer on the U.S. Embassy list– we could be with a lawyer who is known for corruption. Those guys don't want to get you out. They want to keep you in jail because they think that they can get more money out of you and that you'll stick with them. It is very common for lawyers to do that– they're lawyers, they're garbage. There's a likelihood that they are going to try to take the money and run, and not present us with a good legal argument.

I'm being very direct with Diego about what to say to this new lawyer who we have never met.

I tell Diego to tell him, "We expect to go down there and, at the end, walk out. I'm not going down those stairs in front of the clerks. We're going to keep walking out that door. I'm not going back up here–period."

I let him know, "This is what better happen and you better have these things taken care of. Marco, you better have paid the right people." I turn to Diego. "Diego, tell him that. He needs to know that we expect the right people to have been paid with the money we gave him."

At the same time, we start pulling strings through Jeff's mom to contact the lawyer at the top of the U.S. Embassy list. We didn't know what we were being charged with until Friday when we first went to court. This is some serious stuff! We're still thinking this is a misdemeanor and all we have to do is pay and go, but drug trafficking is one to three years. One to three years??

Jeff, through the U.S. Embassy and the U.S. Embassy's list, is working on finding us a new lawyer. I'm also talking to high profile people like Enrique and Julio. I ask them who the best lawyer is for our situation. Lawyers who want to represent us are calling every five minutes. The way these lawyers appear, visually, and how they handle themselves, is a lot different from what we have right now.

Me, Jeff and Diego get together to talk. I say, "Is there enough time to eject? What do we do? Do we have to ride it out with Marco?"

We gave him money and all he had to do was give the money to the right people and we should be out of here. We hope that he's done that. We let him know that's what we expect.

We understand later that he didn't do those things or he didn't think that far in advance. He's in over his head and he realizes he should have done more. He doesn't have much to go on in court and there's no turning back now.

My dad calls and tells me that in the latest version of the case, the charges have changed from personal use to drug dealing. The police are now saying there were 14 grams of marijuana in the car, also. The 14 grams of marijuana shouldn't be a problem because that's within the category of personal use.

The basis of our defense is that 2.95 grams would be drug dealing if there was only one person in the car. But if there is more than one person involved, they have to divide the amount by however many people are there. This is according to their law.

I got a piece of paper and divided 2.95 by the four people in the car and come up with .74 grams per person–way below the drug trafficking amount. We think we'll pay a fine and be out. We think that's the worst–case scenario.

The police officers that arrested us and the guys who handled us and drove us around town in the dog cage come up and say, "You guys should be out. There is nothing there. You pay your fine and go."

Jeff's mom finds a lawyer in the DR and he calls us. We talk to him about Marco. He does some research and calls back to tell us about this really odd DR drug thing we didn't understand. He, as well as other upper level lawyers in the country, doesn't want to get involved with our case because it involves drugs.

He says, "If it was anything else, I'd come down there and represent you guys. If you had murdered someone, we could've done something for you."

We find out later how the law has recently changed. Now someone charged with a narcotics crime gets one appeal. Before that, any narcotics violation meant you were automatically guilty and there was no chance of an appeal.

The government tells their people, "You're poor because people are involved with drugs. If people weren't, we'd have a better lifestyle for everyone in the country. Look at America. They don't have drug problems there. They don't allow it and that's why America is so great." You can say these things to uneducated people.

People are afraid to get close to our case because it involves drugs. I think if someone gets involved with a case involving drugs, people presume they're on the take. It may limit them somewhere else in business. I don't know. I'm guessing.

So the day progresses into the afternoon and my anxiety is growing. We ask Marco, "What's going to happen, how does it go, what do we say?"

Marco says, "Don't worry. Just go in there and tell them who you are, what you do and what you know about what happened that day." Which is nothing.

We finally go to court. It's late at night. We shave and take showers so we look the best we can. We put on long pants and buttoned down shirts–thank God we brought them on our vacation. It is very important there to look presentable. It's strictly appearance there.

They bring the other prisoners down with us to court. Initially, they bring all of us into the same courtroom we were in on Friday. Then they pull all of us out of there and into another room next to the courtroom. A lot of paperwork has to be filled out with our names, who we are, what we do for a living, etc. Everyone has to present identification including the lawyers.

We meet the translator. He's a young guy, a real thin kid who went to school in the States. He wanted to talk to me about what I do for a living, where I work and what he was studying in college. He does a very excellent job of translating. We have a bad translator later when our life hangs in the balance.

After we do all of that paperwork, they take us back to the courtroom. The crowd in the hall is phenomenally large by now. Everyone from Diego's and the girl's neighborhood is there. Even the guards that aren't on duty come in. The guards' big thing is, "We can't wait for you guys to get out. We'll celebrate. We'll have beers outside in the street, *en la calle*."

We're the first ones up. It's a different judge from the one we had previously. This guy looks like the dude on the Uncle Ben's rice box. He looks exactly like that. There's a significant amount of commotion going on because of our case. People that work in the court are coming in and out. We sit in the first pew again.

It goes Diego, the girl, Jeff, me, the translator. There are rows and rows of lawyers in the courtroom. Not all of them are there for us, but it looks like we have the most. One of them is the girl's lawyer. Marco's there and a couple of lawyer guys that we've never seen before.

Marco is overdressed. There's professionalism and then there's flash. Marco wears gold rings, a gold tie and a light blue suit. From a professional standpoint he's a clown. I'm getting this vibe from him. He's dressed like he's in a fashion show. I get the feeling that he put way more effort into his wardrobe than he did for our case. Diego talks to him and he's not getting a good vibe, either.

Marco says, "Hope things work out."

I tell Diego, "No, man, you tell him things better be taken care of. We're walking down that aisle and out that door. You make sure he has a real good understanding of that. There is no other option here."

Diego is visibly upset when he's talking to Marco. Marco is trying to ignore him so he turns and talks to Jeff. Marco knows a couple of things in English, a couple of phrases here and there, but not enough to communicate effectively. Jeff turns into a big crutch for the lawyers.

Marco tells Jeff, "Diego talks too much," which he does. When we give our testimony, he's rambling on. I want that to be Marco's problem, not ours.

Jeff says, "Diego does talk too much. He's crazy," agreeing with Marco.

One of the reasons we have Marco is because he speaks a little English. Me and Marco can discuss the case if we want to, but I don't have the patience for it. Diego's faster. Plus, I don't know the legal terms.

Marco knows that me and Jeff are the golden paycheck. So far, Diego has provided zero funding for this project. At the same time, I don't feel good about Marco, period. This is the DR. Maybe that's how lawyers dress down here.

It doesn't take long for me to realize I'm the smartest one in this room right now. I may not know all the ins and outs of DR law, but I work with lawyers constantly as part of my job. I understand the general legal process and legal system better than these lawyers. If I could speak Spanish, I could defend us and we would walk out the door in a heartbeat. From what I understand, the DR system is similar enough to ours that I could do it.

So a new DA gets up, reads the charges and says, "They are charged with possession, and the volume of cocaine is two point something." Again, it's a different number. Three is the breaking point but the amount they say they have never gets to three. Everyone says the marijuana doesn't matter. The cocaine is where they draw the line.

I'm sitting there and I'm thinking, "How did they weigh it? What about the bag that Marco showed us a picture of? Did they weigh it with the bag? Who has the cocaine? Why isn't it here in the courtroom?"

Any good DA would drop the case immediately, look for a settlement and get the hell outta there. They're not going to try to push it. There's so much lacking here. They never found drugs on an individual person. They say it's in the car, but the car is a taxi. Lots of people ride in it. The volume is so minimal. And we never see a bag, let alone a bag with cocaine in it.

The DA reads the charges off a piece of paper. One of the police officers wrote his notes on the paper saying this is what they think happened. It's three or four sentences. That's it.

I can tell that the person who wrote it is poorly educated. The handwriting is very poor, as well as the part of the Spanish I can read. It's obvious that it doesn't take a whole lot to get a job with the narcotics division of the police department.

They say they stopped the car in this really, really bad neighborhood. They say that when they stopped it, it was in front of a known drug house in a drug neighborhood. They call it a crime of chance.

They say that this is where the arrests occurred and they have visual evidence of us purchasing the narcotics, and that they found the same narcotics in the vehicle. That's what they say, but they never produce visual, or any other kind of, evidence.

Later, the testimony of how the arrest went down and the people involved changes because there's only one officer out of all of them on the stop that said there were drugs. No one witnessed it. This guy comes out of the car and says, "I found drugs." This is the rogue cop on the moped that had a serious problem with Diego to begin with. All of the other police officers there didn't see any drugs; it's just this one guy. He never shows up in court.

This is their case.

Our defense argues the arrest saying, "No. The arrest occurred on the bridge at such and such location." They talk about how the car has moved out of one district and into another, so the hearing should be in this other courthouse. This is the location where it happened so we need to do the court case at a different court.

The judge says, "Okay, let me go back and deliberate over this." He leaves the room. All of the lawyers are happy. They are smiling and saying, "Yeah, good. Good." The judge comes back and says "I don't believe that has anything to do with this case; the merits of the case still stand. We're going to go ahead and run with it."

Whoa! That was Marco's whole case! He banked everything on jurisdiction!

Diego looks over his shoulder at him and so do we and Marco is like–I can tell by the look on Diego's face and the look on Marco's face–they're not going to say anything else. That was it!

Now, we're up. We're back to where the police tell their side of the story and we tell our side of the story. The translator is doing a very good job. At least he can keep up. I even told him later that he did a very good job and he says, "Thank you. Thank you. I appreciate that."

The look on the translator's face when he hears the charges against us tells us he's really dumbfounded and concerned. It's not like he's just doing his job. He has an emotional connection to us. "They're trying to charge you with this stuff?"

Drug trafficking is what they charge us with. In my mind, with all the flaws in the case, and with all the narcotic volume issues, a decent way to go may be to plead it down to lesser charges. The cop admits there were four people in the car. But if anyone does the math, the amount per person is so low it's ridiculous.

I'm thinking they'll work a deal. They'll knock it down to a misdemeanor. We'll pay. Everyone gets their money. The court moves on and they can bring someone else into the jail now because they can clear that room and that's the cycle of life down here. Get your money–get these guys out and eventually we'll get these Americans again the next time they come to the country. Who knows?

To me it's there for the taking. Awesome compromise. Everyone gets what they want. Negotiate down and payout. We're waiting for them to argue some more information and Marco says, "Look. Go ahead and talk and tell them what's going on."

Diego goes first which he does every time. The translator is telling us what he's saying. Diego gets up and starts telling version number two of the story. It's different from the first time he told it in court.

Now he's saying, "These police officers are out to get me because of what I do for a living. These people have no involvement in it. They were just taking a taxi back to their hotel." He's rambling on and on and on and talking about things that have nothing to do with the case.

He says, "No. This is where the arrest occurred. We were on the other side of the bridge, coming down. They pulled us over there."

This is his version of what went down.

"The police officers arrested us and then put us back in the car and I had this conversation." He starts doing hearsay.

"This guy said this to the police officer and the police officer said this back. And then this guy was over here and this one time three years ago the same guy did this and this." He's all over the place. Finally the judge has to cut him off. Whatever possible credibility he might have had is lacking significantly.

Then the girl gets up and she really does a good job the entire time. She says, "This is what happened. This is where we were. I didn't see any drugs the entire time. I am not aware of any drugs. All I was doing was trying to get a ride back to my house." The girl and us have the most honest and truthful statements here because this is all we really know.

She states that she heard the police officer say, "Now I have you," to Diego. Diego says that in his statement and she says, "Yes I heard him say it." She backs that up which really blew me away. There is some credibility there in what Diego says because the girl says she heard the same thing. She has every reason to despise and hate Diego right now for the position that she's in. She says she heard him say it and then he put her back in the car. Then she says, "The police officer said there were drugs in the car but we didn't see any drugs. We didn't know what they're talking about."

The judge says, "Okay." That's the end of that.

Then it's Jeff's turn to talk. Jeff gets up there and I made an error in judgment on my part. I assumed a whole lot about Jeff and I didn't really pay attention to it. When Jeff talks, he doesn't talk like me at all. He kind of rambles and never ends one sentence before beginning another one. And this and this and this... and this and this and this... and that and that and that and this and...

He's trying to say, "We came over here to see the sights and tour the country and we'd only been here like one day. We hired this guy as a tour guide and to give us a ride back to our hotel. This is what we know. We stopped and then the cops showed up with guns drawn on us and they took our wallets and our money and they took us to different jails. Then they brought us here and we've been here for five days now and we don't know why we're here. Today is the first time we're finding out what we're being charged with."

That's what he's trying to say, but he's rambling when he says it. He goes really fast and the translator kid is having a hard time trying to keep up with him and this becomes a huge problem later on. We're at the mercy of this translator and Jeff's rambling and he's not thinking about this guy who has to take everything he's saying and translate it to Spanish and say it to the judge. He's like "Brrr.rrr." and the guy's trying to keep up and Jeff says, "thenthisiswhathappenedandthenwe..."

Bam! The wheels are falling off and I'm sitting there and I'm thinking, "Oh, God, how am I going to save this?" I'm the last one to speak. I have to tie this all together in some way because right now we're all over the place in our storytelling. I try to speak in a slow, thoughtful, manner. I reaffirm what Jeff said about what we do for a profession and this is where we're from and our job responsibilities.

I reaffirm how we went to these various sight–seeing places including what the girl said about the café; we had lunch there and saw the church. We had souvenirs from these places and we hired this guy as our tour guide and taxi driver through the hotel. The hotel recommended him and they knew who he was. Even though Jeff got the recommendation from a guy at work, the people working in the hotel know him and can say they recommended him to us.

This is to reaffirm what Jeff was saying that we were stopped when we came across the bridge by two men with guns. We thought we were being robbed. When the uniformed police arrived on the scene–the two initial guys who were robbing us said they found drugs in the car and from there they take us to jail, take our wallets, our money and our cell phones. No one has told us what's been going on with the situation... and we find ourselves here today and we're confused as to what is going on with us right now. I'm trying to wrap up what everyone said in front of the judge.

I'm pausing for the guy to translate so my story is coming out real nice and clear and sharp and understandable. I'm in an internal panic because Diego went off the deep end, the girl said pretty legitimate stuff and it checked out okay, Jeff went up there and rambled all the way through. I'm hoping he's taking that as "the guy's panicked, doesn't know what he's doing, confused tourist..."

I don't know. I have to try to say something concise and intelligent. At the same time I don't want to come across overbearing about the situation. I'm trying to think quick on my feet because the wheels have fallen off this roller coaster.

The sincerity of the kid who is translating for us is phenomenal. The look in his eyes and his understanding says, "You mean you came over here and all this happened to you in one day?" The look on the translator's face is saying a lot.

Then the judge says, "Is there anything else the legal defense would like to add?"

This lawyer that I've never seen before gets up and starts talking. I don't know where he came from. He says, "I demand that the girl be released immediately and all charges against her be dropped. There is no reason to hold these people."

Then another lawyer I've never seen before–I don't know where he came from either–is saying "These charges are barbarous." The way Dominicans talk is very dramatic, they yell and use emotion and say things like, "This is an outrage!" Drama queen is what it is.

What I figure out later on is the more emotion someone talks with, the more ignorant they are. These guys are not cool-headed or coming across in a professional manner. They're revival-preaching lawyers.

The judge sits back, leans back in his chair and kind of gives us the eye over and he says the most phenomenal thing that I have ever heard in a court proceeding.

"I don't believe what I'm hearing right now. All you Americans are the same. You want to come down here, have fun, meet girls, party and have a good time and you don't have any respect for our laws. You lack appreciation for the laws of this country. Therefore..."

The translator is saying this and I'm thinking, "What the f–––." This has nothing to do with the merits of the case; this is his opinion.

"...you are convicted of drug trafficking. The prison term is one to three years."

There's a "WHOOSH-BOOM!" in the courtroom like the sound barrier broke. Our case exploded into little bits.

The look on the translator's face is shock and horror. He can't believe it. The DA looks over at us, we make eye contact with him and he hangs his head down. Diego is about to jump over the edge of the railing and attack Marco. There is a huge uproar because the girl's family, Diego's family and whoever else is involved, are in the courtroom and everyone is screaming. The courthouse turns into an uproar. The guards are in shock like, "You have to be kidding me!"

That's the whole scenario right there. Later, when I have time to think about it, I think what happened was we had a black judge, who has probably been at this job for years. He probably has a real good understanding of how the world works and he's probably real pissed off at the fact that his country has to kiss America's ass all the time. For years, they've brought these charges upon the Dominican people.

This judge finally has an opportunity. "I got my Americans. I can finally say, 'You know something? Fuck you! For years, you have been taking all of these drugs, doing all of these things and I'm putting my own people away because of the U.S. drug laws. You Americans love drugs up there but you won't admit it.'"

It's a gotcha. I'm guessing he's thinking something like, "How dare these low–level scum lawyers come into my courtroom and talk to me like this. Look at this piece–of–crap driver over there." The judge is probably pretty confident that the driver has something to do with this but he's not sure what.

He's thinking, "Let me send them all away and see who squeezes." Who knows what he's thinking? It's pure speculation on my part, but that is the classic scenario.

This goes back to the perfect storm, everything that happened. This is where me and God are having a whole lot of issues. I had my free ride–three, four, good years where my life was tame. There was no chaos in it. I was a professional, getting my vacation time and I was in a good financial situation.

How can the planets line up like this? You have got to be shitting me. How in the world are we going to prison right now? All of this is running through my head.

Jeff starts bawling like a baby, right? Guess who he's crying in front of? All of the other inmates that are waiting to go before the judge. They're looking at him and I'm thinking, "Oh, God, Jeff is bawling." I'm holding it together, and Jeff is tearing up and he says,

"How come they're not going to let us go?"

All I can think to say is, "What the fuck?"

Now it hits him that this is the position he's been in the entire time. I understood the position and I've prepared myself for both outcomes. I'm ready for either one because I ain't going to do this shit anymore. This becomes an awesome conversation that me and my father have later.

We sit back down on the bench. They clear all the commotion out. Diego's family is out in the hallway now and they're going back and forth.

The first thing Marco says is, "We can appeal in seven days. We'll get a different judge." Then he actually has the nerve to tell me he's going to need more money! That's when I have a really fun Spanglish conversation with him where he's horrified and that's when he becomes Jeff's best friend.

We're still in the courtroom. They put us in the back row to wait while they push everybody else through the court. The girl is bawling, Jeff's bawling.

Diego says, "You know how to do time; you've done time before. Get Jeff straightened out because all of these guys are going to go with us and we can't have this crying bitch with us."

Jeff's a lost cause and he's going to be a lost cause for the next five days to a week. As things progress day-to-day he becomes as much of a problem for me as the whole situation is. It's kind of like living this horrible prison situation twice.

So, I'm sitting there going through the list in my mind and checking things off-shutting them down.

I don't feel this emotion any more.

I don't feel that emotion any more.

This no longer means anything. Boom. Boom. Boom.

I'm looking at a guy and I'm seeing through him as someone who doesn't even exist any more. I have to get there. He doesn't mean anything. If it comes down to it, I'll crush his head into the ground.

I'm running this through my mind and I don't like it. I go there, but I don't want to. I'm really struggling with it. That's going on in my mind, along with what I'm going to do to Marco when I get my hands on him and, once we get to prison, what I'm planning to do to Diego. He's not going to live. If he takes everything away from me that ever mattered, he's definitely not going to have anything that matters to him, either.

I don't know it yet, but this is when having Jeff there turns out to be my salvation. Having him there keeps me from crossing that line. It's a double-edged sword. On one hand he makes everything so much harder than it has to be, but on the other hand, he keeps me in touch with enough of my humanity to keep me from going over the edge and doing something that would ruin my life forever.

The scum of the earth has made its way inside this prison. God knows how bad it is in there. Imagine who even goes to prison in this country? I know how bad a local jail is. Now, let's imagine what prison looks like in this third world country.

I'm thinking, "This is going to be the end of life, the end of the world."

I don't know what I'm going to see but I have a really good idea that it's going to be the worst thing I've ever seen in my life. At the same time, I know I'm going to have horrendous health problems when I get there.

My health system is very fragile. I require a significant amount of medication on a day-to-day basis to maintain it and all those things are gone. I don't have access to them and I know I'm going to get sick. I don't know when but I'm going to be really, really sick in that dirty, unhealthy environment. All of that's running through my head. I know how it's going to end.

They bring us back out of court. All of the other inmates, everyone in front of us who goes in front of that judge, gets convicted. This is the other thing. Marco wasn't smart enough to investigate which judge we were seeing. Just like the States, certain judges act a certain way and with this judge, everyone who goes up there gets convicted. It doesn't matter what you say. We're all going away. We're all going to be riding the bus to Najayo prison.

While I'm sitting there running these possibilities through my head, this guy taps me on my shoulder and I go into killer mode because I have my concept of stateside prison and everything that's going to happen.

"Three months–no problem." That's what this guy says to me. It sounds better than three years like we've just been sentenced to. And the way he said it with this expression like it's no big deal, "Three months–*fue la calle.*"

Another inmate says, *"Mi amigo, no problema. Tres meses fue. Es nada."* My friend, no problem. Three months and you'll be out on the street. *Es nada.* I remember that guy saying that, *"es nada,"* "it's nothing."

I'm thinking, whoa, if I was in his place I'd be pretty upset and this guy is acting like it's nothing. "Going to prison for three months?" It's nothing.

We go back up the stairs. All of the inmates go back in their hole, and we stand around like we usually do. All kinds of people want to talk to us and the phones are ringing. I don't have a whole lot to say. In these kinds of intense situations, my mind is going so fast. I don't want to say anything that isn't important. Everything I say has no emotion in it, it's point blank and it is what it is.

Now that we're in this situation, I could get upset and yell but what is that going to accomplish? Just because we don't like this outcome isn't going to change it. It's over. I had a clear understanding of this possibility.

I told my dad on Friday, "Monday is going to decide it."

We're standing around and Diego is doing his Joe Pesci thing. He's real touchy and he's upset and Jeff is crying and I need to get a phone.

The first person I call is Connor and I say, "I'm not getting out. I could go away for a while. I don't know how long. If you could do me a huge favor I'd really appreciate it. When you get a chance, I need you to go over and pack up my apartment for me. It has to get done by the end of the month if you can. If you want to keep some stuff, go for it. I don't know when, or if, I'll be back. Whatever financial stuff you need to be reimbursed for, go ahead and cut yourself a check. You can work out the details with my dad. Give me a call back when you get a chance and we'll talk about it." I give him my parent's contact information.

It's a real cut and dried conversation–not a whole lot to it–and Connor says, "Well, what's going to happen next?"

"I don't know. I guess we have an appeal date next week and we're going to appeal the verdict but right now this is where it stands."

"Oh man, I feel really bad..."

"Yeah, I guess we can cry about it some other time but if you can help me out I'll appreciate it."

"Right man, no problem, I'll take care of it for you. Anyone that you want me to tell about it?"

"Use your judgment, man. You and me are kind of friends with the same people at work. Whoever you want to tell, feel free. Here's the number. They can call me. Don't know how long we'll be able to talk but whoever wants to can call."

Even though everyone is on stand–by to hear what happened, I don't feel any urgency to make that call. I've already been convicted whether my family finds out about it immediately or 20 minutes later–it doesn't change anything.

I have a conversation with my dad later, after we go back to our cell and I have a different outlook on what I'm planning to do, but immediately after the conviction, I don't think I called him at that point in time. I'm not sure.

Jeff calls his mom and his wife. His family and mine are connected enough now that I know Jeff's mom is going to call my dad as soon as this happens anyway. There isn't a phone available so I'm thinking the verdict will get to my dad.

Marco has this classic smile, kind of like Jeff's. "So sorry. So sorry," is what he says to me!

I say, "Yes, I am very sorry for you, too."

And I don't say it with a smile. I stare at him and he looks down at his phone and he's doing something and he looks up and I'm still staring right at him. At this point in time, I don't care about getting out; I want to blow up Marco's office. I want to burn it to the ground. I want it to explode like the trailer behind our house blew up when I was a kid.

• • •

A couple of things happened when I was a kid that gave me nightmares. Like the trailer blowing up. It just scared me. These things happened at weird times in my life–very difficult times–and this was when my nightmares got really bad and I was scared to sleep. I didn't like sleeping for the longest time.

I was in junior high, maybe 12 years old, when the trailer blew up. It was another difficult time in my life. We moved into a new housing development that still had a small section of undeveloped field across the road. There was a doublewide trailer in the field behind our house with this really poor family living in it.

It was Friday night and I'm watching high school football highlights. My parents were home. I'm sitting there watching TV when all of a sudden the trailer explodes! BOOM! Mushrooming clouds of fire are flying out and it was really close to our house. I could see it out the sliding glass doors to the backyard.

We all ran out in the backyard and the trailer's just blazing. I can feel the heat streaming off of it. I see a rustle in the bushes and this guy is crouching down in them and he looks at me and I look at him. That's it! It freaked me out.

The whole story was that Friday during the day my mom was home while we were at school. And she said there was a huge argument over there and I think the cops came or something like that... I'm not sure. My mom said it was like white trash families living there and a guy supposedly said during the course of the argument, "If I can't live here, no one else can."

That guy saw me and I saw him in the bushes and I had nightmares forever because I thought he was going to come get me. I would wake up and I wouldn't know if it was real or not.

After the trailer burnt down everything was still there. So me and some friends went and checked it out. I'll never forget it. I picked up this doll–a baby doll–and it was half burned from the fire but it was still intact–it was just like–it messed my head up a lot–seeing that.

About that same time, I had a paper route and my dog, Outlaw, that I had from when I was about six until I was 21, would run along side of me. We were down in the riverbed and a pit bull came out of the bushes and then it had Outlaw's head in its mouth! I was just hitting the dog and crying and screaming trying to get him to let go of Outlaw's head and finally it just did. I felt so helpless; I couldn't do anything. I picked Outlaw up and he was really heavy but I carried him back to the house all bloodied up and everything. Outlaw lived but a chunk of his ear was gone.

I was freaked out about that and I used to have nightmares about that pit bull because they looked for the dog and never found it. We tried to track down the owner and all that bullshit. I dreamed that the pit bull came into our house at night. I'm lying in bed trying not to move and the pit bull would come in my room and walk around my bed. I'd lie there, petrified.

There was this window in my room and the light from outside was blinding me. I'd wake up and think "the pit bull's outside" and I went up to the window and I'd lift the blind up a little to peep out the window and that guy in the bushes' eyes would be looking right back through the window right into my face–just like that!

I was always worried that that guy and that pit bull were walking around the house at night. They found him about a month later, but that was some fucked up scary nightmares I was having then.

• • •

I'm still staring at Marco. I'm patient. I have a phone and I have some money. I can touch him from the inside. I'll make a list and start lopping off people backwards. Diego is going to be the last one to go. Diego is going to help me orchestrate everything along the way and then eventually I'll take care of Diego. I don't think he's smart enough to see it coming. He thinks we're buddy–buddies. He'll be the last one to go and whatever happens after that, happens after that. It doesn't matter.

As I get sicker and sicker, and more and more miserable in my situation, the lawyers become very uncomfortable around me. No matter what may be going on, Dominicans are very polite. They say, "How are you? So good to see you." I can't say those things because I don't feel good about anything. I see the lawyers and they hug and talk and everything like that and they come up and they want to do that with me and I look at them like they are not even there.

Jeff says, "Oh, yeah, I'm doing great today. It's good to see you." It's Jeff being Jeff.

He convicted all of us, even the girl. So Diego and Jeff are on the phones and everyone's upset. The girl's bawling, too. She's right next to us. We go back to our area and the inmates are asking us what happened. They're going back and forth. Diego is trying to do whatever he can, to get in contact with everyone he can, and then Jeff is on the phone talking to his mom and his wife and god knows who else. I get back there and we're sitting in our spots and Jeff is bawling is head off, crying. He and Diego have the usual arguments back and forth, "It's your fault this happened." "No it's your fault this happened." That's on a daily basis. It's a really bad time.

I'm struggling with it but in a different context. Jeff is upset about being away from his wife and kids. He's never been arrested and never gone to court before and never done anything and so it's hitting him now exactly what has been going on the entire time.

He kept saying before, "It can't get any worse than this."

I say, "It can always get worse."

Now it's worse and Jeff is dealing with that like a normal human being would and that's the hard part. Because that's what you're supposed to feel. That's what you're supposed to act like. That's what you're supposed to be worried about. I'm not. I'm not like that at all. I'm gone the other way. I'm thinking about all of the possibilities. Fuck it! It is what it is, man.

Various things run through my head. I've always had a good way to deal with fear. It's kind of a trick I learned from my dad, mainly. Especially when I was younger. I can't really give you a perfect scenario but there were things that I was scared of as a kid besides the nightmares. My dad and I always talked through it.

Here's a dirt bike example. When I was a kid, me and the neighborhood crew would build some horrendous death trap to jump our bikes, skateboards, whatever. We had a lot of ingenuity as kids. My dad would come home from work and he'd see some monstrosity that we had been working on all day. Then, when we'd get done building it, no one wanted to ride it. We were too scared!

So my dad would say to me, "What are you really scared of? Are you scared that you might get hurt? Are you scared that people will see you fall? What are you really scared about?"

And then, after I talked my way through it, at the end of it, I'd have to ask myself, "Am I really scared about getting hurt? Well, I've been hurt before. I can take that." You have to boil it down. It's an emotional control mechanism.

Now, faced with going to prison, this is running through my head and I'm using the same mechanism. What am I really scared of? Am I really scared of physical harm? Not really. Most of my life I've enjoyed a certain level of violence.

I'm a skilled pugilist. I boxed for years and trained in a no–frills boxing gym. I've had numerous street yard fights and things like that. I got the skill set there. I'm one of the larger guys.

Am I scared about dying? Not really. Right about now I've had enough of this. The greatest lie anyone can tell themselves is that tomorrow is going to be better than today. In this situation, tomorrow isn't going to be better than today. It's cold-hearted but looking back at my life, I'm thinking, "Well, how much of it really was better?" For every good time, there seems to be more bad times coming.

I did have my break the last two years where I had a great situation in life. It was very stress free, a great environment and great atmosphere professionally. I did an outstanding job and I had a few good friends and did things I enjoyed and this is the payback for that, in my mind. It was like it doesn't matter if there is a good day. After this, there are going to be more bad days waiting for me around the corner because that's the way my life is.

I'm asking myself, "Do I want to keep doing this?"

Jeff is really struggling. He's going through hell and here's the paradox. I'm checking into this person, "bad Corey," but here is Jeff. He is a negative and a positive through the whole situation. That night Jeff is very upset and sad.

When his mom calls him he says, "I don't even want to talk to them."

I say, "Well, do you want me to talk to them?"

He says, "Yeah, go ahead."

I talk to his mom first. She is upset about everything that's happened, obviously. How did it go down? Why did this happen?

I explain to her from my understanding of what I saw. I tell her, this is what's happened. I'm very deliberate and I actually know what's happening.

Jeff isn't doing a good job of communicating with his family and this becomes a reoccurring problem later. Jeff repeats what Diego says and he thinks that's what's going on. I try, but I can't get him to understand.

His mom says, "Well, Jeff said this and I said that."

I say, "I'm not aware of that. I can tell you what I know and what I've seen. Those other things are what Diego has said, and he's not a reliable source. You're really going to have to talk to Jeff and tell him that we're going to have to work ourselves out of this situation. He needs to get with the game or he's not going to work his way through this. What he's doing right now, especially his crying, is very dangerous."

His mom starts asking questions about what went on in court. I say, "I don't think it mattered what anyone did in court today. That judge had already made up his mind that whoever was in front of him in court today was guilty. I believe the mistake that was made was that we went in front of the wrong judge."

She had some other things that she wanted to talk about. I had to kind of cut her off here and there. I said, "You know that's really not important right now. This is what's going to happen in the next 24 hours and this is what we need to do."

I think I said to her somewhere along the line, "I've been in this situation before in the States and this is Jeff's first time and I'm sure he doesn't know what to do. I can't really go into all that right now because we don't have time, but if you talk to my father he can fill you in on what's going on and give you insight into who I am and everything like that." Basically, I tried to let her know that she's really not helping the situation.

Later that night, I talk to his wife. This was the first time I talked to her on the phone. She says, "How's Jeff doing?" I explain to her how he's doing and I share what's going on.

I said, "You guys really need to get him focused on what needs to happen right now."

She says, "Yeah, you're right."

"I don't think he's ever had a bad day in his life from what I can tell."

She says, "No, not really. Jeff has pretty much always gotten everything he needed and wanted."

So this is like the first bad day in his life. Ever. He's having a hard time with it.

I say, "You need to help me with him because it's too much for me to try to keep him alive right now. He needs help. He needs to get focused. You have to tell him there's plenty of time to cry about this later. (He hasn't mentioned his crying on the phone to his wife or mom.) He can't go on all the time about this and how he feels. You need to tell him that he needs to be focused."

Jeff is the complete opposite of me. His life is great. He has a family in place and he has a positive outlook on everything in life. He loves being around his kids and being a father, and his job, and everything he's doing with his life is the opposite of mine. Here's a guy who sincerely cares about the people in his life. Now I'm struggling because it's going to be really, really hard to be "bad Corey" and try to keep "good Jeff" at the same time.

I can trust Diego to a certain extent but I have to keep him in arm's reach. I have to keep Jeff from saying the wrong thing to the wrong person. He never stops. He's so upset at this point in time that he can't think straight.

He says, "Why do you have to be so mean to me? Why are you telling me to stop talking to everyone? What's wrong with the way I talk?"

I say, "You have to think about what you say before you say it and that includes what you say to your wife and family back home."

I start to struggle with who I am compared to Jeff. Even as much as the way Jeff is, I wish I was him because living my life hasn't been a whole lot of fun. It hasn't. The bad experiences in my live have stayed with me. There's no going back and changing them.

So here's Jeff–in my mind everything that's great in this world and positive, and his life means a lot to a lot of people. Then I look at myself how I am emotionally, and how difficult it is for people to be in my life.

I spend a lot of time doing things by myself but there are a few people I enjoy being around. But even with my good buddies I can only be with them for a certain amount of time. If I'm drinking, I can numb myself down and go along for the ride. That's how I deal with relationships. I know this about myself and I accept the fact that I'll live a lonely life. That's the way it is and this is who I am.

I wondered why my friends couldn't be as much of a friend to me as I thought I was to them. It's because being my friend is hard. Things happen to me and if someone's around me, things will happen to them, too. I said this to Jeff before we went on the trip. I said, "If you hang out with me long enough, crazy stuff will happen to you, too."

It's very common. I remember my buddy Brian. Me and him were best buddies through some very tough times in my life and then, when I went back to school, I'd hang out with him when I had a break and crazy stuff happened and I'd say, "Does this stuff keep on happening to you?"

He says, "No, it only happens when you're around."

That's why I tell people it's usually better for me to hang out by myself and do my own thing. If you're with me all the time, things happen. I've seen bad things and I've had things taken away from me. That's hard to deal with.

Sometimes you are who you are and you can't change it, that's the way it is. Trying to be someone else was a constant struggle for most of my life. It wasn't until I was older that I finally said, "This is who I am. I'm comfortable with it. This is everything wrong with me compared to most normal people and that's cool. Most people aren't going to act this way. Most people aren't going to understand that and that's fine. I'm cool with it."

I'm having a real tough conversation with myself about who I'm going to have to become during this process. It becomes an all-out war for me internally.

I've done a lot of work over the last five years to bury the instincts of the person who can go to jail and deal with that culture comfortably and without regard to anyone else. It's a day-to-day struggle for the most part, but I've been able to push that person out of my life and become this productive person.

Your natural behavior for males, in my opinion, between the ages of roughly like 16 to 25 is self-destruction. It's natural behavior. It's a natural thing for us to want to go do dangerous stuff whether it's get on a motorcycle and jump it or drive our trucks and bikes as fast as we can, but self-destructive behavior is normal for us at that age.

I know I did it and everyone else did it. What happens eventually along the way is that you come to grips with that and you have to make a decision:

Do I hate the world and everything in it? Or is there something in this world that is more important than me?

You have to pick one of those or else life doesn't make sense. If the world means nothing to you and you hate everything in it—which a lot of people agree with—then you want to destroy the world and everything in it.

If that's not the case—if there is something in this world that you care about more than yourself—then that's the gist of life. So you want to make the world a better place. That's what you have to come back to.

I decided years ago that I want to make the world a better place and I care about other people. This is a great value that I have along with my education. All the values that make me a good person in my mind, and make me productive... now that I've come to that point in my life, I know I can do so much more.

And now all of that is coming to a screeching halt??

Let's slam the brakes on that and go the other direction. Now I'm going to be in prison, in a world where most of the people that I'll be around are people that hate the world and everything in it and are looking for short-term, moderate, gain.

So now I have to bring all of the negativity back. I have to go back and be the person who hates the world and everything in it. Not only that, but I'll have to thrive in this environment, look for moderate short-term gain at the expense of other people, and devalue everyone around me as a human being.

So I'm thinking about all of that and I feel so guilty about my family having to go through this. Here we go, the worst-case scenario happened. Now I have to become this person that I thought I had gotten rid of a long time ago and I have to bring him back.

I don't know it yet, but you can't keep both sides alive. You have to go with one or the other and eventually one of them has to cease to exist. The difficulty I'm having is mostly internally with me, not externally as much, but I have to start getting my head there. I know all of this, I've been there, and so I know somewhat what I need to do.

I know as we go through this that the things we're going to see, and the things we're going to have to do, are going to change Jeff forever. He's never going to be able to go back to his old life and be the person he was for the people who need him. He'll go back, but he'll go back differently.

We're back in our area now and just sitting there. No one is saying much and it's quiet except the sound of Jeff crying.

We're going to a place where positive doesn't exist any more. I'll have no more positives left in my life and I don't see a way to keep Jeff from being affected by it, either.

I ask myself, "Is there anything I can do right now to keep Jeff from changing?"

I know there is one thing that we have left. I remember a conversation with the Embassy. If they have a dead American on their hands, and CNN gets hold of the story, there's no way they can keep us. There's no turning back now. We could go into court again with our appeal and it may not even matter. We could end up spending a year or more in prison.

So there is one way out, and one way only, that we've still got. There is no way anyone is going to survive around this joint if they've got a dead American on their hands.

We're down to the raw essence. I ask, "Do we still have paper and pen?" Diego leaves and brings them back.

"There is only one way out of here, Jeff, right now. One of us has to own it, admit the drugs are theirs, and everyone else goes, right?"

He says, "Yeah, pretty much."

I say, "Okay, but it might not be enough. The lawyers could use it to confirm our guilt and then we get in even deeper."

Jeff can't talk about this. This is a defining moment in both of our lives.

I say, "I am going to get you out of here, Jeff. I'll get you out."

"What do you mean?" he says as he starts to cry again.

I say, "I'll get you out. What's the one thing these guys are worried about the most?"

"What's that?"

I say, "Having something happen to us. Tomorrow morning when you wake up, I want you to get on the phone and tell your mom to call CNN and every media outlet they can find and tell them that there is a dead American in the jail inside the courthouse where we are right now."

Jeff is still crying and says, "What do you mean?" He's not getting it.

"Do that tomorrow morning when you guys wake up. It might happen before then depending on what time the guards show up in the morning."

He says, "What's going to happen?"

"You don't need to know everything that's going to happen, but you do that tomorrow morning first thing when you wake up and don't let the guards take the phone from you."

He's starting to understand what I'm saying, but he doesn't want to.

I talk to my Dad and give him a concise description of what happened in court. Then I tell him, "They're going to hold us here until they take every penny and every piece of humanity from us until there's nothing left. It could last ten years–it could last forever. I'm not going to give them that. I'm not. Fuck them!"

I tell my dad, "Tell my sisters how much I love them and their kids."

He's very upset when I say this. "What are you planning to do?"

I say, "What needed to be done a long time ago. What needed to be done a long time ago..."

I tell him, "I'm not going to do this anymore. It's not fun anymore. It's not fair. I've lived a pretty good life and I've beat the odds every time and maybe this is it, you know? Maybe it's finally caught up to me. I've been fighting gravity my whole life–pushing the rock up the hill. I'm tired of it. There is no opportunity for gravity to stop." He understands what I'm saying.

I tell him, "There is no way Jeff will stay here if they pull the body of an American out of here. It will bring a whole bunch of attention to our case and anyone with a logical mind is going to read about it and realize that everything that happened is bullshit." I tell him that point blank.

My dad keeps saying, "Don't check out on me! Corey, don't you check out on me!"

I told myself a long time ago, "I'll die before I ever go back to jail again," because you lose a piece of yourself as a person. You lose the essence of being a human being. You get further and further away and this is going to be the worst place ever. I'm done with this shit.

At that moment in time, I feel the most relief I've ever had in my entire life. I was so relieved knowing this was going to come to an end. I'm tired of this. I don't want to do it any more.

That's what my dad went to bed with Monday night; he couldn't reach me again.

Then I went over it with Jeff one more time what was going to happen–not exactly–but enough for him to know and he doesn't say much and that was good that he didn't say much at all.

Then Diego tries to interject, "Ah, Corey..."

"Shut the fuck up! Matter of fact, you don't open your mouth until I tell you that you can. You're going to sit here and you're going to shut the fuck up! I've listened to you for the past five days straight and this is what my life is now and you're going to sit there and shut the fuck up before I come over there and cut your tongue out and shove it up your own ass. You sit there and shut the fuck up. If you want me to say it in Spanish, I'll do it in Spanish for you, too." Diego sits there and he's quiet.

Then we all go to bed. In the middle of the night, while everyone's asleep, I get up. I've been contemplating this for a while and I've pretty much mapped out how I'm going to do it. All the guards' clothes, their uniforms, are in our cell. They have an extra set of boots up there and I take the laces out of the boots.

I go in the bathroom and look at the pipe high on the wall that comes out with a flex hose going into the 55–gallon drum. I jump up there on the pipe and do a couple of pull–ups to make sure the pipe's strong enough to hold me. I have the laces in my hand and I'm standing there looking at that pipe. I'm thinking about everything I've ever done in my life.

This is the longest I have been sober in probably three years so I have a really clear head and I stand there for a long time looking at that pipe dripping water.

There's an off–green glow from a lamp above. I stand there for a while looking at that pipe. Then I start knotting the laces up together to make them a little thicker. I tie them together making little top knots in it so they double up and that's not working too good so I undo it and try again. I get it so it's kind of two slipknots because I need to slide down. I need to stay in there.

I think, "Enough of this bullshit. Let's get this over with."

So I go over and stand on top of this bucket and I'm reaching over to the pipe trying to tie the laces on there and I got problems because I can't reach the pipe. I can tie the laces to it but I'm too far away to get them around my head.

"Shit!"

I need to move the big bucket over to the side a little, and move the little one back, but they are both full of water.

"Dammit! Shit! This is going to piss me off!" I say under my breath.

I have a razor to shave with but I say to myself, "God dammit! I really don't want to do that." I'd rather not lose any blood. If people have to bury my body it would be better if I didn't lose any blood. I don't want to bleed out, either. It takes too long.

So I get back down from the bucket, and I try to pull the buckets of water out and they're so damn heavy that I'm fighting with them. I get one out and I'm trying to walk this one over and it's spilling water everywhere. I give up.

"This is way too much work! Fuck this shit! I'll do it tomorrow night."

So I go back to our sleeping area. Diego and Jeff are asleep along with our guest for the night. I go back to my bunk, take the shoelaces and throw them underneath my mattress and lie down.

I'm thinking, "Well, if we're here another day, I can do it tomorrow night before we go to prison.

So I go to bed and that was it.

Tuesday, June 23

First thing the next morning the guards come by and tell us we're leaving for prison later that afternoon. It turns out to be really late afternoon which is so boring. We wait and wait and wait. There's nothing to do because we could be called up front at any time.

I get up and Diego gets up, and the first thing he says is, "Excuse me, sir, am I allowed to speak?" I start laughing, and say, "Yeah, you can speak now. I'm sorry about that."

He says, "No, you were absolutely correct in telling me that. I apologize. From now on if I'm out of hand or I'm talking too much, you let me know. Pull me aside and let me know."

I say, "Okay, that's fair enough."

He says, "I have the most respect for you of anyone I've met in my entire life. I got us in a bad situation and I'll get you guys out. One way or the other I'll get you guys out."

Jeff is still asleep at this point in time and he doesn't know anything. Sleep is an escape mechanism. I wish I could do that.

He finally gets up and he says, "You're still here?"

"Yeah, I am."

He says, "I'm glad you are."

I say, "Yeah, I figure I can do another day."

Then Diego goes off into Diego mode, and the anxiety is kind of gone right now, but Jeff is still crying off and on.

I tell Jeff, this is one of these hard conversations that we have, and I tell him, "When you're ready man, we're going to have an important conversation about what we're going to do once we get to prison and I really can't do it if you're going to be like this. So when you're ready, let me know, and I'll bring Diego in here and we'll talk about what we have to do now. But as long as you're like this, you're not helping me and I can't help you."

Classic Jeff, he says, "Okay, that's fine. I'm going to go have a cigarette." So he goes to have a cigarette in the bathroom, which is his routine. He comes back and Diego comes back talking about what we're going to eat for breakfast or whatever.

At this point in time I tell Diego, "When you get a chance, we all need to sit down and talk about everything, talk about a game plan and going forward what needs to be done, and come up with a strategy for how we can outthink everything."

Diego says, "I've already started, boss. I got all of these guys taken care of. I've already met the guys that are going to transfer us. We're taken care of while we're being transferred. I told them to tell the guys in Najayo to go ahead and start setting things up. Everything's taken care of for us before we get there."

I say, "What do you mean 'taken care of for us?'"

He says, "We're going to be in the best area that we can get in and have everything waiting for us. We don't have to mess around with any of this shit. They will escort us right back."

I'm confused. "What's going on?"

Diego says, "As long as we have money, we can get anything we want."

I say, "Fuck man, does it get worse than this?" while I wave my hand around the room.

He says, "No. We got big screen TV's over there. We got anything you want. We can get food delivered."

I say, "What the hell are you talking about?"

He says, "Yeah. I didn't tell you this?"

I say, "No, I would have remembered something like this."

"We can get anything we want over there if we have money. I let them know we're coming."

"Well, hell... one thing I have is money."

I'm starting to do a little inventory of myself. There's a whole lot of guilt going back to my family. If I had gone through with what I wanted to do last night, it would have been so unfair to them.

Jeff was really adamant. He says, "We're going to do this together."

I say, "If that's the case, then you guys have to start doing it my way and we have to start working together. When you're ready, and you're done doing what you are doing, we need to talk this through."

He says, "Okay. All right. I'm going to lie down for a while more."

That's how Jeff works! That's one thing about Jeff. I've been in relationships where there are things that you need to address and people aren't always ready to talk about them. I tell my dad about this later.

I say, "I have to find a way to feed the idea of addressing the matter with him so he can think about it before we have the conversation."

Jeff doesn't want to address it, so I say, "At some point in time we might want to think about these things. Let me know if you want to talk about it all later."

About an hour later, Jeff gets up and says, "Yeah, I was thinking about this prison thing."

"Well, we can talk about how we want to handle the bus ride over there and Diego can tell us more about what to expect. Do you want to go over that?"

"No, not right now man. I don't want to think about that right now."

"Okay."

That's what it was like with him. It was so funny. It was like I was in a relationship. He was like my girlfriend or something. I have to throw something out there to pique his interest in addressing something, and then we'll address it. It's going to be uncomfortable and awkward but we have to talk about it and make a decision. It's not going to make a decision on its own. That is Jeff.

This is the beginning of the process of me giving Diego instructions and assignments on a day-to-day basis in prison.

He says, "Hey, boss, we need to talk about business." He really likes that. He's serving a purpose. I need him to translate but I need to use my brain, too.

I say, "I'm not going to tell you how to live your life or what to do, but you should think carefully about what you're doing."

He runs off and does all this other stuff and it becomes a tool later on as things progress but that's how it is Tuesday morning.

I say, "I have plenty of money so I'll go check out this prison thing."

"They've got everything there! You can play sports. You can watch satellite TV."

"Really?"

"Yeah. We can have girls come in."

"What? Aren't we going to be locked in with a bunch of guys?"

"No, man. They bring girls in all the time. Anything you want they will get for you over there. If you have money, you're made."

I'm thinking, "Whoa! This might be one interesting experience we're going to have on our hands."

At this point in time, I shift between "end of the world Corey" to "hood, conniving, street-mindset Corey" because I'll be around street hoods and hustlers.

Eventually Jeff wakes up and Diego's there and I say, "Okay this is what we have to do now. We have to approach this as a job. We have to work now. We have to get ourselves out. We can't trust any lawyers. We can't trust anyone."

Diego says, "Exactly! Exactly! That's exactly what I'm thinking man, exactly."

He talks like this and it's nonstop. He wants to reaffirm everything I say and put his touch on it and interject. I get annoyed with it because he interrupts me all the time, so I tell him he has to ask permission before he says something.

We're constantly doing this thing:

Diego says, "May I speak now?"

"Yes, you may."

"Have you talked to Jeff about that? I have this going and I have that going."

I say, "Great. Okay, Jeff, this is what we're going to do. You have to be with us and we'll work our way out of here but if you are not with us we can't do it."

Jeff says, "Okay, okay, okay."

"I want you to do as much research as you can, Jeff."

I'm making up fake jobs but at this moment in time, this is what it's going to take to get us working together as a team. We have to get some positive energy, or some kind of concept of hope or direction or purpose now. I'm tired of being pushed around here and there–we have to accomplish something.

In some way, regardless of the environment, I can still be somewhat successful. I have to use my brain. I know I'm the smartest person here, but I have to figure out a way to get that to work. I have to think our way out of this. I don't know how. But there is always a way.

If guys can escape from maximum-security prisons, I can figure out a way to get out of this. In this third world country, with these uneducated people, with a lack of structure and the legal system, I can think a way out. I focus all my time and energy on that. We're going to go down swinging if we have to. I get back in the game.

I tell Jeff, "We need to research every legal option available. Look through this paperwork that we got from the U.S. Embassy and see what you can find. Are we missing something there?"

I say, "There should be a public record of our court hearing. We need to get that because now I'm afraid the girl's going to turn on us and roll. Diego, tell Marco he needs to get us a copy of the hearing. It should be public information."

Diego says, "Yeah, it is. Marco should be able to get that." So I assign that to him.

Then I tell Diego, "We need to know everyone who is in here, in jail with us. We need to know who they are, and what they do, and whether or not they are connected. We need to have everything in place when we get to prison or wherever we're going next. I want everything in place. I don't want any surprises. The stuff that we can control, let's take control of. I'm tired of having surprises and not knowing what's going to happen."

Diego says, "Okay, great."

Boom! I send Diego off down the halls talking to every prisoner, talking to all the guards, and doing whatever he's doing. A lot of it's him saying who he is. He gets to assert himself and it gives him a purpose–that's another strategy I use with him.

Then me and Jeff talk, and Jeff says, "I want to kill him. How do we get rid of him? How are we going to do it?"

I tell Jeff, "We need him right now. We're fucked without him. The same person that got us in here is going to get us out. I don't know how it's going to go down. I don't know what he's going to do but I'll figure that out."

I come to understand that I can't do everything because it's too much. It's like how I do my job. I manage the situation. I can't manage every single aspect but I need to know enough details about it.

"We're going to work our way out and keep Diego in sight, but at the same time, distance ourselves from him in some way. We have to figure a way outta here and if that means Diego takes the fall, so be it. I'll worry about that. You do this."

Then Diego and Jeff start going back and forth and I tell Diego, "From now on, if you have anything to say to Jeff, you go through me. I can't help you guys out in an argument because it gets loud and then I get pissed and I need quiet."

"Absolutely, sir. No problem. Corey, is it okay if I ask Jeff about what we want for dinner?"

I say, "Not right now, but we'll talk about it later. Run it by me and we'll talk to Jeff about it." They're fighting over stupid little things like do we eat chicken or not. I'm setting the ground rules and trying to help Jeff.

I say, "C'mon, Jeff. You're a smart guy. You have to start thinking things through with me. We have to work on stuff mainly to occupy your time so you're not sitting around saying 'the world owes me.'" I'm trying to get him in the game.

Me and my dad talk around 8:30 a.m. my time, 6:30 a.m. Denver time. He wants to know what happened the night before. I explain the barrels being full of water and impossible to move. I'm real direct with my dad about my priorities.

I tell him we still need someone on the street making moves for us. This is my number one priority. The way to get money is through an agent. I need a place where the families can funnel money to us. Short term, this could be Diego's family but we also need a contract with them because they've got all of our possessions, including our passports. Diego's family is the only one I have right now working for us on the street.

I'm never able to get someone on the street working for us. They don't understand it. I don't think the concept is that difficult, but somehow I'm never able to explain it in a way that makes sense to anyone. We never get anyone working on the street for us. I have a power play for Diego to get us out of prison, and I can't jeopardize that relationship.

One night I'm lying there and I get this idea that maybe I can take all this money I'm paying out and use it as a tax deduction. I tell my dad, "We have to set up an LLC. We have to funnel all the money through it so all of this money I'm losing, I can use as a tax write off next year when I get out of this. When I walk out of this, I'm not going to walk away empty-handed." This idea goes nowhere.

By noon we have a proposal from a lawyer I like. He will take on the case for $15,000 U.S. for each person we want him to defend. Diego's situation isn't clear. I would like to dump him, but that won't work, so it's $15 grand per person or $45,000.

He tells us, "You have five days to apply for an appeal for the judgment that happened Monday and one day has already passed. Let me know when you want to get started." I tell him we'll get back to him by the next day, that we have a few more lawyers to interview first.

All Jeff wants is someone to come speak to him in English. He says this over and over again. Finally I say, "No one is going to show up and speak English asshole, accept it. All right? It's not going to happen." It never does happen.

Weeks later, toward the end of all of this, he finally comes to understand and accept this fact, but the whole time, he's saying,

"I want somebody to come and talk to me in English."

He has the wrong mindset the entire fucking time and this is killing me. He still doesn't understand the importance of the situation we're in with Diego's family. All the lawyers want to get the passports away from Diego's family. I'm not going to let that one slide because I'm not sure about it.

The one thing I know is as long as Diego is in my sight I have my passports. I still know how to get to his house so if we have to escape in the middle of the night, I know how to get back there to get our things.

I have all of this in my head. The problem is I need people to do what I tell them. I'm here. I'm on the inside. I'm the one living this.

I tell my dad, "Just do what I tell you to. You don't need to know about everything going on."

I only want my dad to know this; I only want this lawyer to know that; I only want Jeff to know this and I only want Jeff's mother to know this.

I have to keep the plan I'm working on in my head. If I let anyone know ahead, I can't trust it because everyone runs their mouth and they don't know when they should shut up and when they should talk. That includes the families as well as Jeff and Diego. I can't knock them for it, so the best way I can do it is give them pieces of information along the way.

I want the number one lawyer that all the drug dealers use to get out. I send Diego on a mission to find out who that is. Diego comes back with Julio, who got beat up really bad. He starts hanging out with us in our area. He's a real goofy guy. He acts really crazy but he's brilliant. Julio has hacked into every bank and financial institution in the DR and stolen millions from them all, so obviously there is no Internet security in the Dominican Republic.

Julio has roughly nine wives and somewhere around 20–25 kids. He's hacked into everything, stolen money from everywhere and transfers money wherever he wants to. He tells us how easy it is because financial institutions have no security. One bank pays him to steal from another bank. He robbed one bank and they came back and said, "We want you to knock off this other bank and you get to keep like 25% or 50% of the money." He refused to do it and they beat him down. So he got himself put in jail, going to prison, to get protection because he's safer inside than he is on the streets. But he's going in there with his computer.

I ask him, "How do you do that?"

He says, "I'll show you. I'll hack into Domino's Pizza and send a bunch of pizzas to the house." He's this phenomenal person. He's a legend in the country.

We meet very important people in jail and prison. Julio hangs out with Enrique. They share a cell. They come down and spend the day with us.

Enrique has a Blackberry that he can use to get on the internet and Julio has his laptop and they go to work for us and track down this lawyer who is the best in the country and Enrique backs him up, too. This is where our networking is coming into play. "He's the best. You can ask all the guards."

Diego goes around and asks the guards. They say, "Yeah, that guy, he's number one."

Here we go, we're doing business.

This lawyer shows up and I love the way he's dressed. He's about my height or so and he's wearing gold metal wire glasses. He has a daily planner with him and he's wearing kind of like a plaid shirt, buttoned down, long-sleeved and he's wearing a jacket over it and he's wearing jeans and a belt with a belt buckle on it and brown cowboy boots. He's not the over-the-top slick guy and he's dressed appropriately. He's a working guy. You can tell he's authentic.

We meet with him and I tell him our story. Jeff stands there and I do most of the talking. The only thing Jeff says, repeatedly, is, "I want someone who can speak English. I want someone who can speak English."

The lawyer can't speak English, but he says, "No problem. I can bring someone to do translating for you guys. I have people on my staff that can speak English. As a matter of fact, my niece and my daughter can translate for you. If you want them to come, we can bring them with us when we discuss anything with you guys."

I feel good about this guy. I really like him.

He says, "I have a lot at stake. I'm very well known."

I say, "What about your fee?"

He says, "Very simple. It will be $4,000 apiece and you don't pay until you get out."

This is what I've been saying all along! We need someone who cares as much about us getting out as we do. I have a good feeling about this guy.

We finish our conversation and he says, "Would you like to retain my services?"

I let him know that we want to make a decision by tomorrow morning and we have some other lawyers that we still might interview.

"Absolutely. Take your time. This is very wise of you. Take your time to make your decision."

His first response isn't, "Here's my retainer and you have to do it right away..."

He has a very business-like approach about it and Diego says, "I really feel good about him."

What I don't know at this point, but Jeff does while we're standing there talking to this lawyer, is that *he and his mother have already hired a new lawyer and that agreement doesn't include me!*

She hires a lawyer for her boy and sends the guy $5,500. I also don't know that when my dad found out they did that, he signed the same contract with this guy and sent him $5,500, too. My dad understands that we need to stay together if we're going to get through this.

If I had known about this at the time, I would've flipped out and killed Jeff. Well, I wouldn't kill Jeff, but I'm really pissed. If we're throwing money around on the outside, we turn into walking ATM's.

My worst nightmare is having all of our eggs in one basket and then we're f'd. We went down that road the first time. I need to have counter-measures in place, and people who have a stake in our interests in more than one area. We end up losing all of that strategy when Jeff pulls the trigger on this. Some decisions are also made–without either of us knowing about them–that make things even more complicated and it gets real messy.

That afternoon, the new lawyer, a dark black guy who is going to represent us, shows up at our place at the courthouse and wants to meet with us. He's reviewing our case.

A guard comes to us and says, "Hey, your lawyer's here." So me and Jeff follow the guard down the hall. Diego is there but he's walking behind us.

We thought it was Marco again because Marco is now trying to bring us food and snacks every second and anything we need because he wants to keep more money coming. So this guy shows up and I'm looking at him down the hall and he doesn't look familiar and Jeff says, "Oh yeah, this is the new lawyer that my mom hired for me."

"What the fuck?!"

He says this as we're walking toward this guy and making eye contact! I have to think quick. I have to come up with something and I was like, "Shit!"

This guy doesn't speak any English. These people right here make our lives hell. They don't get it. Because everyone that comes to see us speaks Spanish! Guess who speaks Spanish for us?

Diego.

So you can't pull a bamboozle on Diego because you have to talk to us through Diego and these people are flirting with our lives now. At any moment in time now Diego can say, "Yeah, I'll go testify against them and I'll say the Americans did it so I can get out of here and they're screwed."

Diego can do that, and they probably want him to, and if he does, he'll get even more of a pat on the back from the lawyers, or the legal system. If there is even a hint of Diego turning on us, we can take care of it quicker from the inside than my dad and Jeff's mom can over the phone with these dumb ass lawyers.

It still makes me angry when I talk about it because our parents are playing with our lives right now and they don't even know it. They're listening to the wrong people. They're not listening to me, first of all, but they're listening to Jeff, even worse, and beyond that, they're listening to lawyers who don't know anything about what is going on.

So he shows up and I was like, "Shit!" and this was as we were walking toward him and he comes up and starts talking to us and I tell Jeff,

"He's from the U.S. Embassy, right? U. S. Embassy, right? *Sí?*"

We convince Diego that this guy is from the Embassy and he's here to help us. In Diego's mind, the Embassy is a lot better than lawyers. We tell him they need our permission to file paperwork requesting an investigation into our case. It worked.

The lawyer picks up on what we're trying to do here. He says, "Yes, I'm from the U.S. Embassy. Here's my card," and he gives Diego his business card.

Diego looks at it and says, "It says he's a lawyer on this. Yeah, he's probably a lawyer from the U.S. Embassy." Diego is buying into what's going on.

The lawyer didn't say a whole lot in this situation. He didn't overstate anything and luckily we were only allowed a real short time to meet with him. We're very busy that day with all of the people coming to see us. Marco is camped out, different lawyers come through, and the girl's family is there along with people from Diego's neighborhood.

The guard says, "Man, that's enough with him–you have to go back."

That was the first of a series of "Oh Shit!" moments. We pulled this one off.

I'm the one making decisions for the group because Jeff isn't capable and Diego is too dangerous. I can't handle all the phone calls, watch what Diego's doing all day, and think about the prison environment we're headed to. It's too much. I have to delegate and monitor the activity. It's mentally exhausting for me. I need time, and quiet, to think.

I go through the process of interviewing other lawyers, even though we already have a new lawyer, to create a smokescreen for Diego. I don't want him to know we have a new lawyer and it doesn't include him. That's why I'm so mad at Jeff. He won't keep his mouth shut and he's talking to his mom about the lawyer and anyone can hear him.

I say, "Jeff, you have to let me know what you're doing."

"Well, I told my mom..."

I'm doing everything I can to ensure our current situation and Jeff's doing everything he can to jeopardize it. No matter how much I try to explain that our situation can get much worse, he refuses to believe it.

"How much worse can things get than this man? We're going to prison."

"Well, it could be worse if we get thrown in with the animals; or they separate us; or Diego's gone and you and I are by ourselves; or you're by yourself. What the hell is going to happen then? Do you understand how vulnerable we are?"

He either won't accept it or he's struggling with the concept of things getting worse, and later on, during the course of a conversation, I'm angry, frustrated and exhausted with this scenario. No one really understands everything I'm doing here. They think they know what's going on. I'm trying to keep Diego in check and Jeff straight, but there's more to it than that.

Julio hangs out with us during the day. He's telling us funny, crazy stories about all of his wives and kids and how his wives, the mother of his children, have boyfriends and how he kicks them out when he comes over so he can have sex with her. We use him all day for information. He's working on his own case and making up fake papers for himself. We don't see him again but he's popular with the people in this area.

Then Denny, a young kid, comes into our room. His foot is swollen bad. I tell Diego to tell him I'm medically trained and ask if I could look at it. So I look at it to see if it's broken and it isn't. It's a really bad sprain. Me and Denny talk a little bit. I do a lot of Spanish with him. He reminds me of myself a lot and if I was there I would probably be like him. Basically, he's an athlete. He plays basketball all the time and he tells me he's real good.

He said the cops came to bust him. The cops and everyone else knows he's dealing drugs. Denny does it because that's the way to make money. You bank it all away, then you go to jail for a while, and after you get out, you go back to work. I don't knock it because there are no jobs.

One day the cops decide to arrest him. When the cops come to bust him, they throw him off the third or fourth story balcony. He landed on his foot and that's how he busted it. He's telling us about it and he had significantly more cocaine on him than what we are accused of. He's going to go to prison with us but he can't walk too good. He ends up staying with us, which turns into a benefit later on.

We hang out back in our area and wait to go. We pack up our stuff and the things that we're going to need. The guards that work in the jail and the courthouse come in to say goodbye to us. The new guards that will be handling us on our way to prison are there as well. There are people in and out all day.

The day before, one of the guards asked to use our phone charger and I told Diego to keep track of it. We can't lose it. We never got it back and I'm pissed at Diego about it. He needs to go get it.

"Dammit we need that for the phone," I say to Diego. "I told you not to let that charger out of your sight." He's also handing out the phone for people to use. We have to buy minutes for the phone and it gets expensive.

"Don't let other people use the phone, or they can use it for a short period of time, but don't let that phone out of your sight. People want to use it and you go handing it out and hope you get it back. I understand what you're trying to do, but don't lose the one thing we have left. If we lose that phone we're fucked."

I have a real stern conversation with him about this and reaffirm that if the phone is for me, he'd better stop what he's doing and give it to me. I don't have a lot of people calling, so when it's for me you better know it's important on the other end.

He says, "I understand, sir. If it rings for you I will stop everything and get the phone to you." He gets good about that, but it turns out that I didn't need to talk about the phone at all because we leave the jail without it.

At the same time, I give him rules to operate under. I give him an assignment, "I want to know what's going on around us at all times, and make sure that we're making connections with the right people."

He needs that kind of structure because he's not a disciplined person and he's a coke addict. He did coke Sunday night, the night before we went to court. You'd never know it, though. When someone does it recreationally they can usually maintain their lives. For all I know, he could have been buying, or doing, cocaine in that really bad neighborhood where we were right before we were arrested. All of those stops he made during the day while we hung around could have been cocaine-related.

Diego needs to be somebody but at the same time, he's networking for us, which is a valuable asset. We can't talk to anybody because of the language barrier, but we need to make sure that we're not perceived as a threat to any other prisoners. They need to see that we don't want any problems with them. We'll be transported later that day. That means we're out of our sheltered area and vulnerable to other prisoners and whatever situation that could come up with guards.

I'm packing up my backpack. I'm trying to put all of our clothes in it. We each have a change of clothes. Diego says he's taken care of everything. He makes sure the phone is going to be there when we get there. We're supposed to leave in the morning but we don't leave until late in the afternoon.

No one knows what's going on. There's a huge amount of anxiety. No one is going to have a way to contact us. We're not going to have access to a phone and for 24–48 hours we're going to disappear off the face of the earth again.

We're also going to be out with the rest of the guys going to prison. Diego says he took care of the bus. He's paid the guards and made sure that we have a seat. You have to buy a seat, everything's money. It's like an old RTD bus with plastic seats. A lot of seats have been removed in the back so they can pack as many people in as possible. It's standing room only. They call it the Grey Goose.

Diego's working all the angles at the prison. We're going to have to figure out a way to get some money once we get there. We don't have that much on us, so we're rationing it out. I tell Diego and Jeff that they've got to quit smoking; we're going to need the money for food and drinks. They never quit smoking, though.

Diego manages the money for the most part. He got the money from Marco. We didn't give Diego any money from our hands which is good because people are constantly asking us for money and we can honestly tell them we don't have any.

I'm constantly thinking, "I have to get control of this situation. I have to think of a way out of this. There has to be a way. I have to get my mind there." I'm running every possible option in my head. I can keep a lot of things in my head without writing them down but it's hard. I'm a white board kind of a person.

When I'm working, my office walls are cover with white boards. There's stuff, like stickies, on every wall including my written notes. People crack up when they see it. When I was in school I wrote on every window and every mirror: what was going on; what I needed to do; what I was studying; chemistry notes.

The guards finally come in and say it's time to go. I have a new white tank top on with the same shorts that I was wearing when we got arrested, mainly because they have a lot of pockets so I can stash a bunch of stuff in them.

We walk down the corridor and everyone gets handcuffed together. Denny, the kid with the busted foot, can't walk too good so me and Diego are together and Denny and Jeff go together. Jeff is a pretty big guy so he can help Denny around. At the same time, Denny is a well-respected hood so we should have no problems riding over there on the bus and going in and out around the other prisoners.

I'm in full calculating mode. If I walk around this corner, this could happen. If I move in this direction, that could happen. If I speak to this person, this could happen and I've mapped out in my mind what my response will be in each situation. I'm doing this every split second.

We get out in the hallway and it's so funny. I have my backpack with all of our stuff in it. All of the other prisoners are hanging around. They've got all of their clothes and everything their families brought them to go to prison in shopping bags. I'm amazed that no one is negative about going to prison. We start to get this vibe that this prison thing is not what we're expecting. The atmosphere is happy. They look happy to go.

Everyone is talking about my hair because it's so long. I haven't cut it for about two years. It's long and in dreads.

Someone says, "Yeah, when you get to prison they shave your head."

That's what all the guys are talking about, *"pelo–no más, no más."*

They say, "The American, his hair is going to get cut."

And everyone is cracking up about it and I'm joking along with them, too.

I say, *"Cuántos pesos por mi pelo?"* How much will you give for my hair?

"Sí, Sí, he's going to sell it."

We're waiting for the bus and joking around occupies my mind. We talk to the other guys around us.

Finally, the bus shows up and they take everyone down the stairs. We go first mainly because we have Denny with us with his bad foot; he's limping down. Beyond that, we're the Americans and the guards are going to take care of us.

We get on the bus and they show us which seats are ours. We sit down and they start bringing the rest of the inmates on board. These are all the guys who don't have money to sit down. Some of them look pretty rough. This kid tells me and Diego to get out of our seat. He's going to sit there.

"I'm gonna cut you with my knife."

He's reaching for his sock or whatever and I'm trying to figure out how to protect us when I'm handcuffed to Diego. But he doesn't have a knife on him so the confrontation ends there.

Diego's against the window and I'm on the aisle and Jeff is on the other side with Denny. Denny has one crutch. We go down the road riding on the bus through the city that five days ago we viewed completely differently. I'm remembering, "That's the park we walked around and we drove by that building. Then the bus gets out on the waterfront against the ocean and I'm looking out at the water.

I'm thinking, "God! What the fuck did I do? How is this happening? I can't believe I'm on my way to prison right now." No one is happy on the bus. Everyone is in the doldrums.

Guys give Diego dirty looks because people from the neighborhood told them what he did to the girl. There's a code even amongst criminals. You don't let women get put in this position. Diego is trying to explain his way out of it.

"That's not what happened. The police did it. We didn't do anything to her."

Before the bus left, the girl's baby's daddy is telling all the guys from his neighborhood about it. He's trying to start some shit. Later, he comes to the prison and looks at us and we look at him. I look at the girl and she smiles at me and I look at him and I shake my head and keep walking.

He basically tells all the guys, "Yeah, Diego got my girl in this trouble." That spreads like wildfire so Diego is trying to explain his way out of it. They see the Americans and it's not helping Diego's case. He's in a whole world of problems he put himself into. It really starts evolving, but this is the beginning of it. He tries to explain his way out of it to all of these guys. Everyone is pissed at him.

It takes about an hour and a half to get to where we're going. Every time we're being transported, I'm anxious. There's an opportunity for us to get split up or be diverted to another jail we don't know about. No one knows where we are right now. We've lost contact with the outside world. We're not supposed to show up at the prison with phones. We find out we could have had them and could have used them while we were on the bus if we had paid the right guy. Diego didn't get all the details straight, but hey, you can only do so much.

We talk back and forth a little bit as we go down the road. This kid's standing there the whole time and he asks me if he can sit down and I say, "no problema." So I slide over a little bit on my seat and let him sit on the edge there. He says, "Gracias, amigo" and he gives me a little fist pound.

There's a guy sitting behind us who says in English, "Are you from the States? Are you American?"

I say, "Yeah, I'm from the States."

He says, "No way, man. I used to live in New York." This is the beginning of meeting people from New York.

"I really like the States. Actually, man, I don't like the United States at all, but I like the people there. The people in the States are really good but the country is the bad part."

And it kind of hits me. Even in this developing country, there is a real understanding that what America does and what the people in America are like, are two separate things. A lot of what America does has nothing to do with the people that live there.

So this guy's really cool and he's talking to me, telling me about himself and where he's been and I'm talking about what I do.

He says, "Man, how in the hell did you end up in this shit?"

I say, "We were riding in a car and the police said they found drugs in it."

"Really? Who did that to you?"

"This is the driver right here," and I lift up my hand that's handcuffed to Diego. I'm not saying anything bad, just the truth about what's going on.

"What the fuck," he says.

Diego says, "Man, the police set us up."

He says, "I don't know how that shit happens."

Diego's telling him in Spanish and in English. He's changing languages because he doesn't want me to know what he's saying. At the same time, I'm starting to pick it up real quick. So he's riding along and the guy is a pretty big dude and he says,

"Yeah, man, this fucking country. That's how they do it. They get everyone, man. I feel bad for you, bro. I can't believe they did that to American tourists coming here. How long have you been coming here?"

"This is our first time."

"No! Your first time here and you get arrested? Well how long were you here for?"

I say, "Less than 24 hours."

"What! You have to be kidding me. That's fucked up, kid."

I say, "Yeah, man, I can't believe it."

"And now you're going to prison. What the fuck? Dude, your lawyer must have fucked something up. There's no way you should be here."

And we hear this over and over again.

I talk to this kid throughout the trip and it's cool because I'm talking to someone other than Diego. We do the Spanglish thing and everyone around us listens to us go back and forth. He tells me about this part of the country and asks about stuff in the States and places I've been. It's small talk but really cool, too.

Then I ask him "Najayo? How do you say it?"

"Nah-Hi-yo," he says.

"N–A–J–A–E–O"?

"No, N–A–J–A–Y–O," he says.

I say, "Okay. That's where we'll be tonight."

"Do you know where you're staying when you get there?"

"No, I don't know."

Diego tells him where we're staying and then he says, "Yeah, we're connected."

The guy says, "My name is___. If you need anything let me know. I'm in Area___." He tells me what area he's in but I don't remember it. "I know a lot of people in there so let me know if you need anything."

Of course, Diego pipes in, "Oh, yeah, that's where you're from? I know such and such from that same area." Diego always has to one-up everyone. It annoys everyone and the guy says, "Yeah, yeah, yeah."

We're pulling into the prison and it's dusk. It's getting dark and the sun is setting. The prison is set back against this beautiful mountain range and what's left of the sun is glowing over it.

The guy I've been talking to says, "This is the juvenile prison right here. This is the women's prison and this is the men's prison. The juvenile prison, that place is crazy man, it's all fucked up. They don't know how to act in there."

I'm thinking, this is going to be an interesting place we're going to.

"It depends on what part of the prison you're in. You guys got money so you should be all right. Because it's all business, man, it's all business. If you have money, you guys will be okay."

"Cool."

They open up the gates to let us in. We come to a circular driveway with grass and trees. There's a flagpole in the center of it. Later we watch as each morning four guards come out to raise the country's flag and salute it, and come back at sundown to lower it. I see what appears to be the main entrance to the prison.

I notice all of these guys hanging out. There are a lot of little doors that open out to the front yard and a bunch of guys sitting outside on chairs and on the grass. They're wearing regular clothes and they aren't guards. There are women and children there, too. It's like a family picnic.

I'm thinking, "What the hell?"

Diego says, "Yeah, man, that's where all the drug dealers, the big rollers, live. Right there where all of those little doors are. Those are private places and their families come to visit them and hang out."

This is prison? What the fuck?

They look like Americans. There are a lot of Columbians sitting out there with their families. They all look white. If you didn't know any better you'd think they were a bunch of Americans.

Diego says, "Yeah, man, in the DR we got every race here."

The bus pulls in, stops, and they bring us out. I'm looking around and I see this woman who looks like a prostitute. They keep saying you can get anything in the prison if you have the money, but we didn't believe them.

By now the sun's gone down and it's dark. It's probably 8:00 or 9:00. I see guards wearing gray uniforms walking around with a stick, pieces of wood. It looks like a two by four. That's their weapon. Some of them don't have anything but most have sticks and they're sitting around here not doing anything. There are other guys dressed in street clothes talking to the guards.

I'm still struggling with my idea of what a prison should look like and how it should be run. I'm thinking, "What the hell?"

I'm trying to figure out what's going on here. They get us all out of the bus and they have us sit down on the curb, still handcuffed. The whole time we're going through this, I'm constantly telling Jeff not to smile. He can't help it, when he's nervous, he has a smirk on his face. It's an ongoing battle telling him not to smile.

"We're going to prison. It's a bad place. Stop smiling." I'm always telling him that. It's not his natural look and it looks funny.

They sit us down on the curb and a guard comes over and he starts talking. I think he's telling us the rules of what goes on in the prison and how you're expected to act. The guards have authority, and at any point in time you don't follow their directions, who knows? He's rambling and I kind of get a sense of it.

So this guy comes out and he's the guy who's going to cut everyone's hair. He's one of the inmates. When he sees my hair, he's got this big dipshit grin on his face and he says,

"Oh my god! I get to cut the American's hair. Look at all that hair!" He's all excited. He comes over and tells Diego that if I want to keep it, it's going to be 3,000 pesos. That's about $100, but you can live off of 500 pesos a day in there.

I say, "Fuck it, man. I don't give a shit."

I look insane. I didn't wash it the whole time we were in the jail. It's down to my shoulders in dreads and I say to him, "Man, I need a hair cut."

Diego agrees, "You said you needed a haircut anyway."

I say, "Yeah, man, we need every penny we have. We'll need to get some more minutes for the phone when we get one."

We're down to under 1,000 pesos right now. We don't know when we're going to get money again, and who we're going to have to pay. If we have to pay when we walk in, what are we going to do? We were told that we have to buy our cells. We can pick out which ones we want out of the ones that are available, and then we buy a bed in that cell. Everything costs money and as long as you have money you're good. The whole time I'm trying to figure out how to get money. How are we going to get money brought to us? Marco had $4,000 on him but I don't know how much he has left.

There are all kinds of inmates walking around out here in front of the prison. These guys are dressed really nice in regular clothes, pretty stylish. Nice Converse All Stars, nice shorts on, hair cut looks nice and they look clean-shaven. They are dressed like they'd be in any mall in America. Some of them are wearing total "ghetto-hood" fashion. Some have hats and some of them don't. The shirt matches the shoes.

I'm looking at all these guys and I don't know what's going on but they're talking amongst themselves and they're looking at us. More than anything else, everyone has their attention on us even though they try not to show it.

These inmates come up and they want to talk to us and we start talking to the guards, too, and they're trying to say something to us and Diego says, "Hey, they don't know any Spanish."

"No habla español?"

Diego says, "No, they're Americans. They don't know any Spanish."

Someone asks, "What are they doing here?" Diego has to talk for everyone, and he keeps explaining it to them. Diego has to go with us everywhere because we need him to translate.

Finally, the guy comes over to take me in to shave my head. All these guys are not allowed to say anything, but the look on their faces when I go is hilarious. He takes me inside and there's a window, a table and a bench. The space is old and narrow, kind of like a thruway. People are constantly going in and out and everyone is looking at me and Jeff. He sits me down on this table and he starts to shave my head. It's so long that I try to help him out while he does it. It falls down and makes this giant pile of hair. It looks like a dead cat when he gets done.

The guard comes over and he's looking at me. It's supposed to be an authority thing. Like, "Yeah, we're going to shave your head and prove you're nothing." He's trying to do that intimidation thing, but at the same time, I'm an American and he wants to be my friend so it's kind of a funny experience.

I come walking back around and I sit with all the other guys and all my hair's gone and they look at my head–even the guards are looking–and everyone is laughing. The guard that's speaking is looking at me out of the corner of his eye. I look so drastically different with my head shaved.

Then a guard does this "Simon says" thing where they have us stand up and sit down, and stand up and sit down. It's kind of like the movie "Cool Hand Luke." The guard's in charge and when he tells you to sit down, you sit down, and when he tells you to stand up, you stand up. "Follow my instructions. I'm in charge." Kind of like boot camp style.

We're sitting on the concrete and we got our heads shaved and they start calling out guys' names and taking them inside the prison.

Two guys keep looking at us and we're looking at them. We find out later that one of them is Alex. Alex is wearing some really up-to-date Converse All Stars and they have a design on them and he's wearing shorts and an Ed Hardy tee shirt. He's wearing all name brand stuff. He's watching everything going on. Eventually he approaches Diego and they talk. Alex looks like a light–skinned Hispanic. He has this goatee and wavy hair and is probably in his 30's to 40's. He's a skinny guy. I figure he's gay from looking at him.

The other guy is Fidel. He's a dark skinned guy with a shaved head. He's in his 40's or 50's, I believe. He's wearing an orange shirt, khaki shorts, and orange and blue Nikes that match his shirt. They both approach us and Alex speaks a little bit of English.

It's finally time to go through the "Door to Hell." We've done everything we could to delay it but it's time. The guards take our handcuffs off before taking us through. In front of us is a long hall with men standing around. Some of them are talking together but a lot of them are just standing by themselves. It's very dark. The prison was built of concrete and cinder blocks and the halls have no windows. There are a few naked light bulbs in the ceiling but they aren't turned on. It's too expensive to run electricity.

We come to the first gate. They have a lock on everything. There's an inmate, like a trustee, whose job it is to man this gate and open it for people and the guards. The guards never open any of their own gates. It's funny. Why work when you can get someone to do it for you? Every time we go through a gate, they want money, like a couple of pesos, to open it for us. This becomes a chore later on.

We stop at the first iron–bar door on the left and Alex points at it and says, "Look." Diego tells us Alex wants us to understand that if we can't pay for our cells, this is where we will end up. We are horrified by what we see.

How the Prison System Functions

Looking into that room is our first experience of just what we are facing at Najayo prison and much of it is so much worse than I could ever have imagined. The prison doesn't provide anything for the inmates. If you're a nobody with no money, once a day you get a bowl of gruel. It's the nastiest crap I've ever seen and smells disgusting. There's no telling what they use to make this stuff, but if it's the only food you get all day, you learn to eat it. Everything else, you have to pay for.

All of the "rooms" we see as we walk through the prison are called pods. Each pod is rectangular, made of concrete, with an open area in front that lets air in and openings to the outside with iron bars in the concrete in the back to provide some ventilation. Even so, it's sweltering hot inside no matter what anyone does.

The cells are in the back of the pod. In our pod, there are eight cells with four on each side. Each cell is designed to hold from three, to however many inmates they can cram into it.

Each pod has its own organization, called a syndicate, with leadership and rules everyone in the pod lives by. If there's some kind of dispute between inmates in the pod, the syndicate boss steps in and sorts it out. Some of these syndicates function better than others.

The syndicate is responsible for keeping their area clean. Some of the cells are disgusting and some of them are as clean as they can be considering the circumstances. Ours is one of the best ones we see and we're grateful that we are allowed to stay there. That is, as long as we can get some money. Me and Jeff decide if we have to stay here a long time, we're getting our own cell, put in a dish and watch football all day long.

Even though a judge sentences you to a certain amount of time in prison, you have to pay the warden to get in. Then you pay the guards. Then, unless you want to stay in one of the cages, you choose a pod and which cell in the pod you'd like to stay in. You have to pay the syndicate boss to get into the pod, and the guy who owns the cell to get a bed. If you don't have money, out you go into the general population, and possibly, a cage. Then, when a judge releases you, you have to pay the guards and the warden again to get out.

The prison doesn't provide anything. Not food, first aid, cleaning products, medication, personal hygiene products, bedding or anything else, so you either have someone you know bring it in or you have to buy it inside. You can get anything in prison that you can get outside. Each syndicate provides a special service or product. They have little stores like concession stands you'd see at a ballgame, in the front part of the pods.

There's a trustee who works for the guards in the prison. He coordinates all of the different food, toilet paper, soap, clothing, books, magazines, towels, etc. coming into these stores. He sells each product to the syndicate that handles that particular thing. Some of what he makes goes to the warden and some to the guards. Then, when the product is sold to the inmates throughout the prison, the syndicate makes money. It's a giant business.

There is constant noise. Walking down the hall you go from one boom box playing one station to the next boom box playing something else. On top of that, the guys in the hall are yelling at each other. Guys standing around in the halls are constantly touching us, begging for money. The guys who are not allowed out of their cell are pushed against the bars with their arms outstretched begging for money. Some of them are banging things against the bars. It's so loud and discordant I literally can't think. I'm a person who needs to be in a quiet environment. Constant noise and confusion just stirs up my ADHD and I get more and more stressed out. This is one of the hardest things for me to deal with while we're in Najayo.

It's a flea market atmosphere. You go to the fruit guy and say, "What do you have today?" and he says, "I have bananas and papaya." The next guy makes Johnnycakes, the next guy makes rice, the next guy fixes shoes, another guy fixes electronics like TVs and boom boxes. Everyone has a purpose.

There's a little garden out in the front yard and this little guy grows vegetables that he sells to the inmates who cook the food for the inmates to buy. The juice guy makes the best smoothies because it's all fresh and organic. It's only 40 pesos, a little more than a dollar, and you could easily sell it in the States for $8 a pop. People go nuts over it. It has all kinds of fresh fruit like mangos and papaya. And that's this guy's thing.

There's a paint crew that will paint your cell, a construction crew that does concrete work the whole time we're there. There's an electrician that will put in another fan for you. He'll hardwire it in. He'll put in another line so if the electricity goes out—which it does all the time—you have a backup. Some of the guys have satellite dishes and they can watch anything they want.

Certain inmates are assigned to take care of the common areas in the prison. They make sure the offices that the guards use are acceptable, but with the immense overcrowding, the halls are packed day and night with dirty, stinking, disgusting human beings and it's virtually impossible for them to keep those areas clean. There's dirt and trash all over the floor, along the walls and in the corners. Bugs crawl around looking for bits of food the inmates just drop on the floor.

The stench is overpowering. It's the smell of an open sewer worse than any Porta–Potty you've ever been in. There is no septic system. All of the waste goes through a pipe lying on top of the ground and empties into an open field. Imagine over 2,500 men and how much waste moves through this "system" if that's what you want to call it.

Of course, open sewers attract and breed flies and mosquitos. There's nothing you can do about it. Flies land on you all day long and while you sleep. There are flies in your food, sometimes they're alive, and sometimes they're dead. Mosquitos bite and draw blood, then move on the next person. From my EMT training I know they can't spread HIV, but they do spread malaria and dengue fever.

There are sick inmates wandering around everywhere. They cough without covering their mouths and my vivid imagination sees billions of bacteria and viral organisms being spread throughout the population. There is no medical care unless you can pay for it so most illnesses go untreated. A large number of inmates are HIV positive and many of those have AIDS. They're supposed to be taken to clinics to receive treatment but, again, if you don't have money to pay the guards to let you out and the bus drivers to take you to the clinic, you aren't going anywhere.

For a lot of people, life inside the prison is better than outside. On the outside they're homeless, there's no work. But in prison they have a skill. They like being there because they get to be somebody. There's no welfare in this country so this is the closest thing you might get to welfare.

The thing is, anyone can come visit you three days a week. They can bring you anything you want. They have conjugal visits, too. There are times when me and Jeff can't get to our cells on visiting days because the guys are taking turns. With all of these privileges, a lot of inmates prefer to stay there than to get released.

Tuesday, June 23, continued

When Alex points at the door and says, "look," me and Jeff walk up to the front and look in. It's completely dark. I stand there until my eyes adjust to the darkness and then I can't believe what I'm seeing. I'm looking at Hell.

It's an open cage made out of bars on three sides, about 25' x 25' with a concrete floor and ceiling. A mass of 40–50 naked men just stand there. This cage reminds me of what I saw in the jail, only so much worse. There are so many bodies stuffed in there that it's impossible to have any kind of personal space. They're connected by the lack of room. The temperature, with no ventilation, has to be well over 130 degrees.

These guys are slowly starving to death. Nobody cares. It's just one less person to take up space so they can put someone else in there. They get one bowl of nasty gruel a day. They tear up newspaper and stir it into the gruel to make it bulkier so they feel full. They stand around in the cage and I can count their ribs and the vertebrae running down their spines. They all have these little potbellies that you see on starving people around the world.

There is no toilet and no water inside the cage. If someone wants to use the toilet, they have to have money to pay a guard to let them out and money to pay someone else to use it. The smell that comes out of this cage is indescribable. It's a stink like nothing I've ever smelled before. With no toilet, the men have no other option but to defecate and urinate on the concrete floor. Then they walk in it and it gets spread around. Guys are standing in the feces. They're sitting in it, lying in it. They're covered in it; it's in their hair.

Added to that is the smell of unwashed bodies. If you don't have money to go into an area that has water, you're never going to get a shower. And even if you pay to get into one of those areas, all they have is a hose you can use to rinse yourself off. There's no soap; that costs extra. The heat and humidity amplify the sickening odor.

There are flies and mosquitos everywhere. I see flies landing on men's faces and bodies. They are so used to it they don't even swat at them anymore to get them off. One guy has a fly in his eyebrow. He doesn't seem to notice. He's staring at me straight in the eyes. I watch as the fly leaves his eyebrow and lands on his lower lip. He doesn't even twitch. I have to turn away.

Some of the inmates are ill, their vomit lying on the floor just inches from their mouth. Someone moves past the cage close enough that I can see black sores on his back. AIDS–related Kaposi's sarcoma. It doesn't surprise me that there are men in the prison with AIDS. It's just another thing to keep in mind. This dangerous situation just got even more deadly. If I was ever forced into a fight with someone I could get infected. I feel like I'm going to be sick.

Jeff is standing next to me and I glance over at him. He has a look of horror on his face that I've never seen before. His mouth has dropped open. He's stopped crying. I give him a nudge and he jerks a little like he's waking up from a very bad dream. He looks at me and closes his mouth. I see his eyes well up.

Throughout our time in Najayo, every time we have to go up front we have to walk past the cage with the dying animals. As many of them as possible have their arms sticking out begging for money. It's no accident that this is the first "room" you pass on your way in. The warden and the guards want you to see where you will end up if you can't pay or you get out of line.

These guys don't have 10,000 pesos (about $300) to pay the warden to get into prison so they're not registered as being there. If the judge gave them three months and they've been there three months, three years or thirty years, they still haven't served their time because as far as the system goes, they were never there.

And even if they can figure out a way to get around that problem, they still can't get out. They can't show up to court naked and covered in filth. And if, by some miracle, they are able to take a shower and somehow get dressed in a nice pair of pants and a button down shirt, they don't have the money to pay the warden to get released.

Their life is over.

My professional life is based on helping people and I feel my anger rise.

Why doesn't the Dominican Republic's legal system do something about this? They can't possibility not know that men sentenced to these prisons are being forced to pay their way in and out. They can't possibility not know that men are "living"–if that's what you want to call it–under these appalling conditions. Are there no humanitarian organizations in the DR? Is there not one Dominican man, woman, politician, priest, nun or business owner who cares? Other countries, including the United States, send missionaries and money to the DR. As far as I can tell, none of the efforts of missionaries or money are directed at the prisons. Does no one care about the conditions in there?

The men in the cage have been reduced to something subhuman, to mistreated animals. Before they got to prison they could have had a family they loved and people who loved them. They had someone to put their arms around, and laughed at kids playing silly games. They hung out with friends, joking around and trying to make the best of their situation.

Now there is no love. It doesn't exist. No one visits them. Even if they have a family, they can't afford the transportation to get to the prison. These inmates have no human contact unless they're shoving someone out of their away. No one is hugging anyone in the cage. There is no laughter, no friends, no life. Life has been stripped away and all they can do is wait to starve to death. This is worse than my worst nightmare because it's real.

I've seen the end of the world and it's a place where people don't matter. This is the definition of Hell. Watching people starve to death in front of you, day-to-day. It's that raw.

The guard opens the door and some of the guys go inside. They don't resist. They don't hesitate. They know there's no point.

We get to a certain point and the guards stop. They don't go any farther. I'm thinking, "Oh shit, why aren't the guards coming with us? What the hell is going on now?" I'm looking around and every possibility is running through my head.

We continue walking with Alex and Fidel through all of this filth and humanity, the stink, the flies, and the disgusting look on people's faces and how dirty everyone is. There's trash on the floor along with what looks like discarded food and other things I can't identify. Things I don't want to identify. There are rat droppings and cockroaches skittering around in the dark places. I don't want to think about what else is roaming these halls.

I'm still thinking, "What's going on?"

The whole time we walk, Alex is saying little bits of English to us. He looks gay to me and he keeps asking me if I want a bath, "Would you like a bath?"

I'm thinking, "I'm not taking a bath with this guy." That's going through my head. I really want a bath because I'm covered with hair from getting my head shaved, but not with him.

We get to the end of the hall and there are stairs that go up to the second floor. We walk up to the pod on the left, right before the stairs, and look inside. This is Area X, our future home. Area X has no bars. There is plenty of circulation. The cut out spaces in the back that help provide ventilation are the only things that have bars on them.

We've been walking through the prison and all this filth, and then, all of a sudden, there's this area that is really clean. Nice. The walls are painted mauve pink. Everyone there is really friendly and happy and smiling. They look nice and they dress nice. It's a real ethnic mix. White people, black people and everything else, all mixed together.

Area X is laid out the same way the other pods are with a large open space in front where the guys can hang out and eight cells in the back, four on each side. In theory, each cell is designed to hold three guys. In reality, overcrowding means a lot of cells have six, seven or more men living there with some pods housing 50 guys or more in the same amount of space. This pod has about 25–30 guys. The open area has two benches and a table where guys play dominoes. A prison guard that the syndicate hires to protect them usually stands in this open area. There's a little concession stand in front.

They've got music going but it's turned down. There are guys playing dominoes at the small table and guys talking on their cell phones and a couple of guys are lying on mats. It's very relaxed and tranquil. They don't do that crazy stuff. There's a guy standing there. His name is Mano Negro, "Black Hand," pretty big dude, big shoulders, and he likes me a lot.

There's a mural of Jesus on the wall. There are fans in the front and back. There's a fence with a gate that separates the two areas. Anyone can come in the front area and visit but to go to the back, you have to have permission from someone who lives there.

When we walk in, the guys standing there want to shake our hands and meet us. I'm trying to say hello to everyone as we walk in, to acknowledge their existence, and show them some respect.

"Hello, how are you?"

"*Bueno, Bueno,*" I answer.

"*Americano?*"

"*Sí, Americano.*"

"*Americano!*"

Everyone's excited and all of a sudden someone says,

"Where you from, man?"

"What? New York," I say.

"New York! We have someone from New York in here."

That's Rocky.

He has a shaved head, he's lived in New Jersey and he speaks perfect English and Spanish. He's the first person in our entire experience who can speak fluent English. Rocky becomes one of my right hand men along with some other guys. He's the first guy I hire to work for me.

Everyone offers us some food. Here's some bread. They want to show us the cells that they have and what's available. By now, I'm mentally exhausted.

The guys are very metro-sexual in their appearance and the way they act. It's very common for that culture; it's really odd and something that I don't get. If we saw the same guys here with their mannerisms and the way they talk and dress, we'd say these guys must be gay. But it's the way everyone dresses. It doesn't make a statement like that. So what are we doing with a bunch of gay guys? What the fuck? I don't care. I'm thinking, "Man, I'm way too good looking for this." Everyone keeps staring at me.

"Oh, strong American. Look at him."

Alex brings us into the back area and he's talking to all the guys who live back there. All I know is that we need to stay in here, not in any of those other hell-holes we saw. I don't care how much it costs. It doesn't matter about the court case or getting back to the States, we need to survive because if we don't survive, none of it matters. My primary objective is to get in here, and stay in here. We need to get this taken care of. I don't care if we have to pay five grand and we're only here for two nights. That's fine.

Most of the cells have three people. Each cell has a bed, a bathroom with a shower–that's just a spigot coming out of the wall–and a toilet that's in the shower. There's a tiny kitchen area with a mini-fridge. Some guys have flat-screen LCDs, some don't. There are a couple of five-gallon buckets that the guys sit on. And they've got fans going, blowing air.

The building has a high ceiling, so what they do is frame in a crawl space above, and someone can live up there in that area. They make a ladder out of two by fours. That person will have another TV, their clothes and fans going. It covers about the same surface area as the one below. It's a short ceiling but I could sit up without bumping my head.

This is the closest thing we've seen to civilization in a week. Everyone looks clean and nice. They don't look like trash. They don't look sick. They keep everything looking nice. There's the store in front and someone lives above that, too.

It's 10,000 pesos to register in the prison. All of that goes to the warden. Then 5,000 pesos go to Alex because he's the syndicate boss of Area X. After you decide where you want to live, you negotiate the cost of living there with the guy who owns the cell.

We don't have this money on us. They're acting like money's not a big deal. They know how to get money and we don't, so I'm not sure how I'll get the money to pay everything. Again, that's why I need someone on the street making moves for us. Otherwise, we're dependent on Diego's family.

We need to pick out where we want to stay depending on what's available. We go into the first room. Alex lives on the top and Daniel and Joey–who are Hispanic looking–are on the bottom. Everyone has a birth name, a street name and a name in jail. Most of them adopt an American name either on the street or in jail. So Daniel and Joey are names these guys picked. Joey doesn't have any money so he's Daniel's servant.

Daniel is very feminine and Joey looks totally gay. I'm looking at the bed and thinking they must share it. These guys all look like pussies. They're not tough at all. They'd never last a day in an American prison. All three speak some English. Alex tells me that he used to be in computer software. I never asked him why he's in prison.

Even though it looks like the room is full, they've got one guy sleeping in the bed and they pull out mattresses to sleep on the floor. They tell us they have room for Jeff. They're really super friendly.

Diego asks me what I think. I say, "I don't know, man. I have a good feeling about these guys, I trust them. I think it would be good." I trust Diego's judgment on this one, too. He agrees that would be a good place for Jeff.

I say to Jeff, "Go make yourself comfortable with these guys."

Diego and Jeff are in the room, but I stay out in the hall trying to get away from everyone. I'm trying to think. I'm super tired by now and there are guys in the hall and it's noisy. I'm keeping to myself. Diego's doing the talking.

Me and Diego go across the hall to the room where Samuel is. He's shorter than me, kind of stocky, a black kid, knows a little bit of English, has braces on his teeth.

He says, "Whas–up man!"

In his room he has two skinny kids up above. One's light–skinned and one's dark–skinned. I would've sworn they were gay. They're totally feminine but later on, they have the hottest girlfriends I've ever seen. We make fun of them because they're gay all the time, but they constantly say they're not. None of us guys believe them. They have a poster of Winnie the Pooh on the wall!

Winnie the fucking Pooh!

Samuel turns out to be a pretty tough, hard-core dude. He has room for one person but I'm not ready to commit. Diego is talking to everybody and he goes all the way to the back and he's talking to Fidel. Fidel only has two people in his room. Fidel lives on the top and this older man, Javier, lives on the bottom. Javier speaks English. He's an older guy in his 50s to 60s. This place is spotless! I haven't seen anything this clean since I had the misfortune to land in this country.

Diego says, "He's got room for two people on top." So we check out the top area and it would fit two people easy, with Javier on the bottom.

Fidel says, "Do you guys want to work something out?" He wants to do a deal.

I say, "Yeah..." I have the look of exhaustion on my face.

He wants 50,000 pesos because I will buy the room. That's about $1,700.

I say, "I'm very, very tired right now. It's been a very long day with all that's gone on and I don't think it's the right time to make a decision about where to stay and what I want to buy. Would it be possible to negotiate a price tomorrow?"

Fidel says, "No, no problem. Please stay." Fidel and Javier are nice guys and we become friends. Fidel says we can stay the night and pay him for the one night if we don't like it later. It's 1,000 pesos to stay one night. That works out to about $30 a night.

It's been a wild ride. We made it through the bus and we made it through the population. Now we're back here and we have a little sanctuary here. We can breathe. I never expected to be met with kindness in this situation but there it is.

I have all my stuff and these guys have nice stuff too. You get to their little apartments or cells, and they have TV's and nice clothes. I'm thinking, "Well, we don't have to worry about these guys stealing from us." They have nice things, too. It's as close to civilization as we've seen so far.

I say, "This is awesome."

It's been a week now that we've been in a hellhole and every second or every minute someone is asking us for money. We don't have to worry about people stealing from us here but we need to get food.

They have a little store in front. The guy that runs it says, "I'll set you up on credit. What's your name? You can pay us when you get a chance. Here, have a couple of sodas and some food."

This is its own little society here. This is the best we've seen since we've been on the island. That's what Diego was talking about. We have to pay. Everyone is taking care of us right now. There's an even nicer section than this where you can get anything you want but it's a little too much. We want to keep a low profile. Those guys up there are going to ask us for money every single day. Here we pay once and we're done.

They didn't try to tax us harder and we end up negotiating a better individual amount than anyone else but, again, they want us there because we're Americans. They like having us. It's really welcoming. Even though it's business. It's always money related but at the same time, for everything that's going on, this is the best situation we can get.

Everything's running through my mind. How do we get money? Our current financial situation is the most important thing right now. We need to take care of this and I want to do it so I can start taking things off my list of things to worry about. We haven't heard from our families. It's been 24 hours now. What's happening with our appeal? Is Jeff going to be all right? Along with all of that, there are all of these housing options.

I decide to call my dad before we go to bed and let him know we got here all right and that I'm going to need him to send some more money to me. Fidel lets me borrow his phone because he wants us to get the money.

I call my father and after I explain, briefly, what went on that day I say, "Hey, I need you to send me $3,000 dollars from my checking account. You can wire it to Diego's father-in-law. We'll have him bring the money along with our passports. Here's the information you need to wire the money."

He raises his voice and says, "What do you need $3,000 for?!"

"I need it to pay for prison."

I've already explained to him what I need it for but he won't send it. He's doing this move on me because he has listened to everyone else except me. It's the classic story of my life.

I say, "Why don't you listen to your son for a minute? He's very smart. He knows his way around."

The lawyers are telling him not to do it. "No, don't send the money to him. Send it to us."

Well, of course they want the money sent to them! The lawyers tell them all kinds of lies and if they can get more money out of us, that's even better.

They say, "Yeah, they have a cell phone at La Victoria."

Oops! We didn't go to La Victoria. We're at Najayo. The lawyers don't even know where we are! They don't find out until later when our families tell them.

I say, "Who are you listening to?" He stumbles around telling me who is telling him not to send it.

I say, "People from your church? Oh, that makes it okay, then."

I don't know who the fuck is giving him advice. The families don't do a good job of figuring out who to trust and who not to trust.

They say, "We can trust these lawyers like we trust our lawyers here in the States."

WRONG.

And it becomes more and more of a struggle.

We find out later that we can Western Union money to ourselves in our own name and then the runner from the prison will go get it for us.

Instead, I'm thinking that we need it brought to us and we can get the passports at the same time. I'm orchestrating all of this in my head.

I tell my dad, "All you need to do is send the money, and everything is great. Send it to Diego's father-in-law. Here's his name and Diego's name and here's what to do. Here's my new cell phone number. Call me back and give me the confirmation number so I can get the money."

He doesn't call me back that night.

So what if I'm out three grand? That's where I'm at. If it was $30,000 I would have paid $30,000. Money doesn't mean anything in this situation. I don't know if I'll even get out of here to spend it. Surviving and staying in this nice area that we found where we're secure and protected and there are guys that speak English–that's the most important thing right now.

I need $3,000, which is about 96,000 pesos. Jeff asks for less, but he ends up paying more. My $3,000 covers me and Diego and there's extra money left. Jeff's room deal is more expensive than mine. I'm working every angle. I'm a businessman and that's what I tell everyone.

They say, "Yeah, Corey is a business guy. You want to talk business with him, he'll do business with you. You know how he is."

Later on someone will come to me and say, "Hey, Fabio wants to talk business with you."

I say, "Okay we can talk business. Let's find a good time that we can sit down and talk. What is it that you want to talk about so I know ahead of time?"

"Well, he says he can get a larger variety of food if you're tired of chicken and rice."

"Okay. That's fine. Don't come to me with some bullshit about someone wanting cigarettes or money or stuff like that. If you want to talk business, I'll do business."

Everyone respects that and likes it and it evolves tremendously later on.

Who knows how long we're going to be here? We could be here for the next three months to a year, or longer. Who knows? And these guys have welcomed us with open arms and limitless hospitality. They've said we can stay here until we get our money. They're providing us with soap, water, towels and food. All the things that we don't have. And they are letting us use their phones; they want to help us out.

Meanwhile, I'm dealing with a certain level of fear of violence in the prison population. I don't know how bad it can get. When we were back at the jail I heard horror stories of contract murders, men getting maimed over a drug deal gone bad and other violence. Going through the halls just now was a nightmare because of how crowded they are. We heard a lot of yelling and verbal fighting while we walked down the halls. When a bunch of guys are arguing and we walk right next to them, what's to keep us from getting stabbed?

I also see the potential for a fire. In addition to open flames, there are matches and cigarettes. If someone fell asleep with a lit cigarette and caught his bedding on fire... There's no fire safety equipment, no exit policy. Nothing. Fire prevention and containment is not a high priority in the DR prison system. The prison is so overcrowded that if a fire did break out, there would be a stampede for the front door and people would be crushed against the locked interior gates. Everyone inside here would go up in flames. I try not to think about it.

The hall we walked through is the only way in or out of our pod. During the day the hallway is packed. It's dangerous every time we leave, especially when we go back and forth with Jeff. After awhile we don't let him out of the pod. He tells his wife how scared he is to go out there because there's no protection. We have to have security from our syndicate travel with us in case there's a problem. Toward the end, I walk everywhere by myself. Everyone knows who I am.

Now we have a guaranteed place to live and we're safe, and if we give these guys payment we're good, we're golden. We have some security and that's critical because the scariest thing is that every second you don't know what's going to happen next. They could move us somewhere else. We could go to a different prison, or they could put us in the general population where we have no amenities like a toilet, water or anything like that. At any moment it could be the end of the world.

Here we have some security. We have locks on the cell door. The guards don't come in there unless we ask for them. We have food and toiletries that we can use until we can buy our own. Until we got to Area X everything was minute to minute and second to second. I still have the anxiety from when we got arrested, and now going to Najayo. All of that is still fresh and real.

So we go to sleep on top that night and there's me, Diego and Fidel. This is the worst night of sleep in my entire time here. Diego's snoring like hell. I punch him three or four times during the night. Fidel snores, also. It's hot, it's miserable and I can't sleep at all. I'm losing it. I have this look of desperation on my face and everyone can see it.

Wednesday, June 24

We wake up the next day to the sounds of music. The guy to the left of us has a huge stereo and all day long the music is going. We're trying to figure out what's going on and get oriented. We're working on getting a phone and putting some minutes on it so we can find out what's going on back home.

Me, Jeff and Diego are trying to figure out the money. We have to pay these guys to stay here so we're trying to come up with a plan. I'm trying to assess this situation. How can we get food, something to eat? People want to talk business, talk money, because that's what it's all about.

I have my shoes but I don't have laces for them anymore. The guards took them when we were in the narcotics holding cell. I climb downstairs and this older black guy who sleeps in our area comes to me with shoelaces in his hand.

I say, *"Muchas gracias!"*

That is really nice of him, and people are saying hello to me, and good morning. I'm trying to take in everything right now.

Rocky is up and moving around. He says, "Good morning."

Fidel and Javier are very hospitable, especially Javier. He's always offering me food.

"How are you today?" Javier says in English.

I say, "Very well."

We spend time together and talk about all kinds of stuff. It turns out that being with Fidel and Javier is very advantageous to me in this situation.

Everyone wants to make a deal, wants to do business with us. I tell Diego to go find out what everyone's deal is because I don't want to take the first one. I want to see if we can negotiate something down. No one's going to take advantage of us because we're American's.

We're looking at business deals and Fidel asks me who I want to stay with.

I say, "What we did last night is not working out. We have to come up with something else."

Fidel says, "I want you to be comfortable. I can tell..." but he doesn't know me well enough to finish the sentence.

The guards interrupt us and tell us we have to go up front, that there's someone here to see us. I'm thinking who's here to see us? No one knows we're here. They drag the three of us through the maze of all that humanity. It becomes really annoying to have to go up front to meet with the lawyers about nothing. Eventually, if there's nothing to talk about, we send Diego up there. We walk around the corner and it's fucking Marco! He came to see us.

Marco says, "Hey, guys! How are you doing?"

I'm looking at Marco like I'm going to kill him.

I look at Diego and he knows what to do. He raises his voice and says, "You want to know how we're doing? Why don't you come on back here? Why don't you come on back here and see how we're doing?"

I'm looking at him like he's a piece of shit. He and Diego start arguing back and forth. Whenever that happens, Marco wants to talk to Jeff because Jeff doesn't get upset and yell.

Jeff says, "Yeah, we're all right, and uh, ah, and ah."

Marco says, "We're supposed to get you guys phones. Your parents said to get you guys some money and phones so you can talk to them." He gives us a couple hundred pesos or a thousand pesos, some bullshit like that. A minimal amount of money. Our appeal is for next Friday so we're going to be in here for more than a week at least. That money isn't going to last long.

Then Jeff blurts out, "Yeah, did they tell you we're going to have a new lawyer?"

He says that out loud to Marco!

Marco says, "What?!" Then there's a lot of confusion and I let Marco know exactly what I thought of him.

I say, "Jeff, man. Why the hell did you tell him that for?"

He says, "I don't know. We're getting a new lawyer aren't we?"

Diego's says, "Fuck him, man. We're done with him anyway."

Diego's still in the mindset that we're going to get a new lawyer. He has all of these business cards of the lawyers we talked to.

Diego says, "Yeah, we need to get a phone so we can contact them."

We go back through this sea of people to our cell area.

Fidel says, "We need to get you guys cleaned up. Do you have a change of clothes?" We don't have towels or anything like that. I have some soap that I brought from jail in my backpack and we have a change of clothes.

Alex cleans up our haircuts because the guy did a very bad job. He does the best he can to make the most of what's left. From there we get familiar with the bucket shower system. I take a five-gallon bucket and fill it up from the big barrel. I dump that over my head and the cold water in this heat feels so good! Then I soap up and dump a couple more buckets over my head to rinse off.

Fidel's cleaning up after we're done. I'm trying to get a feel for how he likes things to be done so we can be respectful of his place, especially since we're staying there as guests.

The three of us talk about how we like where we're living now, how nice it is and how much money we have on us. We tell Diego to get us some drinks and other stuff, and we're talking about how we're going to get a phone so we can start making some calls and how we're going to get some money.

Daniel and Joey come over and they feed us. Daniel says it's 3,000 pesos (about $95) per person for all of your meals for 30 days. It came out to be really, really cheap. They do the cooking and all we had to do was chip in for groceries.

Then two guards come back and bring us up front again. There are guys with a different syndicate. They tell the guards, "We'd like to show them what we have." We've already kind of made a deal with the guys where we're at, but we want to see all of our options.

We walk over there and shake hands and meet everyone. Their syndicate is the one that looked like they were having a family picnic out front when we arrived. The rooms are a little nicer. They have air conditioning units in them. They have a stove. They show us their store and it's the best one we've seen.

It's a lot more expensive than the arrangement we have now. They want 100,000 pesos or more per person to get in and then you're on your own. You have to continue paying a lot of tax every day on top of the 100,000 pesos. It isn't as welcoming as where we are, either.

After we go through the tour, they ask us what we think. I tell them, first of all, "Thank you very much for your time. The last 24 hours have been very stressful for us. I don't know if we're ready to make a decision at this time about where we want to stay. We'll have to get back to you."

"Oh, yeah, we totally understand that you want to think about it." As we're leaving, they tell us to come back anytime.

Where we are now is more than a syndicate. There's a family atmosphere instead of everyone as an individual. They tell us later that if it ever comes down to it, and we have to fight another clique, everyone in the syndicate will get involved. In Area X we're part of a community. It's starting to register with us. We offer some advantages. I'm thinking, "How can I use that for leverage?" Nothing comes to mind right then, but I file it away for another time.

The whole thing takes 30–40 minutes. Guys from our syndicate aren't allowed to come into these other guys' area. So they're waiting for us and kind of monitoring the situation while we're gone. Fidel tells me later that they were a little worried that we might stay there. They really want us to stay with them.

When we come back to our cell, everyone is saying, "*Amigos, amigos,* our friends are here."

We tell them we want to stay with them. They feel good about that. We still haven't given them money, and we want to stay, but we haven't made final business deals yet.

"We're glad you're still here. We'll make you some food. I'll cook up some rice and chicken for you guys. We're so happy that you're going to be here with us," Fidel says.

Something I find out later is that the guards can never touch us. No physical contact whatsoever and there is an extra layer of security for the syndicate if they have the Americans with them. The guards can't get out of control there.

If the Americans get in the middle of something and one of them gets hurt, that guard has a huge problem. God knows what's going to happen to him. Knowing the guards can't roll up on the guys who do business with us is a great buffer. If we're all hanging out and the guards come in and want to do a shake down, they have to ask permission and be very courteous to the Americans and not upset them. We don't know this yet but we figure it out eventually. It's easy to see why this group wants us here. In addition, we're kind of celebrities.

"We have the Americans with us–not like the Dominican Americans–we have some real Americans. They don't even speak Spanish or nothing."

We're sitting around talking and it's mid–morning. All of a sudden there are guards at our door again. This time they only want me and Jeff, not Diego. They say the Embassy is here to see us.

So we go to the front for the third time that morning. We don't know it yet, but they put us in the warden's office. Everyone is watching us. I'm thinking, "Whoa man, this is a big deal." We don't know what's going on.

We walk in there and there are two guys and a girl sitting at a table. There's a third guy standing in the back. The girl is young and really cute. One of the black guys is who we met initially at the courthouse jail. I'm guessing he's the new lawyer that Jeff's mom hired. I told Diego he was from the U.S. Embassy. I assume the other guy is one of our lawyers, too.

Our new lawyers don't speak English. They never do. Never. NEVER! Jeff won't stop saying, "I want someone to speak English to me." That's the whole point as far as he's concerned. He keeps bringing that up and I keep telling him that it's never going to happen. And it doesn't.

During this meeting, the girl speaks English and acts as our interpreter. She went to college in the States. She's someone's niece.

We sit down and then Jeff says, "Yeah, they told me that the lawyers were coming up to meet us."

I don't know when he was planning to tell me what's going on. We're in the warden's office and I'm thinking, "Oh shit! Do we need lawyers right now for something I don't know about?"

We don't know if we do or not. We haven't seen these people before and our parents didn't tell us ahead of time what's going on. Jeff's mother may have told Jeff something, but it comes out all fucked up all the time when Jeff talks because he misses the details. Neither one of us really knows what's going on. Who knows if this person is who he says he is. Who knows if they are actually our lawyers?

We're not sure if our parents really hired them or not. We don't know if they are even lawyers. Maybe this is a whole set-up and they're trying to get information from us. Anything's possible. We can't trust anyone right now.

When people on the outside make decisions without telling us first it creates a huge amount of confusion. We need to tell our parents what's going on because every time they pull this, it jeopardizes our safety. We have to know about their plans before they do them, because they don't know what's really going on.

Our main focus is to get our money. That's the most important issue. These guys want to talk about our case but we don't know who they are and we're trying to have a discussion through this girl.

When we were in jail, Jeff tells me his mother hired a new lawyer for him as we were walking down the hall toward the guy. We needed Diego to believe this guy was from the Embassy. The guards didn't give us very much time to talk to him. By the time we were done, I still had no clue who he was. If he was our new lawyer, he never said it because he was going along with our Embassy story.

So now he shows back up. I still don't know who he is. We're going back and forth through the translator and they don't understand why we aren't happy to see them.

They say, "Hey, how are you? We're here to help you."

Me and Jeff are very stand-offish.

I'm thinking, "I don't know you from anyone."

I say, "Jeff, what the hell?"

He says, "I don't know, man. One time when I talked to my mom she said she would get me a new lawyer."

I say, "Well, what do these guys want? What are they doing here?"

The girl is doing her best to translate back and forth, but the lawyers don't know that our families haven't told us that they've hired them. It takes the first 20 to 30 minutes to get to that point.

I tell them, "We don't know who you are. Our families didn't tell us that they hired you."

They try to explain, "Oh your mother is such and such... and then they contacted us and hired us as your lawyers to represent you." And we're going back and forth but after 20 or 30 minutes of awkwardness we're in a panic.

I say, "I don't know what you want. Did you bring money or a phone with you?" They don't have either one of those things so as far as I'm concerned, they don't mean anything to me right now.

What we need to do is talk to our family. We don't know what's going on. We need to talk to them but we still don't have our own phone. We're using inmates' phones to call our families to see what's going on with this money that we need. Who cares about the court case? I need to get my housing situation set up. I need a place to stay. Right now I'm on borrowed time...

We're trying to get that set up, and one of the guys starts in on the passports this, the passports that.

I tell them, "I don't know who you are, man.

He says, "We need your passports."

"Our passports are fine."

"Well, we need to get them from the driver's family."

I say, "We'll take care of that."

He says, "Well, where does he live?

I say, "We'll get them for you. You're going to fuck up everything I'm working on right now, bro. You know what I'm saying?"

This turns into a very antagonistic thing. They finally do what I say and it works perfectly when we get the passports. It is smooth as could be. No one thought the wiser of anything that happened. It was a happy time for everyone involved, but until then it was nothing but chaos.

Suddenly the guy standing over in the corner pushes himself off the wall and walks over to the table. He turns out to be the warden and he says in English, "You guys need to settle down!"

So the warden speaks English. Very interesting.

He says, "Do you guys need a phone? You can use my phone. Go ahead."

I call first. I'm on the phone and get hold of my dad and say, "Hey, I really need you to send me my money."

He says, "Okay, okay, okay. Yeah, I'll take care of it."

"We really need that money. That is the most important thing right now. You have to trust me now more than you've ever trusted me in my entire life. Send the money. I can explain it to you later. You need to send the money. I don't have time to explain it right now. Send the money."

I'm not going into the specifics with him because you can't say you need the money so you can pay for your room, and that some of it goes to the warden. You're not supposed to say those things and we don't want the other inmates to start saying, "Yeah, they said they needed money for a cell and how much the warden charges." See what I'm saying?

My father wants details but I don't have time to explain all of this. Time is something I don't have. I have all of these lawyers right here, and the warden's right there. We end up having a relationship with this warden. We go through three wardens while we're there.

Wherever we go chaos ensues. It's proof to me that in my life it doesn't matter where I go in the world, if you hang out with me some crazy stuff will happen to you, including the warden.

I ask my dad, "Who are these guys? They tell me their names and I repeat them to him.

He says, "Yeah, we talked to Jorge."

Do they think Jorge is going to show up and talk to us at the prison? We never see Jorge. Jorge doesn't even exist as far as I'm concerned, but to our parents they think he's real because that's who calls them. It could be a guy in India.

My dad says, "Yeah, Jorge's there."

I say, "There's no one here named Jorge. There are two guys. One guy says he's our lawyer. I don't know who these people are."

"Well, Jorge said they were going to come visit. They were going to come talk to you guys."

Okay. Neither one of these fuckers can speak English. I don't know what the hell is going on right now and neither do they.

I say to my dad, "All right, well, I don't know about that. What you need to do is send the money. We can worry about this later." And I hang up.

Our new lawyers say, "We're going to be your new lawyers and we need to file this paperwork for your appeal next Friday and we need your passports."

I keep saying, "I can get the passports. You need to get me money first. Once I have the money I can deliver everything that you want but I need the money. Send the money. If you send the money I can take care of everything." I keep telling them that.

Me and Jorge have it out later on the phone. They talk to Jeff so they think they have notified us but Jeff is blind to the world, he's clueless about everything. He doesn't know what's going on. He's never been in trouble in his life.

I'm the complete opposite in that I'm making moves and I'm thinking ahead. I think these guys are impersonating lawyers.

One day I finally ask my dad, "Have you explained to the lawyers who I am and how smart I am? Do these guys understand this?"

And he says, "I've been telling them repeatedly to run everything by you before they do anything." This never happens.

We're sitting in the warden's office and I talk to my dad again, "So this is what needs to happen..."

"Yeah, well, they're supposed to be bringing you money and phones."

"These guys showed up and they don't have any money or any phones."

I ask them, *"teléfono y dinero?"*

"No, no, no." You're useless to me then.

I ask the girl doing the translating, "What are they going to give us?"

She says, "They're going to give you 500 pesos apiece."

"That ain't going to help me!" Who the fuck are these lawyers? They don't know shit.

This is where we start having conflict with the lawyers. They don't get us and there is nothing for us to get from them.

I say, "Why are you here?"

They say they want to talk about the case.

They keep asking, "How do you know the driver? How do you know the driver's family?"

I explain the whole story to them and they say, "Oh, oh, okay."

And they want to talk about the circumstances of the court case. I explain what happened. The warden listens in the whole time.

I say, "The driver took us there and this is what we were trying to do."

"What about the girl?"

"I don't know anything about the girl."

"What were you guys doing there?

"Well that's where the driver took us. We didn't know where we were going."

"How do you know the driver?" I explain it over and over again.

I say, "We don't know about any drugs. We never saw any."

I'm doing most of the talking at this point in time and later on Jeff says, "Well, I want to talk, too."

I'm being very concise now. I'm telling them, "This is exactly what happened. This is true. This isn't true. This is what you need to know. I don't know about that."

Jeff wants to talk but he wants to ask them open-ended questions that they can't answer. Like, "What do you think about our case? Do you think we're going to get out?"

I'm talking through this girl and me and her have little side conversations between the two of us that she's not repeating to them.

I'm asking her things like, "Does it make sense when I say this?"

And she says, "No. What about..." and "Okay now that makes sense."

So she turns to me and we have an English conversation and then, "Okay this will make better sense if you tell them this."

I go into the case and tell them point blank: "We don't know anything about drugs. We never saw any drugs."

They say, "Okay. Well, that's very good. Make sure you say that when you go to court."

I say, "That's all we know. It's the truth. It's easy for us to remember it. That's all we know."

The girl says that and she's laughing when she says it to them and the guy shakes his head and he starts laughing and we make a little breakthrough with the lawyers. We go back and forth and they want to know exactly what transpired. That's what they are trying to do. They want to know exactly how it went down.

Even though that's not what we're interested in doing, that's why they came so we spend the time doing that even though we said the same thing in court.

The lawyer finally explains the problem with our case and why we didn't get released. He tells us, "They say your stories, yours and Jeff's, didn't come out the same way during the translation in court. They say you guys gave two different testimonies." This goes back to Jeff rambling and not being concise.

They keep saying, "Your stories don't match up."

And I'm thinking why our stories didn't match up and finally I say, "Everything's through a translator. I think this is the problem. Jeff was speaking really fast and he'd start a new subject before he finished with the first one. He was all over the place. So when the translation went through, I think that's where the errors became evident, where it didn't sound like we saw the same thing."

I figure this out because the lawyers keep saying, "What were you doing on the bridge?" That keeps popping up over and over. Then, beyond that, if someone isn't using basic, simple, English and the translator can't keep up, this can happen. As much as I say it to Jeff, it isn't clicking and it doesn't click for a while. We end up having argument after argument about how he needs to talk.

He says, "Don't tell me how I need to talk, man."

I say, "Dude you need to work on this. This is serious. You can't get up there and ramble on and talk about whatever comes to your mind." This is a conversation I have with him later after I figure it out.

That's why the lawyers keep saying we each told a different story. So I have to figure it out again, like everything else.

What did Jeff say? What did I say? What did Diego say?

We're in the warden's office going round and round with the lawyers and one of the lawyers says, "These charges aren't a big deal in our country. It's nothing. This is no problem, man. It's business."

"Crap."

And he says, "Don't worry, man. This is nothing."

"If it's nothing, how the fuck did I get to prison, asshole? You telling me that it's nothing doesn't help my situation. That's what Jeff wants to hear, but don't tell me that. Tell me what you're going to do and how you're going to get me out. I don't want to hear 'No problem. It's business.' We need to get out."

The warden is listening to everything and he says, "You guys have to pay me some money. What area are you in?" He knows exactly what area we're in.

"We're in Area X."

"You should be safe there. I can keep you safe up here but once you're back there I have no control over that." He's saying this in English so the lawyers don't understand. He's talking to me and Jeff. "Have you guys gotten your money yet?"

I say, "We're trying to. That's why we need a phone."

He says, "From my experience you guys need to get comfortable back there. You might be here awhile. Get comfortable. Stay close to your driver, eventually you might have to take care of him."

Of course I don't trust anyone. I see through everyone but I don't know what Jeff thinks. There are these bits of truth in everything everyone says. I have to pick it apart. None of the truth is ever direct and I know this.

I know I can't say anything directly that involves political corruption. Everything is indirect and circumvents the truth. I'm taking in every single word that everyone is saying and watching their body language. The warden and the lawyers are mainly talking to me. It's obvious Jeff's not with it. The kind of words I use when I speak to them and the tone I use is very deliberate. I'm sizing the warden up and he's sizing me up. He's engaging in this conversation because he's putting out feelers to figure out who we are and what he can expect from us.

While I'm having this conversation with the warden, I'm sizing him up from his responses to what I'm saying. I'm choosing my words carefully and he is also being careful about what he says to me. He's doing broken English.

He says, "You need to stay close to your driver and get comfortable back there. That would be my biggest suggestion. Get used to that environment. Like I said, get comfortable."

What I hear is, "You're going to be here awhile." We're still in the mindset that any minute now they're going to come get us and take us out of here, or the lawyers are going to make something happen.

He says, "Keep an eye on your driver, the guy that put you here. You're going to have to pay some money." He's letting me know that we're going to get taxed.

He's talking business and I'm picking up on it. I see it. I understand what he's saying and he's letting me know how important money is. "You're going to need some money, kid. You're going to be paying throughout your stay."

He thinks I'm an ATM machine and he's going to try to squeeze as much money out of me as he can. I'm not going to let him do it. So I file that away in my mental filing cabinet along with other stuff I'm figuring out.

Now I'm aware that I have to be judicious and deliberate when I handle my financial arrangements. I don't know how I'll do that, but I have to do it in a way that we don't look like walking ATMs. How am I going to work that? I see people later on that are handing out money every second because once you get started you can't stop. You have to somehow establish a boundary there.

I file this away from what the warden said: you're going to be here awhile; keep the money coming; stay close to your driver because eventually you're going to need him to take responsibility for this. The warden's telling me the rules of the game and what's going on, but this is all happening very quickly; he's talking very fast.

Meanwhile, we have lawyers here, and we're trying to get a phone. I look out the window and I see the girl come off the Gray Goose bus. The girl that was with us. We haven't seen her since we got here. We thought she might have rolled on us. Oh my God! What are the chances? I'm sitting there in the warden's office looking out the window and I see her and she can't see me. There she is! And the whole time the three of us were wondering what happened to her. We want her to testify for us.

Boom! Now I have that going on, too. I need my money. I worry about it getting to the prison and how it's going to work once it gets here. I have these new lawyers going on and on. I don't trust them. I don't know what's going on. I need to get our passports from Diego somehow. The workload, the list of shit I have to get done, is getting longer and longer.

We get done with these guys and we go back to our area. We've been gone almost two hours. There's a big commotion around us all the time. There's paranoia circulating around the guys that we may have told the warden and the U.S. Embassy they're trying to extort money from us.

Diego's waiting for us. "What's going on? What's going on?"

I tell Jeff to tell Diego it was the U.S. Embassy. They came to check on us and that's what they wanted to talk about. I'll wait to tell him that I saw the girl because I feed him information as I need to or have to. So I have to think. If I say this, he's going to jump to this conclusion. If I say that, he's going to react that way. I can't tell him something until I've thought it out.

Alex's nervous. The first thing he asks us is, "You guys didn't say anything about having to pay us money for your room?"

I say, "No, no we didn't say nothing."

Alex says, "Good because you can't say that. Whatever you do man, that's going to mess everything up and make it worse."

I say, "Don't worry, man. We didn't say a word. We didn't say anything of that nature." It's kind of funny. Everyone knows about these taxes, including the guards and the warden, but nobody says it out loud.

They keep asking us what we've been doing the past two hours.

I repeat, "It was the U.S. Embassy. They came to check on us. We were in the warden's office."

"Oh, the warden. They said you were in the warden's office." There are no secrets. Everyone knows where we go. Other inmates see us and tell people, "They're in with the warden. Yeah, with the guys from the U.S. Embassy."

"Ah, yeah, yeah. That makes sense. That's why they went into the warden's office, man."

At the same time, the other syndicate has already asked if we want to go stay in their area. So all the guys in our area are working that out. "Man I don't know. The guards might move them out. If they don't stay with us, man, then they're going to stay with the other syndicate."

Now I'm starting to use my leverage. I'm tired of being a victim in this situation. I tell Diego, "We have to give the Embassy our passports, man, because they're worried about their safety."

Diego says, "Your passports are safest with my family. The lawyers have already tried to come to the house to take them. I told my family, 'Don't let them have them.' When these lawyers showed up, my father-in-law refused to give them up. I told them don't give them up unless it's the U.S. Embassy, or they have a signed letter with your signature on it saying that they can take them."

We didn't know this was going on.

I say, "Perfect. Good job."

Our lawyers are demanding these passports. They're the property of the United States. They can't hold them; it's against the law. At the same time, I can't jeopardize our relationship with Diego's family.

I need to leverage them, but at the same time, if we take those passports and things go wrong, Diego could think he's getting a raw deal and he could roll on me and Jeff. He could say, "Yeah, it's the Americans who wanted the drugs. They hired me to do this." This is how it goes; it's the classic set-up.

The attorneys need our passports to file a motion in court to get us a bond to get out. So if they have our passports, they can make copies of them and ask the court, "Give us a bond. Let these guys out. They won't leave the country."

The passports are important to get us out, and we need them in a safe place. They aren't really in a safe place with Diego's family. I don't think anything would happen but who knows? They could use them to extort money out of us forever.

At the same time, I tell Diego that the U.S. Embassy needs them to file a motion. This makes sense to him.

There is no one we can trust right now. We can't trust any lawyer, we already got screwed over by one. We need to get a new one–well, we have a new lawyer–but Diego thinks the Embassy is going to step in, and Diego trusts the Embassy because they're looking out for us. And if he's with us, and we're with the Embassy, he thinks he's good.

I have everything running through my head. At the same time, there's a little bit of uneasiness within the syndicate because we met with the warden.

They say, "God, I hope these Americans didn't say nothing."

"Don't fuck up our business."

We keep saying, "No. No. No. We didn't say nothing..."

While we were gone, meeting with those guys, Jeff's mom called back. We don't have our own phones so she calls the phone that we're using in those guys' room and she asks for Jeff.

Again, more chaos ensues. None of them speak English and she wants to talk to Jeff so Diego gets on the phone.

She says, "Where are the boys?"

"They're up front."

"Where'd they go?"

For some unknown reason, Diego says, "They moved. They're up at the front."

She says, "They got moved?"

"No the guards came and took them up front."

"Well, where did they go?"

Diego says, "I don't know," because they don't know where we are and Jeff's mom is panicking by now. This is awesome! Let's add fuel to the fucking fire.

She says, "Oh my God! They're gone and you don't know where they're at?"

She was calling Jeff back to say that she had wire transferred his money to him because Jeff called while we're in the warden's office right after I got done talking to my dad. He gets hold of his wife and tells her, "You need to send this money. Whatever you do, wire transfer it to me."

That's when I find out that I can wire transfer my money to myself and I'm the only one that can touch it.

Diego says, "I don't know where he went."

She says, "What do you mean you don't know where he went? I sent him money."

She got done with the lawyers and they tell her, "They're trying to extort money out of the guys. Don't send them any."

It's not like he's going to get it right then and there, it's not like an ATM machine, it takes three days but she doesn't know this.

She says to Diego, "So you're trying to extort money out of him and now he's gone."

Jeff's mom is very upset and she goes off on Diego. The guys know enough English to know when someone is saying something bad.

She says to Diego, "What are you doing to my son? You're trying to extort money out of him. How dare you!" And she insults all the guys while we're gone.

After his mom gets done insulting all the guys in the area, she calls my dad and says, "I don't know what's going on. Some guys showed up. They keep asking Jeff for money, and I sent it to him, and now Jeff's gone. They're getting extorted."

My dad is horrified, "Oh no!" Both of their imaginations are running wild back in the States.

When we come back, the guys are all talking, repeating what she said.

"Yo, man, this is what your mother said." These guys are very offended by it because they are trying to be nice. They've taken care of us and I'm thinking, "Oh, fuck."

This is how people make your life harder than it already is.

So that happened while we were gone and we come back to that and they're all upset about it and they say to Jeff, "Your mom said we're trying to extort money out of you."

We have to put this fire out now. Again, the lawyers didn't tell our parents that they were going to visit us. They show up and we don't know what's going on. The lawyers keep telling our families that they're going to bring us money and cell phones but they show up without either one and I need them now.

I say, "Jeff you need to call your mother back right now and tell her that you're fine and you were up front talking to the U.S. Embassy and you need to ask her to personally apologize to the guys if you can.

So he calls his mom back and calms her down and says, "This is what happened." She apologizes to the guys in the pod and everyone settles down.

I guess the reaction back with our families is that the lawyers are telling them one thing and we're telling them something completely different, which happens to be what's actually going on.

My dad says, "Well I don't know who to trust." And he's not going to trust me. He trusts people he doesn't even know. I can't believe the shit this fucker pulled.

Jeff starts talking about crazy shit. According to Jeff, the lawyers say they're coming to get us in the middle of the night, tell everyone we're sick, and take us to the hospital.

Here I am like, "Oh shit."

Now animosity is growing. There's concern within the syndicate that these Americans are going to cause us problems, man. They're out there with the warden and the Embassy and if they find out that we're taxing them, or we're trying to get money from them then we're in all kinds of trouble. This is the way it is, but you don't say it out loud. That's the way the whole country is.

When we get back to the cell, we put out two fires, their suspicion of us and Jeff's mother's meltdown. I'm going around re-establishing our relationships with these people who are uneasy around us. Things are getting back to normal, whatever that is. Everyone's cool now.

As the day goes on we're taking everything in. Late afternoon, we get a phone up and running. I'm mentally and physically in a different place and everyone can see that. At the same time, I'm trying to be polite to people, asking them how they are.

By now, I'm getting into play-maker mode. I'm starting to figure out a way that we're getting out of here and Diego is going to stay. Not only is he problematic for us, but there's a whole bunch of people asking why we're here. The people who can speak English are really bothered by the story.

Diego is annoying Javier because they like it quiet in there and Diego is a non-stop talker and won't shut up. Me and Javier are talking about something and Diego comes in and interrupts. He's always got something to say and he disturbs people.

Diego is beginning to wear on me. Everyone's concerned about me because they can see periods where I'm outgoing and then times when I'm blank. They can see me crash whenever Diego's around.

The people in the pod are concerned for me. They like me because I'm respectful, I say thank you whenever anyone does something for me, and I try to speak Spanish every time I can. That's how I act and I'm mindful of it because we don't have any money to pay these guys.

Jeff's money is on its way. When you set up the transfer in the States, you get a confirmation number. You give that number to whoever is handling the transaction on this end. Then they call and check to be sure there's an account with that confirmation number. So they do that with Jeff's transfer and the confirmation number checks out so it is a legit transaction. We got Jeff's situation all squared away and now back to me.

I call my dad again and say, "Here's what you need to do. Send it to me. Send it in my name if you don't want to send it to Diego's family. Put it in my name." Then I explain all the details on how to do this.

And this is when he starts being "The Asshole."

"Uh, I don't feel good about doing this. I don't think it's a good idea. I can't really send you money. You're going to have to convince me to send you money."

I say, "Look, this is how it works here. There's no food for inmates here. You have to buy your own food. You have to buy your bed in a cell. They don't provide you with anything. If I can't buy a place in a cell, they'll put me out in the general population and I'm dead."

"The lawyers are telling us that if we start giving you money now they'll keep on asking for more and more and more money later."

"Who the fuck cares? It's my money, I'm not asking you to send your money!"

"I'm not going to do it."

I say, "You have to be kidding me. Jeff's mom sent him money. Talk to her."

"Yeah, I talked to her. She said that she didn't feel good about doing it but she did anyway. So I'm not doing it. I don't think this is the right thing to do because my name is ___ and I'm an honest Christian."

This side of him shows up right now after I told him before. I said, "We may have to make deals with some drug dealers and we may have to pay some bad people in the world but that's what it's going to take to get me out of this. If you ever want to see me again, these are the things that we may have to do that we don't like. So everything that you know about right or wrong, forget it."

Obviously that conversation didn't stick in his head when I said it because now he's listening to a bunch of people who aren't in this prison. I am and I'm pleading with him on the phone and everyone is watching me on the phone because they know I'm talking about the money. This is not good.

I say, "Please you have to do everything you can to send me the money."

And there are guys watching me who can speak English and I've worked hard to gain their respect and now they see me begging my father for money.

I say, "You have to trust me on this."

He's still refusing to send it.

I'm trying to be cool about it and trying to be smooth, but I'm like I was the other night–ready to erupt in rage. I say, "I swear to God if I ever get out of here I'm going to kill you if you don't send that money!"

"I don't feel good about doing it."

My dad and mom are in a conference call with the lawyers about all of this shit at the same time! They're talking to whoever, and the lawyers want to talk to my parents while me and my dad are having this conversation. It's totally bizarre.

My mom picks up the phone and says, "Oh, your dad's on the other line."

I say, "Mom, I need that money. You need to do whatever you can to send that money. Promise me. Promise me that you're going to send me the money. Mom, I've never asked you to promise me anything in my entire life–ever. Promise me that you'll send the money."

"Oh, I will. I will. Yeah, your dad says he's going to send the money."

"Great. Tell him to call me back as soon as he does it."

Hours go by and hours go by and I call him back. He still hasn't sent the money. He's lying to me now.

"Dad, you need to send this money. You don't understand how important this is."

"Oh yeah, yeah. I'll take care of it."

I call him back again and he says he sent it.

I tell him I need the confirmation number for the transaction. I say, "What is the confirmation number?"

"Um, I don't know where it's at. I have to call you back."

So I'm catching him in a lie when my life is on the line. I'm riding the roller coaster of emotions inside. I tell him to hold on and turn to Jeff and whisper,

"Jeff, I need your help. You need to tell your mom to convince my dad to send the money."

"Dude, I can't do it. He's not..."

I say, "You need to help me, Bro. Jeff, do you understand how serious this is? My dad won't do it. I have $30,000 in my checking account alone. I'm just asking him to send me $3,000 of my own money."

Jeff whispers, "Thirty. Thousand. Dollars?"

"Who the fuck cares? They may never see me again."

"I'm back. Dad. I don't know what else to say. I need the money to stay alive in here. I've explained what I need it for. You need to send me that money."

Then my dad says, "I don't know if it's the Christian thing to do."

The motherfucker!

He's not honest. He thinks he lives a righteous life, by the way. He thinks he's a God–fearing person. Everything he does. A week later, when I realize we aren't getting out of here anytime soon, I ask him to pay my bills for me. I don't have a lot of bills, but I don't want to get charged late payment fees. I give him access to all my accounts and I ask him to go in and pay my bills. Here's what this fucking, bullshit, asshole says:

He says, "Yeah, I'm feeling uncomfortable about this. I'm forging your signature on some of these things."

I say, "What the fuck? Just do it."

We get to the point where he won't forge my signature. So, while I'm in prison, I take the time to set up my bank account so he can transfer money directly from my account to his so he can use his own account. He doesn't like that, either.

He says, "My value system and commitment to being honest is really taking a beating right now, you know, because I'm having to say I'm you, but I'm not!"

I lose it and I say, "Of all the other things you've done in your life, you're going to grow a conscience about this? Seriously, of all the bad shit you've done to your kids and everyone else in your life, you're having a problem paying my bills? You've lived a lie your entire life and you're gonna have an issue about this when your only son's life is on the line. This is the kind of shit you're going to pull?"

I just hang up. I can't stand hearing his self–righteous voice spewing even more lies.

So Jeff gets on the phone and he says, "Mom. You have to do whatever you can. You have to tell Corey's dad that he needs that money. I'm good. I'm set. His dad needs to send that money."

So then we go back and forth on the phone for hours.

He finally says, "Fine. I'll send you your goddamn fucking money. You want your fucking money? It's yours." And he starts cursing me out on the phone.

By then, I'm back to being cool and calm, "Please. Please send me the money. I need it. I need the money so I can buy a cell so I have a place to live, so I can pay for food, so I can survive this."

"Well, your sister told me not to do it."

"Well, tell my sister to fucking call me!"

So I'm dealing with all this. In addition to that, I have all this other stuff going on. I have Diego to keep under control. I have the passport thing going on.

I have the lawyers to deal with. I have my roommates. The stress is taking a toll on me mentally and physically.

Then he says, "Fine I'll take care of it." We hang up.

So I turn and everyone is asking, and I say, "Yeah. It's being taken care of."

Wednesday night Jeff has the confirmation number he needs for his money.

Me and Jeff are sitting there and I say, "God, I hope that money comes. We need it bad." We're borrowing to eat and running up tabs and people are providing their own personal belongings for us.

We meet some of the nicest people in prison. It's the culture. It's family. If you have something, you do whatever you can to help people out. On the other hand, my own family is fucking with me.

The other guys in there feel bad for us.

"You guys got a raw deal. You shouldn't even be here. They set you up."

And they're looking at Diego like, "I can't believe what he did to you. He put you guys in this situation."

There is a huge amount of empathy toward us from everyone. We don't belong there. It's not fair. They shouldn't be doing this to us. And that feeling gains and gains momentum over time.

I'm worn down by everything that went on that day and it shows in my face. Usually I'm good for a couple of jokes but I'm worn down, exhausted, and I have a million things on my mind that I'm trying to get a grasp on.

Mostly, I'm still trying to process what I went through with my dad earlier in the day. I'm not surprised. He's been like this my whole life.

When I was a little kid, like five years old, he'd get mad at me and hit me with his fist. He would say it was because I didn't behave in church, but the reaction was way out of line for the situation. A lot of things he had to deal with were taken out on me. He denies it to this day but I lived it and I've never forgotten. This is just part of the same pattern.

I probably had that look like I've had enough of everything. This situation is more stressful than everything else I've ever been through. Making sure everyone is set up in a comfortable place, getting the necessary funding, and trying to control things around me in this environment is the most stressful thing that happens the entire time.

This isn't the environment to be a street hustler like Diego but he doesn't know how to not do that. In the end, his personality does him in. What I'm doing now is winning people over by saying very little. I'm projecting an image. Jeff has that look about him. He's along for the ride. People like being around me and I end up befriending a lot of guys along the way. They have a genuine concern for me and they see that Diego is the person causing the negativity around me.

Diego's disgusting and he's wearing on my patience. He's a disgusting person. He eats with his mouth open and talks with his mouth full. He goes through this routine every morning where he has to clear his sinuses and blow his nose and he makes the most disgusting sounds when he's doing it. He has no self-awareness. He has no idea how inappropriate what he's saying or doing is and how disgusting he is. He doesn't have any boundaries. This becomes a problem because of the people we're staying with.

Now it's Wednesday evening and we're getting ready to go to bed again. There are a million things to think about and we're still talking about where we're going to stay.

Throughout the course of the day this is coming to a head. I say to Fidel, "I'm really sorry but it's too hot up there and the snoring is too loud. I'm sorry."

Fidel says, "No, no, no. Please stay. I will sleep on the floor. I will pull out one of the mattresses and sleep on the floor with Javier."

I go back and brush my teeth and clean up the little bathroom area and make sure it's dry. Diego goes back there and starts doing his disgusting routine to clear out his sinuses. There's paper towels and toilet paper back there but he does a farmer's blow where you lean over and blow with no toilet paper or anything to catch it and he blows snot all over everything. All over the toilet area and on the wall right after Fidel finished cleaning all of it.

I look at Diego and say, "What the fuck is wrong with you? You're disgusting! You don't do that!" I'm really mad at him.

Diego doesn't understand what he did wrong.

I lose it, "I can't do it! I can't spend so much time with you. You're killing me, man. You're killing me."

We're arguing and Fidel and Javier are visibly upset. Then there's this moment where the world changes. I'm very upset. I'm saying, "I can't do this" over and over.

Diego walks out of the room. I sit on Javier's bed and apologize for Diego and I say, "I'm sorry, I'm sorry about your house."

Fidel's telling Javier to ask me what's wrong with Diego and how much disrespect he has. He says more, but he's speaking Spanish and I can't keep up with it.

Javier says, "He is such a problem! I do not like him whatsoever."

Javier is a very well respected man, very wealthy, comes from a wealthy family, traveled all over the world. He told me his favorite hotel is the Plaza in New York City across from Central Park. Later on he tells me he has nine Porsches and he asks me which Porsche is the best. I tell him, "I don't know, man, I've never driven a Porsche."

He says, "The Carrera is the best," while nodding his head.

Javier is talking to Fidel and he's saying how offended they are by Diego but how much they enjoy having me there.

I say, "Okay, okay, I am very sorry. I will take care of it."

Diego comes back in the room and I tell him point blank, "You're making my life harder than it has to be right now."

He says, "I'm so sorry..."

I interrupt him and say, very quietly and calmly, "No, stop. You're making my life harder than it has to be right now and I can't take it. I'm losing it. I need some quiet. I have to get away from you, man. You're making this situation with these people harder than it has to be. They have been very hospitable to us and I don't have any money to pay them. They're offering us food and the use of everything they have.

"What you're doing is very offensive to them. You're showing them a lack of respect and it's reflecting badly on me. I'm asking you. You need to help me now. You either need to be aware of what you're doing and change the way you are–I'm not saying you have to–but if you're going to be around me, you're going to have to change the way you're acting or you can't be around me all of the time because it's very hard on me right now. I'm trying to take care of Jeff..."

He interrupts me, and he talks real fast, and he says, "I know exactly what you're saying. I'm trying to take care of Jeff, too."

"Diego, you're doing it right now.

"I'm sorry, I'm sorry."

"I have enough on my mind right now. I have to figure out what to do with Jeff, I'm trying to figure out a way to get out of here, I need to get these lawyers..."

"I'm telling you, these lawyers, man, you can't trust any of them."

"I know that Diego, but I also have to worry about what's happening on the outside with our families. I have to figure out a way to get money so I can take care of all these things. Right now, it's up to you. I'm not going to tell you how to live your life, but if you're going to be around me, this is what needs to happen.

You have time, you don't have to decide right this moment, but this is a decision you're going to have to make. Do you understand that?"

"Yeah, man, I understand that. I'm very sorry."

"That's fine. You need to understand what you're doing to me right now."

"Okay. Enough said. You're absolutely right, you're absolutely right. I was trying to do what I can."

"Yeah, but there's a time and a place for it. I need a break."

Before Diego leaves the room, he cleans up the bathroom and apologizes again to my roommates and says to Fidel and Javier, "Do whatever Corey needs to help him out. I'm worried about him."

After he leaves, Fidel and Javier say, "Are you okay? Do you want something to eat?"

"No."

I didn't eat anything Wednesday. I didn't eat anything because I have so much anxiety going on and I'm not feeling well. I have too much on my mind.

"Tranquilo. Tranquilo, aquí."

Tranquilo means tranquil. It's tranquil here. I can relax. I can think.

They see how concerned I am. They can tell how upset I am. They don't want to see me that way. And these are strangers! I haven't given them any money at all yet and they offer me the use of the shower and a towel and everything they've got. They're talking amongst themselves about how bad they feel for me and what's happened and what kind of guy Diego is and what they think of him.

Diego comes back in and he says to everyone in the room, "I apologize. I am very sorry if I offended you." And he apologizes to me and says, "I think it's probably best if you have your own space. Why don't you stay here. I'll go stay somewhere else, there are other guys out there."

"I'm not trying to kick you out, I want you to know."

"No, I think that's what's best," he says.

What happened in that short sequence of events was Fidel and Javier really wanted Diego gone even though they had offered us this business deal. I take Diego out of the picture for them. They're thankful to me for doing that and they're very happy having me as their guest even though I still haven't given them money.

Fidel says, "You take the upstairs and I'll stay downstairs."

I say, "No, that's your area."

And he says, "No, no, no, please take the upstairs."

I end up with the whole area upstairs to myself. Fidel and the old man are on the lower level and I have exactly what I need and what I wanted all along.

Fidel takes out some of his clothes and folds mine and puts them on a shelf. Fidel has a raspy voice and I have a hard time understanding him. Later on, he starts writing to me and I write back and we communicate in Spanish that way.

Fidel keeps his place very clean and orderly. There's not a lot of traffic coming in and out. In the other cells, people from other parts of the prison, and the guards, wander in and out. Our cell is at the end of the hall so we have very little traffic. It's an escape, kind of. The only people who come in are people we know. We have a really good routine and open communication about everything.

It's quiet and peaceful and I finally have a place I can think.

Wednesday night I sleep by myself on top with the fan going and it wasn't too hot. I sleep really good. Most of my life I've had bad nightmares. I never wanted to go to sleep because of the nightmares. Starting there, in a Dominican Republic prison, the nightmares stopped and they've never come back.

Daniel sees Diego lying out in the hallway and tells him to come into his room. They have another mattress. So Diego stays in Jeff's room. There are four guys on the bottom and Alex sleeps on the top. It was supposed to be temporary but it ends up staying that way. Everyone in that room starts hating Diego.

So that's Horrific Wednesday.

Thursday, June 25

Visiting day gets under way and all of these people are coming into our area. We're trying to figure out what's going on. Of course, they want to see the Americans. For the most part we sit out in the hall.

I call my dad Thursday morning and he has a very different attitude. All the emotion is gone on his side. He tells me he cried all night. Whatever he dealt with Wednesday night about himself, I'm sure some of it had to do with his relationship with me. He had to be honest about a whole lot of things in his life that he never wanted to address: "Do I love my son and want to do anything for him I can or do I not?"

I don't know. Maybe that was it. I can't say for sure. That's what he tells me. Who knows what the deeper, underlying issues are. I talk to him and he says he sent the wire transfer.

I say, "What's the latest with this? Were you able to get the money sent through?"

"Yeah," he says, "I sent it. Here's the confirmation number."

He went through with it and sent the money.

He says, "I took care of it."

I say, "Thank you so much. I appreciate that. I love you for doing that. I needed you to do that very much."

He says, "Great. No problem." And he gives me the confirmation number again.

"Great."

A courier goes to check on the money that day. I call it in. He gets it from Western Union using the confirmation number. He goes down Thursday morning and comes back late Thursday afternoon. These couriers deliver the exact amount of money that's there and they're very honest about it. You tip the courier after you get the money. They pick up a lot of money and one of them could run if he wanted to but there is a tremendous amount of honesty in this prison and an expectation of doing the right thing. There's a code of ethics here and you don't steal even though you're working in a corrupt country and there is a corrupt practice in place.

When the courier shows up, we go up to the front to get our money. What's going through my head is what if he only sent me $5.00? What if he only sent me

$500? What if he lied to me again? Maybe my father's lied to me again on this one. Everything is going through my head.

We get up there and this guard is calling out names. All the inmates are standing around in a group. Everyone, including other syndicates, is standing there waiting for their name to get called. Guys are getting 1,000 pesos and 2,000 pesos and more. This happens every day. This is the practice. So we're standing there and guess what? Jeff's name is there. He gets his money but my name isn't on the list.

I say, "You're sure?"

"No it isn't here."

We're standing there and I'm trying not to lose it.

I ask him to please look again.

He says, "No, I don't have your name here. What's the confirmation number?"

I give my confirmation number to the guy and he calls it in.

He says, "No, your confirmation number isn't right."

I swear to God if that motherfucker gave me a fake confirmation number and didn't send the money, this is going to be real, real bad. I use Fidel's phone and get through to my dad.

"Okay, they say the money isn't there. Did you send the money?"

He says, "I sent the money."

"What's the confirmation number?"

He says, "Oh, what did I do with that piece of paper?"

I'm thinking he's setting me up again.

"Let me see if I can find it."

I'm standing there and all the guys from the syndicate are standing around me trying to figure out what's going on.

My dad says, "Here's the number, A–B–C–D..." and one of the numbers got backwards when he read it over the phone. We hang up.

I tell the courier, "Okay, here's the number."

The guy calls it in and he says, "Oh no, you can't get it. They're saying it takes 24 hours to get it."

Oh shit. We're going to have to wait until tomorrow to get it. And so we come back to the cell and Alex says, "Have you got the money?"

Everyone's waiting on the money. It becomes this huge problem.

I say, "No, I don't have the money."

"How come you don't have the money?" Alex is very upset and says, "The warden's been on me about the money."

I explain the problem with the confirmation number and that the account won't release the money for another 24 hours. Alex is not happy.

During the day the warden comes to Area X to visit us. The warden never comes into the prison. He comes down to our area and he says, "I wanted to see how things are."

Everyone's like, "Whoa, dude, these Americans are so important that the warden came all the way down here to see them."

That afternoon, Diego says something that shows his lack of understanding of the situation we're in and it just floors me. He says, "Man, ever since we came to the prison man, ever since we got here, it's been so good for my nose. It's been healing up so much, man. I needed this to heal my nose."

I sit there, and Rocky is standing there, and we look at Diego and then I say, "Well, I'm really glad that we got to come to prison so you can get off cocaine long enough for your nose to heal up. Thank you!"

Rocky is laughing so hard he's got tears coming out of his eyes and I'm looking at Diego like, "Thank you for bringing me to prison so you could heal your nose you sonofabitch!"

And Diego is trying to justify his ass and he's like, "Excuse me. I'm sorry. I didn't mean it like that."

I say, "No, I heard exactly what you said, asshole." By now, I'm calling Diego names every time I can. I'm miserable so I use all the profanity that I can think of all the time, like "Old man get your fat ass out of my way you smelly bastard." And I'll push him and stuff like that.

And he gets all mad, like "What the hell are you doing?"

Rocky loves it so he repeats the story to everyone and they're like, "You've got to be shitting me."

They're just as appalled by him saying that as we are and that helps to develop the animosity toward Diego during the time that we're there.

Also on Thursday, after the money fiasco, this guy, Franco, shows up to see us. All three of us go up there and this dude introduces himself as Franco, the runner for the lawyers. He has cell phones for us.

He says, "Here you go. Here are some calling cards."

He's trying to be discrete about it. He can't speak any English so he has to go through Diego. We have a short conversation about his role in our life. He's responsible to make sure we have the money we need and to get anything we need that we can't get on the inside.

I'm picking up Spanish at a rapid pace by now. It's total submersion so I focus and concentrate and try to understand it. I get to a place where it starts to click and I'm learning fast.

That's Thursday. Each of us has his own phone. Now, if I can only get my money.

Friday, June 26

Friday comes along and I'm thinking, "All right. My money should be here today and I can get all of this mess cleaned up." I'm really tired of it hanging over my head. I go up front and find the courier. I ask him if he has my money.

No fucking money on Friday, either. The courier doesn't work on Saturday or Sunday so it looks like the money won't be here for another three days. My stomach is in a knot.

I walk back to the syndicate and pull Alex aside.

I say, "We have a problem. I ain't got any money."

Angel says, "What do you mean you ain't got any money?"

"I don't know. The courier says it's not being released."

"It's not being released? What's going on?" By now everyone in the syndicate knows there's a problem.

And the confusion is back. Like how come we can't get our money?

"It has to be released. How much is it?"

I never wanted to tell anyone how much I'm getting because now they will think I'm a walking ATM. I don't see any way around it, though. I tell them that it's $3,000, which is a little under 100,000 pesos. That's a huge amount of money.

Someone says, "Oh, man, the government might be watching it then because it's such a large amount of money. They might not release it."

Everyone in the syndicate is involved with this now. I call my dad again and he says that he sent it 24 hours as a security thing. With everyone working together, we finally figure out that since it's a 24–hour post, I have to call Western Union with the confirmation number to get them to release the money. So I call Western Union and grant the release and they say it will be released in 24 hours. Since the courier doesn't deliver on Saturday, I'll have to wait until Monday to get the money.

What I find out much, much later–it's a good thing it was much later–is that my dad had two ways of sending the money. He could send it overnight and I would have had it Thursday or he could pay a little more and send it to arrive 24 hours later with a hold on it. According to him, with the weekend coming up, he didn't think it made that much difference, so he sent it the 24–hour way. In my mind, it was a "gotcha!" He didn't like it that his son was telling him what to do and that was his way of getting back at me.

We stayed with the syndicate, in the nice area, for four days without paying. Through trial and tribulation and everything else. I am overwhelmed with burdens at this point in time because I have the passport issue as well. I have Diego. I also have the court appeal that I haven't even started to think about, and the lawyers are saying, "We need the passports."

So I get on the phone and I'm trying to orchestrate the passport situation. I begin to wonder if I could pay the courier to go get my money on Saturday. I run that by Alex and he thinks it's a good idea. We can always try. So Diego and me find the courier and ask him if he will do that for me. We negotiate a price and he agrees.

Later that day, the Embassy shows up. There are about 15 U.S. citizens in Najayo. Once a month, the U.S. Embassy comes to the prison to check on everybody and bring them a magazine and a bottle of multivitamins. This month it's National Geographic.

Me, Jeff, Diego and the rest of the group walk down this hall past the warden's office. We need Diego to translate while we're moving through the prison. We get to this room where they process new inmates. This is where we wait for our turn with the people from the Embassy. There's another room a little farther down the hall where they talk to the inmates.

They call each person in individually and ask him the same two questions they ask everyone. Have you been physically harmed? Are you being extorted? Everyone has the same opinion: "It doesn't matter what you say. The Embassy is useless. They don't do shit for you, man."

Even if you show up and you've obviously been beaten they can't do much. A guy in the waiting room says, "Yeah, the guards were beating on me. I was having a problem with them about some shit and I told the Embassy about it and all they did was 'request that an inquiry be made into your situation.' What a joke."

They call my name and there is this lady and the same Embassy guy, Chandler, who came and saw me and Jeff in the courthouse jail. I'm already annoyed.

"How are you doing?" Chandler says.

"I'm in fucking prison for some shit I didn't do. What do you expect me to say?"

"Have you been harmed or threatened in any way?"

"No."

They asked me how I was feeling and a bunch of other general bullshit. Then the lady says, "Do you have a phone? Do you need us to contact anyone on your behalf?"

I tell them I have a phone.

They are aware of our case because it's so messy and it doesn't fit. The other Americans in here look shady. If you saw them on the street in the States you wouldn't think they were doing anything positive.

Then Chandler says, "Is there anything the Embassy can do to help you?

I say, "No, but I'll tell you what you can do," and we have this conversation.

"What you can do isn't for me. What you can do is make sure this never happens to anyone from the States again. That should be your responsibility right now. Nowhere on the travel web sites, all of our hotels, all of our reservations, did it state anything about the possibility of this happening to us."

This lady that sits next to Chandler speaks pretty good English. She says, "I understand, but we can't bad mouth the country on the travel web sites."

"If I was a professional representing this country, and I had someone else going through what I'm going through right now, I would feel very responsible that I made an error somewhere in my job and didn't warn people that this could happen to them if they get in a taxi and travel in the city."

She says, "I can see your point."

"I would hope so. Other than that there is no point in us talking right now." I was very direct and at the same time I let them know that there was nothing they can do for me now. They could have done a whole lot for me before.

She says, "Maybe we can go to the travel web sites and notify people to check the Embassy web site to ensure safe travel. Basically put a disclaimer on the travel sites: Please see the Embassy travel web site before you come to the DR."

I say, "There should be a list on the Embassy website of what to do and not to do like don't ride in taxicabs. A friend of mine went on a site and said there were nightmare stories that are exactly like ours. Americans are taught that the first thing you do if you're in trouble is to contact the U.S. Embassy in that country."

I travel all the time to other countries. I take my friends' recommendations if they were there recently. I was mad at myself. I wasn't smart enough. I didn't go and check the fucking web site! I didn't check what could happen there. Anyone can check the website for different countries and it's the same thing.

I'm being very direct. Just like a business operation. My country can't do shit for me in this situation and my country knew that there was a very high probability of things like this happening. That wasn't being effectively communicated. All of the U.S. companies that own resorts and hotels down there are making tons of money. They aren't telling people about the possible dangers. They don't want people to be afraid to go to the DR.

The whole point is don't believe what you see in the movies about the Embassy. They ain't shit and they will never do shit for you. Why we even have them I have no idea. We have a couple of glorified cases where Congress and political people get involved and the Embassy appears to be something more than it is, but for the average U.S. citizen going to other countries, the Embassy ain't going to do much but watch. And let your family know when you're dead, I guess. I mean fuck! That's your tax dollars at work again.

Saturday, June 27

About mid-morning two of the gatekeepers come back to the syndicate and tell us we need to go to the front. Jeff doesn't really need to come, but he wants to so I let him. The three of us are pretty excited, thinking that we're going to finally get the money.

This whole thing about getting my money, and the day-to-day anxiety, is almost impossible to live with. Today's supposed to be the day.

Going up there, I say, "God, I hope it's $3,000."

Diego says, "What if it's only $300?"

What if this is all a set-up and bullshit?

The guy who coordinates the money is there and we watch while he counts every peso. I thank the man for his time, give him a tip and then tip the courier on top of our negotiated price.

When I get back to the syndicate, I go to my cell and sit down to count all of the pesos again. Then I find Alex and give him the money for me and Diego to stay in the syndicate. The most important part of the money was to get the 10,000 pesos that we each have to pay the warden. I pay that for me and for Diego, too. Alex says he'll take it to the warden when he comes in on Monday.

Alex offers to have me come live with him up in his area but that puts me back in a cell with Diego and Jeff again. I tell him what I need.

I say, "There's too much traffic over here. I don't want to be involved with this. I need tranquility but thank you for offering.

Alex says, "I understand. That would be good for you. Javier is very good. You're welcome to come spend time with me up here if you like." He acts semi-gay but he has a wife and kids that come to visit him.

By now, me and Fidel have spent quite a bit of time negotiating the price of the room.

Fidel says "Well, if you want the whole upstairs by yourself..."

I tell him I don't have to have it. He says, "No, I want you to have it."

I say, "How about this? I'll give you 6,000 pesos for staying here this week without paying."

We agreed on 1,000 pesos a day on Tuesday night, four days ago, when we first arrived. To stay in the upper area by myself will be more expensive.

"The way I'm figuring it out, we should be gone next week after our appeal in court on Friday. At the most, we might be here for another week. Everyone's saying, "Oh, you'll be out next time you go to court. So I'll probably be gone next week. If not, the week after. And if I stay longer than that, I'll give you an additional 6,000 pesos at that time."

Fidel nods his head.

I say, "So how do you want to do it?"

He says, "Well, I'll take your money now, and when you leave, I'll give you the 6,000 pesos back because basically we had an initial contract in place for you, Diego, and me in that area up top, right?"

I say, "Well then, I don't want to be up there with anyone else–I want to be up there by myself."

He says, "Okay, that's going to be a extra."

We work back and forth and negotiate down. By the end of the day, I have the entire upstairs to myself and I get Diego out of their cell, so there are three of us. I get all of that in the ballpark of something like 70,000 pesos, about $2,200. Jeff paid somewhere in the range of 80,000 to 90,000 pesos for his bed and everything like that.

I have some leverage in place during these negotiations because the other syndicate also wants us to come live with them. The prolonged issue of obtaining the money helped negotiate the price down also.

• • •

In the meantime, the lawyers come up with all of these extravagant plans. "We're going to move them out of Najayo. We're going to have them get sick and then we'll move them to the hospital. That's how we'll get them out of prison."

I say, "No way. We're going to stay where we are until we leave. Period. I'm not going to another prison; I'm not going to the hospital or anywhere else."

Their worst idea is, "The boys are in too nice of an area. It will look better in court if they're staying in the general population."

"Fuck you man. I have to stay alive!" These lawyers are saying all of this random shit to our families.

At the same time, I'm working everything from where I am. To be honest, trying to manipulate everyone, dealing with the lawyers, and getting my money is so stressful that it's worse than any job I've ever had and I've had some pretty desperate jobs. I arranged with Diego's father-in-law to bring the rest of our stuff and the passports later that day.

Franco shows up again presumably to pick up our passports. Here's another one who only speaks Spanish. Diego translates and after a few minutes he says, "This guy says he's with these other lawyers."

Four lawyers show up with Franco. They're standing together in a little group,

I say, "These other lawyers?"

Diego says, "No, I mean the guys from the Embassy."

I say, "Oh, okay, the guys from the Embassy."

Franco isn't keen on everything he's hearing. He says, "Yeah, we're the new lawyers for you guys."

Diego doesn't know we have new lawyers at that point in time.

Diego says, "What the hell's this guy talking about? He says that we need to bring the passports from my family and have them brought here, to us in prison, and that he's with your new lawyers. And he says it's illegal for my family to hold your passports. What is he talking about?"

I say, "I don't know man. This is who we talked to. Who knows what's going on with the families? Let's get on the phone and try to figure it out."

I'm trying to play Diego at the same time so I whisper in Franco's ear in Spanish. I tell him to shut up. *"Cállate por favor"* and I grab his face and say it again, *"Cállate por favor."* He doesn't know how much Spanish I understand. I can pick up on his conversation with Diego. He's working for the lawyers our family hired and he's waiting for the passports I've arranged for Diego's father-in-law to bring today.

Diego's father-in-law shows up with our passports. Everyone, including Franco, is there. Saturday is a big, busy, visiting day. He's happy to see us. He's a big teddy bear. He calls me his son.

He says, *"Oh, mi niño."*

I call him my father. *"Papá, mi padre."*

They think this is funny, so we embrace. He really likes me a lot. He talks to me. I give him a hug. He hands Jeff his backpack with his laptop and all of our clothes. Then he pulls the passports out of his pocket and hands them to me.

I say, *"Gracias, amigo."*

The lawyers have been threatening to go get them from Diego's father-in-law. I tell them over and over, "I'll take care of it. I'll hand them off to you. Let me handle it." I turn and put them in Franco's hands. Once the lawyers have our passports, we're no longer dependent on Diego.

I ask Franco, "Can you give him some money for driving out here? For all of his efforts–he kept our passports safe and brought us all of our clothes." Franco only gives him 500 pesos.

I tell Diego to tell Franco, "You're making me look bad, Franco. I shouldn't have to ask you to give him more money. It's embarrassing for me."

So Franco gives him some more money. It's roughly 1,000 pesos for his time and bringing all of our clothes to us. It's a nice warm thing. It's a "we're all here to help each other" kind of thing.

Of all of the things I have on my list of things to manage, I can take these issues off. I still have a lot of other things going on but the list is shorter.

After everyone leaves, and thing calm down a little, I have a huge argument with Jorge on the phone. He's supposed to be our main lawyer but we never see him. He has it out with me. He's trying to tell people what to do and it's coming back to bite him. He's clueless.

I keep telling my dad, "You need to tell this guy that I know what I'm doing here."

My dad finally tells Jorge, "Run everything by Corey before you do whatever you plan on doing. He'll take care of it."

Jorge says, "We'll have Franco at the prison in case you need anything."

I say, "No. We need the other guy who originally met with us, the first lawyer. Diego thinks he's from the Embassy." We go round and round about what I think needs to happen.

Jorge says, "We have to get you away from Diego. The whole defense is to prove that you and Jeff are separate from Diego and the girl. You guys having your own attorney will help a lot with that. We'll get you out. We'll represent you and then Diego will be the fall guy."

I tell Jorge, "I'll take care of this. I don't even care what your lawyers do anymore. I'm done. You go do whatever the hell you want to. I'm cool where I'm at now. What me and Jeff have gone through to this point has been hell. I got this situation under control now."

Eventually, my plan is to put Diego in a position where he's going to do whatever he has to do to take the fall and say, "Yeah, those drugs are mine." That's the direction I'm headed. I hate Diego for putting us in this position but I have to play it cool. I can't let that affect me. All I know is we're going to walk out of here and he's not. If this is the last job I have, I'll take care of this.

After I finally get the money from my father to pay everyone, and I get done with the passport hand-off, I have about 9,000 pesos (about $280) left over to live on. I can live like a king off of 500 pesos (about $16) a day. I'm set.

After going through all of this stress, the people, playing the lawyers, all the lawyers trying to fuck up what I'm doing, getting away from Diego, dealing with

Jeff telling him what to say and what not to say, I finally have a spot where I can have my silence. I'm good.

Then I start thinking of something: Maybe I don't want to get out. Maybe I want to hang out here and relax for the next couple of months. After all that hell, maybe I'll kick back here and get people to leave me the fuck alone. Everything worked out the way I wanted it to. I'm good here. I'm protected here. I have a place to stay for as long as I need to.

I have something stable right now. It's not chaotic anymore and things have been taken care of. I have enough to live off of. I have time to breathe and I need time to think. I can think my way out of this. What do I need to do next?

I don't know it yet, but I have more to come. This is just the first round.

The guys are very concerned about my well-being. They understand that they need to keep Diego away from me. I have moments when I'm not stressed out and they can see the change in me, the joking and laughing. Before this happened, I was making jokes and having a good time. I was being me, saying smart-ass shit that people find hilarious.

Now, in this prison environment, I slowly die as a person. Each day that goes by I get further and further away from the good in me. There is more hard coming. The hard stuff coming is mostly mine from here on out. It's me and Jeff working through it.

• • •

At some point in time, what I've accomplished in this situation finally clicks in my dad's head. I explain a situation the way it happened and my dad says, "Why did the lawyers tell us that it happened like this? That's not true." As much as my dad thinks he knows, he has no idea what's really going on and how very bad the situation is.

My dad finally recognizes what I'm doing on the inside and the–I don't want to say "trust"–but it's more like the respect that we have for each other gets stronger. The ability to keep my head clear at a time when everything else is chaos, and focus fully on the task at hand, these are the things I think he gets an appreciation for a little bit more.

From that day forward, the relationship with my dad changes phenomenally. When I finally make it home, he says, "I love you son. I'm proud of everything you're doing."

His appreciation for who I am and what I do is an amazing change from my mom's constant disapproval of everything about me. She's told me how much she disapproves of me throughout most of my life and my dad kind of backed her up.

My dad disapproves of me from a religious standpoint–the God stuff–because I don't go to church. But I have a real–life relationship with God that goes way beyond the superficial that most people have and are happy with. Most people think they have a relationship with God if they go to church every Sunday. If that's the basis of their relationship, they don't have one. I talk to God and ask for His guidance all the time. I pray on a regular basis.

I see through a lot of stuff from my past. For example, I've loved alcohol most of my life. Nowhere in the Bible does it say not to drink. You know what I'm saying? The only thing you can come up with is, "Don't be a drunkard." Right? That's the only verse that's out there.

There's a huge problem with wine and religion, especially Christianity, but the Bible doesn't make a distinction there. Why does God turn water into wine? I don't know. He wants people to have a good time. I think it was Ben Franklin who said, "Beer is proof that God loves us and wants us to be happy." It's a true saying.

When I got back home, my dad apologized for the money issue. He said he was sorry, and that he was way out of line and he shouldn't have done that.

My dad is surprised by how many people care about me. Even his own sister. My aunt is worried sick about me. She's more worried than my parents. And she's not a religious person at all. She doesn't believe in God.

My dad repeats this conversation to me while I'm still in prison:

He and my aunt are talking on the phone and she says something along the lines of, "I've been praying for Corey every day."

And my dad says, "Really? You're praying? Do you even know who God is?"

He said that to her! It's a very insulting thing to say and he repeats it back to me.

I say, "Did you hear what you just said? I don't know what kind of relationship you have with your sister, but here she is, she's not a faith, believing person, but she's so sad and concerned about my situation that she's praying, and in the midst of that you say that to her?"

Again, he's acting like, "Look at me. Look at me. I've always gone to church and I'm very religious."

I don't know what else to say. Then he repeats it to me again and I say, "You seriously said that?" He didn't get it and I say it again and it finally clicks in his head and he says, "Oh, yeah. Yeah, that was probably inappropriate."

And I say, "You think, dude?"

I told my dad how much I appreciated what they did for me but for some reason, he doesn't tell my mom that. After I'm back, she says, "You know you should be more appreciative for everything we've done for you in this situation."

And I said I am and I say it repeatedly. I've apologized and told her how much I appreciate what she went through for me on numerous occasions. My dad heard it.

I said to him, "Did you not tell her that that was the first thing that came out of my mouth?"

All these things. These family dynamics. Maybe she doesn't want to hear it. I can't explain it any other way. I don't know what else to do. I want to thank everyone and I'm trying to visit everyone who called me, prayed for me and played a part in my life during this time.

The bottom line is I appreciate everything they did, and that they were willing to help me, but compared to how Jeff's family embraces him when we're released is phenomenal. His mother and sister get on a plane and fly to the airport where we're going to land so they are there when we arrive. They're so happy to see him; it's the complete opposite of my family.

I don't know if I'm out of line because I don't have a child, but if my child was going through this situation, I would be happy every day that person was around and be grateful that I get to see him again. That's how I would be.

I feel really bad that they had to go through all of this with me but, I don't know, should I have not called them? Should I have had my buddy Connor take care of everything for me? Should I have not called them at all? Would they have been better off if we had done all that and not even involved my parents? Bad things happen, but I mean, "Do you not want me to contact you?"

Right?

That is the question.

• • •

One day, me and Jeff are randomly talking about how dirty everything is. We're surrounded by so much humanity–most of which is unwashed–rotting food and other debris, flies, mosquitos and bugs. We keep our cells as clean as possible for the situation, but it's a challenge.

And then there's the odor from the filth. It reminds me so much of pictures I've seen of Africa on TV. There are flies and mosquitoes everywhere, constantly. It's hard to get clean because there are so many people.

Everyone touches everything. People touch you constantly. You have to shake hands. There's no way to keep anything clean because people handle it all the way along the line. So, it's constantly dirty. I remember me and Jeff sitting there talking one day. I was like, "Man, I want to get a giant vat of hand sanitizer and take a bath in it."

The water isn't clean. They don't have a water purification system. When you take a shower, you do the best you can but you're never really clean. I try not to look but, at times, I see how dirty the guys are who are handling the food I'm going to eat. There's no such thing as washing your hands after you've used the bathroom. There are swarms of flies, and where did the meat come from? How old is it? What kind of deal do they have going on with this rice? Eating questionable food that was not prepared well is just one of those things we have to do every day, but it also wears on my health day to day, especially when I was getting sick.

One day Rocky says, "I got this guy, Keith. I think you'll really like him. Let me introduce you to him." Rocky's a great source of information. He shows me around all the other places in the prison. He shows me the gym and he's telling me stories about different people in prison.

"This guy over here, look out for him man. He cut this other guy's arm off one day in the yard with a machete." It's all crazy stuff. All kinds of wild information.

We go and meet Keith. He's an interesting kid. He grew up in Atlanta. His mother is still there. That's where his family is from. He played high school football and stuff like that. He's very similar to me. We have the same interests and we really like hanging out together. Keith is one of the nicest people me and Jeff meet while we are there.

He was sentenced to 20 years in Najayo for drug trafficking. He wanted to make some fast money like everyone else. So, according to his story, he made a body package of cocaine. He was going to smuggle it to Spain. Someone snitched on him and the police got him before he could leave the country.

A body package is a suit that has drugs in it like cocaine, or heroine, or whatever you want and it fits your body. It conforms to your body so you walk right through security and get on the airplane with the drugs on your body. It's the best way to go. Supposedly, drug dogs can't smell it.

The appeal, the rush, and all the things they talk about when it comes to smuggling drugs into a country. You can understand it, I guess. I'm impressed by his attitude in this situation. He's honest about it, deals with it and it is what it is, "I'll be here awhile. So be it."

If I had to be there long term, I'm pretty confidant me and Keith would end up getting a cell together because we're very similar. He cracks me up. He's always asking about the latest music and what's going on in the States.

Hanging out with him is the closest thing to being normal. He lives up in the real nice area in the front of the prison, where those guys came and took us up front to see their syndicate. He's living up there with two other guys.

One day the issue of cleanliness comes up and Keith's like, "Oh, man. You guys need to protect yourself. There are so many germs." He gives each of us a little bottle of hand sanitizer. It was awesome. We were so excited.

I put that hand sanitizer on my hands and I rubbed it on my face. I brought it all the way back to the States with me. It was hand sanitizer from a Sprint golf tournament or something like that, wherever Keith's mom picked it up.

• • •

I always get sick when I'm in a dirty environment like this. There's a huge problem with my face. I've broken my nose several times and now I can't breathe out of it. If I don't have the things I need to maintain a clean sinus tract, I end up getting a sinus infection, and the mucus and infection travel down my throat and start filling up my lungs. I get bronchitis and from there, if I don't take antibiotics, I get pneumonia. It's a five day window as soon as it starts and I know it's coming. I can't explain how miserable I am when I'm sick. It's hellacious for me. It's the sinus headache and feeling so tired I can barely move. Eventually, I get a fever and feel like I have the flu.

I know what I need to do to prevent it, and not being able to do the sinus rinses, and mix and match the medications I need, is so frustrating. My body's vulnerable. I had a staph infection before I went to the DR. My immune system is already pretty damaged and it's a constant job trying to keep it from going down.

Once I get sick, I'll stay sick. I need to start all these medications before I get sick. I need to get Franco to bring them to me. My mom knows exactly what I need. She e-mails the list to the lawyers. Stupid fucker, Franco, keeps showing up with a bottle of Tylenol Extra Strength.

I tell Franco, "This is not what I need."

Finally, Franco brings me some amoxicillin. Amoxicillin will keep me from getting sicker, like getting pneumonia, but it's only going to hold the symptoms where they are. I'm not going to get better on amoxicillin.

It only lasts a week. As soon as the antibiotic runs out, I'm back to being sicker than I was before the amoxicillin. Not getting my medicine in this situation is making me miserable. It's driving me closer and closer to the edge, hating every single day, every moment. For me, when I'm sick like that, it comes to a point where I'd rather be dead than be sick anymore. It's that shitty for me. If I can't do the things I need to do to maintain a healthy life like exercise, eating well and maintaining good hygiene, and all I am is sick, my life is over as far as I'm concerned.

At least if I'm healthy, I can go exercise. I can go out on the softball field, walk around and play catch with the guys. There's a prison softball team that we end up getting involved with later on through Diego. The first couple of weeks that we were there, we were actually playing games with them.

Diego is friends with the guy who runs the softball program and he introduces us to him. It's kind of cool because he invites us out to the practices and we can go out to the grassy part of the field with all the players. We walk around and it's quiet. We get our own space. It's fresh air. Other inmates can't do it. Even guys inside our own cell can't go out where the softball team is. Only the guys on the team can go out there.

The first week passes and I'm doing all right; second week, I start feeling sick, and I'm telling them to bring me my medicines. Finally, the third week they bring the amoxicillin. The last week we are there, they don't want to give me medicine because their strategy is to make me look sick.

Once I get sick, I'm miserable and it gets progressively worse. I start losing weight. My body's trying to fight off the dysentery along with the bronchitis. I look like shit. I feel horrible.

Because of all the time I spend in the gym and running, I have very little body fat, maybe 1% to 2%. My body's constantly fighting dehydration from the dysentery. When you get dehydrated, your muscles release acids and you start cramping. Eventually, when there's no fatty tissue left, you body starts going after the protein in your muscles. It feels kind of like what I imagine arthritis feels like. Your body's cramping, and you're sore. That's why me and Jeff are drinking as much sugary stuff as we can; a body can maintain itself at a certain level if it has enough sugar. But still, for your body to process sugar, it needs to be well hydrated.

I think about how Jeff's constantly saying, "It can't get worse than this."

All of this pushes me over the edge. I hate everything around me, I'm pissed and I start getting a real animosity toward the lawyers and I let them know it.

One day when the lawyers come to visit us I can't stop coughing and trying to clear my throat. This lawyer tells us his strategy going into court. He says to me, "Oh, that's very good. Can you do that when you go to court?"

I say, "You have to be fucking shitting me. You're telling me to look sick when I go to court? It's good for our case?"

The lawyers say, "Don't give him anymore medicine. We want him sick when he goes to court." This is our fucking lawyers' strategy when it comes down to it.

I say, "You motherfuckers."

That's when my family starts getting a real understanding of these lawyers, what we're dealing with, and everything I've been saying all along. You can't trust anyone down here. These lawyers don't know their head from their ass. They screw up everything they touch. Even though my family stresses the importance of this to our lawyers, I never get the medicine I'm asking for.

Sunday, June 28

On top of being sick, I'm anxious and frustrated. Now that I have money, I'm not at the mercy of other people and I have some control. I pay Diego's way into the syndicate and as far as I'm concerned, I'm done with him. I wash my hands of him and over time, I let everyone know that in subtle ways. I have new translators now.

Diego rubs everyone the wrong way. He isn't the kind of person that would normally end up in this particular syndicate and he doesn't like the guys in it. He wants to go into a different syndicate and he talks about it constantly. I'm not paying for that and, presumably, he doesn't have the money to do it himself. There are a lot of guys who speak English and Spanish in the prison. These guys are telling us, "Dude, this guy is a set-up artist."

Geraldo shows up in Najayo. I thought he was going to La Victoria but it's good to see him. It's been awhile since we spent time talking back at the jail. He's a pretty bright guy. He used to live in New Jersey. He's in Najayo for writing bad checks. This time he sits down and tells me how he really came to be here and it had nothing to do with shooting someone.

Geraldo says the police finally came to arrest him for writing bad checks. He was in his car at the time. They pull him over, but when they get out of their car, he starts driving away. He tries to outrun the police and they end up shooting out the tires on his Cherokee!

Then the police try to get him out of the car, but he's a really big guy and he's on his phone talking to everyone in his family, so the police have to wait until he's done. He finally gets out of the car and the police tell him that they are arresting him for writing fraudulent checks, or whatever the charges are.

He says, "I was going to give them my car. Like, here man, take my truck and let me go."

But the police officers say they have to take him in especially after they had to chase him down and shoot out his tires to get him to stop.

At least, this is his current story. Then Geraldo looks across the room at Diego and says, "There is no way that guy can know as many people as he knows in this prison and not have been here before."

Our lawyers checked, and he has a clean legal record. There's no evidence that he's been in the jail or the prison. Even so, people are constantly coming up to us and saying, "That guy you're with, Diego, he's shady. He set me up before with the cops."

I can't believe everything they say. We don't know if people are saying this to create confusion. We can count on about 90% of everything we hear being a lie because it's a prison, but there are elements of truth there, too. I learn how to filter through it. It seems like everyone wants to get close to us so we have to be careful all the time.

Fidel tells me, "Yeah man, be careful going anywhere. If someone pulls a knife on you, run and try to get to a guard as fast as you can so they don't shake you down."

I don't want to deal with the guards directly. That's what I have Diego for. So when the guards approach me and ask for money, I act like I don't speak any Spanish and I don't know what the hell they're talking about. They don't see us walking around with cash or see us handling money. The only person with money is Diego.

It doesn't take long before everyone realizes that the Americans never walk around with money and if you want money from them you go through this guy, Diego. He functions as an awesome buffer. Diego enjoys the role as well. He gets to say, "I'm with the Americans." Throughout the course of day-to-day life, I give Diego tasks but at the same time I'm making business deals with other people.

Rocky is my first business deal after negotiating the cost of my room. He wants to earn some money by providing services for us. He doesn't have his own cell. He sleeps in the pod right next door to us, which is a big step down. At night, those guys lie down on the concrete in the front of the pod curved around each other, packed in like sardines, until it's full. They have a certain amount of space and the guys who have some money can get a little cubicle or cubbyhole to keep their things in. The only thing the other guys in that cell have is what they're wearing.

Rocky's a drug addict. He must have gotten hooked on drugs to end up in Najayo because he speaks very good English. He used to work in the Free Zone so he had a job, and he's an awesome translator. He really understands how the inflection in someone's voice can change the meaning of what they're saying, and he can communicate effectively in Spanish and English.

At the same time, Diego feels threatened by him and that's good because now I have checks and balances with Diego. I can do some things without him. He knows about some of them and some of them he doesn't.

220

Rocky is a beggar but I tell him that I don't do handouts. That's not how I handle things. He says, "I need a thousand pesos so I can get my own room." I tell him about a person's guaranteed money and how you don't want to mess with that money trying to get more money.

I say, "Don't fuck up your guaranteed money. I don't know how long we're going to be here, but this is what we're going to do. I'll give you a thousand pesos like you asked for but you're going to provide laundry service for me and Jeff every day, and along with that, I want two smoothies every morning, one for me and one for Jeff, and either bananas or Johnnie cakes for us. That comes out roughly to less than 100 pesos a day for all of those services that we talked about. However you go and negotiate this deal on the backend is up to you. It's roughly 100 pesos a day for the services you provide and you get all the money up front. If we get out earlier you get to keep the money.

"We're going back to court next week and everyone thinks we're going to leave. We can do it that way or we can work it out at 100 pesos a day to get a thousand. Ten days or two weeks from now you'll have to work all the way through and keep providing us with services." He has all kinds of hustles going on to make that 100 pesos.

Rocky says, "Yeah, man I'll do that."

He's getting a place to sleep and who knows? My thousand plus the other money he's saved up? He's moving up from this bottom level to the next level.

I say, "Now, this deal is between us. You know how I expect you to handle it."

He says, "I understand Corey. I totally respect you. I love how you handle yourself. It's business."

"Right. It's business."

I say, "If we have a problem later on, and you can't provide me with these services, you're going to owe me money. Do you understand what I'm saying? To not owe me money, you're going to have to find someone else that you can work another deal with. If you can't provide all of these services for the allotted time period, or you come up short or you don't provide any of them, I'll make a deal with someone else and let him know that for him to get payment, he's got to get the money out of you."

I say that because I don't want to have anything to do with strong-arming. There are enough desperate people here–they'll do anything.

This is the beginning of the business deals and they start calling me, *"Tigre Americano.* This guy is sharp."

So I make the business deal with Rocky on the down low. It's between him and me. Diego doesn't even know about it.

From then on, I wake up every morning and Rocky is out doing his thing. He gets up before I do. He gets up at the crack of dawn–as soon as they open the gates.

One day, I'm up and he says, "Corey how are we doing this morning?"

"I'm good."

He says, "What flavor of shake would you like? Do you have any laundry for me?"

I say, "I'm cool, go ahead and take care of your other customers. Whatever work you have to do. When you get a chance, sometime, bring me two mangos and I want to do bananas today. Bring me two bananas." It gets to the point where I tell him, "You don't need to check. Bring me whatever you want."

We never have to do anything for ourselves, me and Jeff. People are always on stand-by. "Oh, I'll go get you a drink."

"I'll take this bowl back to the guy who fixed you guys dinner."

If we mention we're hungry, someone says, "Oh, you want something to eat? I'll get right on that." There are people around constantly, but at the same time, I want to handle things appropriately.

I can't walk around with all this money on me because then I'm a target. I don't want to keep it all in one location, either, so I need to stash it in various locations. The people who hide money in their cell for me know about it, but at the same time I don't want everyone to know about it. People begin to feel like they're playing a role, but at the same time there's a level of secrecy and it's in their best interests to look out for my best interests. This is what I start using Rocky for. I use Rocky and Diego against each other all the time. They dislike each other, which is even better.

Initially, part of the reason why I picked the cell I did is because it's safe and Fidel doesn't do a whole lot of business out of there. The front room where Jeff is has people running in and out all the time because they're selling all kinds of crap out of there. Alex mainly runs whiskey. There's so much traffic in that cell that you don't feel safe leaving anything around. These people may be nice, but they are still thieves.

Javier and Fidel are real straight guys. Back in my room, Rocky translates for me and Fidel to fill in the gaps when we need to have a conversation but we don't have the patience to write it all down and work through the English language. I'm very articulate and Rocky is awesome at translating. He conveys it exactly the way I say it.

I tell Fidel, "You know I made a business deal with you about this room and I expect you not to come back later and ask for more money. I'm trusting you, so if you don't feel like you can keep our business deal between us, you need to let me know now."

Everyone is interested in how much I ended up paying Fidel for my room. They ask him, "How much did you sell your room for to him? How much money does he have?"

I say, "If this is something you feel that you can't handle. If you can't keep our business between us, you need to let me know now because I'm trusting that you can handle this in a professional manner."

I'm saying this very respectfully, but at the same time I'm letting him know that I have a whole lot of expectations that he needs to live up to. If he doesn't think he can keep our interests between us then I need to know so I can find another place to live. It's a constant leverage pull.

Fidel says, "No, it's between us." He'll take on the responsibility and Fidel becomes one of my primary banks.

Then I leave some money with Jeff. He knows how much we have in his cell, but he doesn't know how much I have in mine. I'm worried in case Jeff gets diarrhea of the mouth, or something goes wrong, or we need a backup if we get into some kind of extortion situation. Jeff's roommates are aware of how much money we have there, too, and they're going to watch it. It's a delicate balance all the time.

• • •

I get up early and usually do my routine, pushups, pull–ups, whatever, and then hang out with these older guys that get up early, too. We congregate out in the hallway in a recessed area that has a cinder block window and a little pull–up bar.

We hang out there and read the newspaper together. It's quiet, tranquil and relaxed–the way we like it. They like me because I'm quiet. They like it quiet. Diego gets up and he wants to talk to me. He starts in and I say, "Hey man, it's too early in the morning."

He says, "I'm sorry. I'm sorry," and he wanders off to go do something else.

The older gentlemen say, *"Gracias. Sí. Sí."*

Someone brings us a little coffee, too, like a little shooter of espresso. They are five pesos or something like that. That's the way we like it early in the morning.

Rocky starts to show up every morning with smoothies, coffee, bananas and things like that, but they never see me hand him any money. That starts people talking. Rocky does the laundry and provides breakfast. I tell Jeff about the deal. Jeff makes another deal with the guys in his cell so they get some business. They provide us with lunch every day, but it's not a whole lot. It's rice and some nasty meat and a little bit of beans. It's shitty food.

This black guy, Kobe, who is a pretty respected gangsta, cooks burgers and sells them for 50 pesos. They put mayonnaise and ketchup on everything they eat there–not mustard, nothing spicy, but mayonnaise. If we want burgers one night, we talk to Kobe and he hooks us up for fifty pesos.

I have credit with Kobe, or he gives us the burgers for free. One night I tell him I only have 100 pesos on me. That isn't enough for the dinner we ate. Kobe calls me *"blanco"* which means "whitey."

"Blanco, es nada."

He likes me but he has to be a tough guy about it–he's a street guy. One day we get into it. He brings me a girl and I don't want her and he gets really angry with me. We have it out but nothing comes out of it.

Sometimes, if guys are talking about something important, I'll chime in with something in Spanish and they say, "See, I know he knows what we're talking about." They realize that I'm a reliable person if you want to talk to someone; I'm not going to snitch to anyone because there's no one for me to talk to. Sometimes if someone thinks they have a good idea, they want to tell me about it and see what I think.

At the same time, some of the guys I'm talking to and even the guards want to use a little bit of their English, and they want to know why I'm here. I explain it again and they see Diego and they say, "Oh yeah, the story fits."

This is the classic story where people tolerate him but really don't like him that much. Then pressure starts coming in at him and by the second week, the Columbians, and other groups, are coming to me.

It starts with: "Your taxi driver, I can't stand him, man."

Then they're saying, "Hey man, we'll take care of him for you for X amount of money."

And then it's, "We'll take care of him for free."

And then it comes down to, "Can we have your permission?"

Diego feels this coming in on him. He realizes that he's in a bad spot where he can't roll on us because if we're still in prison and he's out on the street, he's a dead man. The hotel he works for knows what happened. We're connected enough on the inside now that I can touch him even if he's on the outside. And I have money and he doesn't.

My personal happiness is now Diego's daily objective. It becomes a burden for him because he sees me slipping each day. At this point in time Jeff is doing what he can to get by but I have Jeff taken care of. He's scared to walk the halls; he's vulnerable. He can stay in his room and watch movies all day.

Toward the end of our stay, I walk the halls by myself all the time. I talk to people along the way. I meet more and more people including kids from the States.

I finally tell the Columbians, "I need Diego for my case."

Jeff finally picks up on this and says, "Yeah, you have to keep your enemies close."

"The time will come." That's all I keep saying, "The time will come."

The last thing I say to the Columbians about Diego is, "When we go to court and you see me come back, there's a problem. As long as you keep seeing my face, there's a problem. Once you don't see my face anymore you can do whatever you want with him."

As long as people see us here, and know that he brought us here, there's a huge code of ethics in the prison that makes him a target. He gets to the point where he will say the drugs are his. He'll take full responsibility. This is what I planned.

I have my plan in place; it's there for the taking. I talk to a lawyer on the phone and tell him what Diego's going to say. He says, "No, no, no. Our strategy in the case comes down to it was a police set–up. There were no drugs involved. If we volunteer anything else, it makes you guys look like there is some admission of guilt."

I'm thinking, "What the fuck? This doesn't make any sense. These lawyers don't want to get us out; they want to keep taxing us." Eventually we go full circle. The final strategy going to court is that the lawyers agree to handle it the way I said all along.

All three of us sit down with the lawyers before we go to court and they say, "Each of you will get up and say who you are and what you do for a living. Then we will present evidence backing up what you said and show the judge that you don't have criminal records. Then Diego, you need to tell the judge that it's your responsibility. If there were drugs in the car, they were for your personal use."

And this whole time, the lawyers tell our families a completely different defense they plan to use. They change it all at the last minute.

Even my dad says, "Holy shit. Corey is right. He said he was going to figure out a way to get out from the inside and now it's going to happen."

I put everything out there. I deliver the case. I finally get control of the situation and it has nothing to do with money. The lawyers tell me, "You have to pay Diego to do this." No. He's ready to fall on his sword because of the pressure of the environment. You can only dance for so long and the music is running out on him.

The girl ends up getting out before we do. They give her bail. If she makes a statement that changes from what she said when we got convicted, the convictions could be overturned. That's the first thing that we have going for us. If she didn't give a statement at all, and she's out, then why did she get let out and we're not since we all got convicted together?

Denny, the guy with the four kilos who got thrown off the balcony gets out before we do. If you're Dominican, you post bond and they let you go. The problem here is that there are Americans involved. With their system, the quickest way for Diego to get out, is to get us out of the picture so it's just him. He's Dominican. He'll get bond and get out. They don't want to give us a bond because they know we'll leave the country.

Before we can go to our next court–appointed hearing, on July 2, the lawyers have to get all of the documents and letters of recommendation from our families to prove who we are. Then the lawyers submit them to the court where certified translators translate them into Spanish. We have to pay for the translations.

Thursday, July 2

This time when we go to court we have a better legal team than we did with Marco and they have a list of all the violations that happened: You arrested these Americans. You held them for five days without charging them. You never provided them a translator, and on and on.

The thing that I keep telling Jeff is, "Getting out of this depends on what we say in front of that judge."

I keep going over this with Jeff. I'm still thinking, "Why are they saying there are two different accounts between me and Jeff?" And I go back to the fact that we're at the mercy of the translator.

The lawyers tell us, "Oh yeah, you're going to get out. Worst-case scenario, you get bail bonded. Otherwise you get released and there won't be a money bond."

Best-case scenario, we'll be out the next day, on Friday, and on a plane back to the States. Of course everyone says, "They'll be home for the 4th of July, Independence Day."

Diego, without me asking, says, "I'll get you guys out of here. I can't do this anymore. You guys need to go."

He needs to save face. He can save face now if he says, "Yes, I said the drugs were mine. I got the Americans out."

He earns his respect back and becomes honorable with the syndicate and the prison. He did the right thing. He also needs that when he goes back. If we all come back together and he's there and he's bringing the Americans back, it's not good for him and he knows it and it becomes an ongoing pressure situation for him.

• • •

The night before court, I went over everything with Jeff again.

"You have to be really careful when you're in court. You have to talk very slowly and deliberately. The translator has to be able to translate and you have to understand that. You have a tendency for rambling on when you talk."

He takes it personally and doesn't like hearing it. I may not say it in the right way, but at this point in time, we're down to the basics.

"This is it, Jeff. This is how serious it is." I say this to him over and over.

"Don't say what you think Diego told you. Say exactly what we know which is how this situation transpired. Don't say anything about the police or the law.

You don't want to offend the court. All you have to say is this is who I am and this is what I'm all about. I had no intention to use drugs and I don't do drugs. I can't do drugs. My job doesn't allow it. This is what I do for a living. I have security clearances and work with government entities. These are the responsibilities of my job and what's at stake."

We also talk to the lawyers on the phone that night. I'm very specific about what I want to know. I don't want to hear, "Everything's going to be okay, everything's fine."

I want to know how it's going to happen. These are the steps that are going to take place and then there is X, Y and Z. I want a play–by–play breakdown of what is going to take place.

When I talk to my dad that night everything's in place. All of my friends back in the States know what's going on. My dad has been updating everyone. The families sent all of the requested documents to the lawyers.

My dad talked to the lawyers that night, too. He says, "What is your plan of attack in court? What are you going to say to Point A, Point B and Point C?"

Me and my father have a conversation after we've both spoken with the lawyers. He says, "These guys are not answering my questions; they are not being direct."

I say, "Dad, they're a joke. If they were in the States I would have fired them a long time ago." My dad agrees.

They are not delivering what I asked for and I have serious doubts going into this court hearing. They are saying all of these things and giving guarantees before we go to court.

They feed everyone the same line on the phone, "They'll be home by Monday at the latest, probably this weekend. We're going to get them out. No problem. Worst–case scenario is a money bond and they'll be out Monday, or we'll get them out before that. Best case scenario, the court drops all of the charges and they walk out of the courtroom free men and they can leave the next day."

That was the atmosphere leading up to the courtroom on Thursday. Obviously everyone in our cell area and everyone in the prison are saying, "Yeah, these guys are going to go as soon as they go to court." The guards feel that way, too.

I'm restless that night thinking about court the next day. Everyone is going to bed but I can't settle down so I decide to do another workout. I go over to the small area where I hang out with the old men in the morning.

I do my pushups and then I'm doing my sit-ups. It's weird. I'm lying there on the floor and I look up and I can see the full moon through the holes in the cinder blocks. It's traveling and I keep inching over to watch it and the phone rings. It's this girl who was my assistant for a year and a half on another job. It's hours earlier where she is.

I'm talking to her and I say, "It's a full moon tonight."

She says, "Yeah, you're right."

And this sounds so corny, but here's this small piece of beauty connecting us. Here I am, living in a this filthy, disgusting shit hole, and then I can see the same full moon that everyone in my family and everyone else on the outside can see.

• • •

The worst part about going to court is getting up at 5 a.m. to get ready so when they open the gates, we can go out to the front area. While we take showers, shave and put on our nice clothes, word gets out that we're going to court and before we leave, a bunch of inmates are standing around asking us,

"Will you give me this before you leave?"

"Will you give me your phone?"

"Give me your clothes?"

"Can I have this when you leave?"

"Oh, the Americans, this will be their last day. You guys are going to go to court and you're going to walk out."

This is the big day, our only appeal of the drug trafficking conviction, our day to get out or settle in for one to three years. There is this 4th of July mindset that the lawyers start by telling everyone we're going to get out on July 2 so we will be home by the 4th of July. Independence day! Everyone thinks this is what's going to happen. The lawyers tell the families that it's going to happen.

Every time we go to court, we end up spending about 1,000 pesos. We stand outside by the flagpole and wait and wait until finally the bus shows up.

The 24–48 hours leading up to court is a very stressful time period as we go over everything that we want to say and need to say. At the same time, every time we go to court we travel into the city and it's this huge event. So it's a coordinated effort. We have to make sure the guards get their money. We're going to pay for a seat on the bus.

When we're in transport we're vulnerable but it's also a great opportunity to escape and we're sizing those options up as well. These become Plans B and C later on. The guards on the bus aren't really that protective for the most part, and we stop to pick up their friends and give them rides along the way.

All of the sitting around doing nothing and waiting for hours, or days, for something—anything—to happen is a big part of what makes prison hell for me. I'm used to doing stuff. I'm working, or I'm at the gym or running. I don't spend time just sitting around. There are times I think I'm going to lose my mind just out of boredom.

The head guy that runs the bus–the transporter–has already transported us from the jail to the prison, so he knows who we are and he's happy to see us.

He smiles and says, *"Hola! Americanos! Mis amigos."* We're his friends.

I talk to him all the time. He's a hard-nosed guy and he dislikes the other inmates and the guards but he likes us and he wants to take care of me and Jeff all the time. Me and Jeff get handcuffs put on us and we get on this shitty-ass bus. It's about 7 or 8 or something in the morning and we ride along the waterfront through San Cristóbal, which is the capitol of the San Cristóbal province located on the south end of the island.

The guy who is handcuffed to Diego is from New York and speaks English. He turns to me and Jeff and says, "I don't know who this guy is but he's saying he wants to go in front of the judge right now and take full responsibility and that these Americans had nothing to do with it. I don't know, man, I don't know how you guys know him but he wants to do anything to get you guys off."

At this point in time I'm thinking, "There you go. Everything's in place. We're going to go up there and say who we are. Diego's going to say it's all him. The judge is going to have nowhere else to go. If they convict us on this then..."

There are different courts located throughout the city. Once we're in Santo Domingo, we take a different route. Everyone who gets on at the prison gets dropped off at various locations. We're always the first ones to get dropped off and the last ones to get picked up. We sit there all day. We don't get on the bus to go back to the prison until four or five in the afternoon.

We get to the appeals courthouse. It's a very old Spanish-style building. They pull us off the bus. I'm anxious and trying to figure out what's going on. I can tell right away that something is wrong. Our lawyers aren't out front to meet us and we don't see the court-appointed translator. All we can do is wait to find out.

The guards take us into the courtroom. It's similar to the last one but a lot larger. There's this weird-ass mural on the wall behind where the judges sit that doesn't make any sense at all. Me and Jeff try to figure it out. We sit on these hard wooden pews and we wait.

The court-appointed translator shows up and this dude is a shitty translator. He sucks. He's trying to translate and he's not doing a good job at all. Finally, the two lawyers come out. The black lawyer is the one that we convinced Diego is from the Embassy. The other guy is new, kind of a lighter skinned dude. I'd say Puerto Rican–Hispanic looking guy. They are the two lawyers for me and Jeff.

Before they can say anything, Diego tells our lawyers, "We have to do whatever it takes to get these guys out today. They need to leave. I'll say the drugs are mine. I'll take responsibility for everything that happened." If all of us go back to prison that night and we're not getting out, it's very bad for him.

When Diego is finished, the black guy says, "Yeah, well, we didn't get all of the documents translated in time. We didn't get them to the court early enough."

These dumb-ass lawyers didn't get all of the documents submitted in time! These are all of the letters our parents collected and sent to the lawyers. These are recommendations from past employers, personal recommendations saying who we are and that we don't do drugs, letters from important people giving us even more credibility. All of these documents have to be translated from English to Spanish by a court-appointed translator. Our parents worked their asses off to get the documents to the lawyers, but the lawyers couldn't find time to get them to the court early enough.

Since the documents aren't ready for the judges, we're not getting out today. The only thing the lawyers can do today is identify themselves as our legal representatives and file a motion requesting that the girl come to the courthouse at the next hearing. When we got convicted, the judge gave different verdicts for each of us. The lawyers request that they represent me and Jeff together so whatever the verdict is, it will apply to both of us. Then Diego can get a different verdict.

Everyone has to have legal representation, and even though we're paying for it, our lawyers get a low-end lawyer for Diego. It's a set-up. We know this is going on but we're trying to play Diego at the same time.

We try to get comfortable on this wooden bench while we sit there for hours watching inmate after inmate go before the judges. Finally, they call our case and we walk up to the front. The look on the three judges' faces is worth a million dollars. They're looking at us and looking at all the lawyers and there aren't enough chairs for everyone and the translator.

Again, I have to point out that I'm reading people's body language and expressions on their faces. This is a skill I learned and practice through my work. It's especially helpful when I have meetings with corporate lawyers.

The judges look at us like, "What the hell is this? There is something seriously wrong with this. What are these Americans doing in this courtroom to begin with?"

Then they start looking at the files for our case and seeing what we're charged with. They start having a conversation together and their expressions are like, "Oh, man, this isn't good. What are we going to do now?"

The only thing me and Jeff can do in this court proceeding is go up there and say, "This is who I am. This is what I do for a living. I'm not this kind of person."

Thankfully, the fact that we aren't getting out hasn't hit Jeff yet so he's able to go in front of the judges and say what we've been practicing.

Then one of the lawyers says, "During the arrest, the police officers violated the Americans' rights X, Y and Z." That's all our lawyers are going to do today.

Diego and his lawyer go up there and say something. I'm not sure what it is. The translator is useless.

The judges and lawyers coordinate their calendars and we're scheduled for a new hearing a week later, Thursday, July 9.

Knowing we have to go to court again, I'm thinking, "Classic set-up job. They want more money so they'll drag this out as long as they can. They don't want us to get out."

It's tiring. We sit there all day. I'm sick and I'm pissed. It's like, "What the fuck?"

The emotional side of everything that goes on when we go to court is like, "Okay, this is it. You have everything in place, and here are all the things that can go wrong, and are probably going to go wrong."

I don't want to get my hopes up even though Jeff does every time and when it doesn't work out, it sucks.

We're back to not having control over our situation. We're frustrated. It reaffirms my opinion of our lawyers. These lawyers don't know shit. I'm going to have to figure our way out of here. Diego is begging to go roll on himself. I'm thinking, let him roll.

What really pisses me off is why didn't they know about this problem last night when we talked on the phone? They must have known they didn't have this in place. They should have told us last night that we weren't going to get out. They could have said, "We're going to court to file a bunch of papers."

I would have asked, "Do we have to be present to file papers? Can't you do it without us being there?"

Again, no one speaks English so it doesn't really help Jeff at all. He's pissed off and he's asking me to ask them these questions, and what are they saying and what are they talking about? At this point, I'm getting better at understanding what people are saying. I can tell what's going on. I can't talk back in Spanish very well but I know what they're talking about.

Finally, the lawyers say, "All right, nothing is going to happen. We have to wait until next week. We didn't get all of your papers submitted in time."

I'm like, "Whatever." I expect it now. This is how this country is.

Jeff is exploding like someone shoved a stick of dynamite up his ass. I'm already there so I don't have a whole lot of emotions right now but the biggest thing is Jeff not understanding why this isn't happening. He was planning to escape Friday night and then he was going to go do this and he was going to take his kids shopping at the mall.

I say, "Dude, whatever."

That's his world.

We sit on this wooden bench handcuffed to each other and the guards are constantly, all day long, asking me for money.

I decide to fuck with all the guards now, "I gave the boss money. You didn't get any of it? You need to go talk to him."

And they're like, "No, no, no" and I'm doing Spanglish with them. I mess with these guards all day long and they love it.

Diego says, "They want to talk to you."

I say, *"No hablo español."*

The guard says, "No speaka English."

We go back and forth and he says, "Man, give me money, give me money."

I say, "All right. Here's what I'll do. When I get out, I'll buy you a beer."

Diego translates for me. "All your friends and people in your neighborhood. I'll buy you a beer the day I get out."

He says, "Okay."

Later on, we see the same guard back in the prison, and he asks me for money again.

I say, "Hey, if I give you money now, how can I be able to buy you a beer when I get out?"

I'm doing that all the time and the guys love it. Sometimes I'll say stuff in Spanish and other times I won't. I'll act like I don't know what they're talking about and I'll get a translator and I'll say it through him. Then they get confused.

"Is he *Americano*? *Columbiano*?"

They see me with the Columbians, hanging out, playing soccer with them. My skin is pretty brown. Some people know what I am, but for the most part, I blend right in.

We ride the bus back to Najayo and it's packed by the time we get on it because we're the last ones to get picked up. It's not only the other inmates coming from court, but it's all the guards and women getting a ride home from work. I'm waiting for a chicken to get on the bus–you know what I'm saying?

It's standing room only and me and Jeff are standing there and a guard is sitting there doing his paperwork and all of a sudden he notices us standing there and says, "Oh, no, no, no," and he gets up out of his seat.

The head boss says, "Sit down."

I say, *"No necesito."*

"No, no, por favor." Please. Please. So we sit down in the seat right behind the driver. Diego has to stand. And he's handcuffed to the same guy on the way back out.

We're riding through town, dropping people off and the bus is packed and we're driving by the coastline again looking at the water. Jeff comes up with the perfect escape plan. "We've got to jump off this bus. Jump in the water. We'll throw some scuba gear on and go get an underwater, motorized scooter thing. Basically you hold onto it and it has a propeller on it and you go under water and it pulls you around. Then we'll have Victor waiting out there with a boat and we're gone. These fuckers don't know how to swim anyway. They're not going to jump in that water and get their heads smashed against the rocks. There's no beach. We just need to run and jump off of the cliff and hope Diego has some scuba gear waiting out there and we go under water and..."

Me and Jeff have all kinds of ideas. We're riding all the way back and it sucks going back to prison. Every time we get away from our cell or we're not in our cell it sucks, but the only chance we have to get out of the DR is to get on this bus and go to court.

Guys are getting sentenced for like 10 years, 20 years and when they get back on the bus, they have the same attitude they did in the morning. Some guys get off. They get bonds so they're all excited. We talk to everyone around us. We get back to the prison and they take the handcuffs off and we come walking back in.

"You guys aren't leaving?"

"No, we have to go to court again."

"You have to be kidding me–why not?"

"Well, our lawyers didn't get all of our documents translated."

"What kind of fucking lawyers do you guys have?"

And so, right then and there, it finally hits our families in the States what's going on. These lawyers are lying about what's going on. They're telling our families what they want to hear even though it's not true. I've been saying it all along but no one believes me.

My dad tells our family members and Jeff's mom, "I told you Corey said these lawyers don't know what they're doing and Diego was ready to roll and say it was all on him. He wanted to do it and he was going to take the fall like Corey said he would. He had everything in place. There's pressure from the syndicate because they want to kill Diego and they're waiting for Corey to give them the word."

My dad is telling them all of this and now they say, "What?"

Jeff reaffirms this. He says, "Yeah. Corey had everything ready to go."

And now our families are pissed at the lawyers.

The next appeal is scheduled for Thursday, July 9.

Jeff's mom finally calls me. She asks, "What actually happened in court today?" So I explain what happened and how the lawyers screwed it up.

"That's not what Jeff said."

"It's never what Jeff says."

"Okay."

Jeff tells his mom, "Yeah, I don't know. They said they didn't get the paperwork from our parents."

I tell her that's not what they said. They said that they didn't get all of the papers submitted to the court translator. That's what the problem was. And it made sense and checked out.

Jeff takes something away from it that is completely not the way it happened.

I tell Jeff's mom, "If we err on the side of caution, we'll make sure that we get out even though we don't have every bullet in our gun. I want to know that everything is in place before we go to court. We only get one appeals hearing. It's not like you can appeal and appeal and appeal. You only get one shot. This time it better be right. They better make sure that the next time we go to court we walk the fuck out."

Jeff's mom says, "I've been getting a different story."

I say, "I understand that."

"Do you mind if I call you?"

"I don't care. If you want to hear exactly what's going on, you can call me and I'll tell you."

Jeff is still emotionally not there. He keeps talking about what he's going to do when we get out. We aren't out by a long shot but he doesn't want to acknowledge that. I'm realistic about it.

• • •

Friday morning, the disappointment of court the day before sets in and I stay to myself, trying to think everything through. Even though I had my doubts that we would be released, it's still a disappointment. Any way I look at it, the results aren't good. I have trouble seeing anything positive in this situation.

No matter how hard I fight it, my reputation in the prison is growing. I'm getting further and further away from the person I worked so hard to become, and find myself becoming someone I don't respect. I'm getting too comfortable with it and it bothers me that I can go there even if it's only in my mind. Living this way day in and day out, in this environment where men are treated worse than you'd treat a dog, is eroding who I am as a person.

I get more and more angry each day and it's becoming my primary emotion. The sadness and loss I felt when we were first put in jail isn't there anymore. Anger has taken over. I lose caring, empathy and concern for others. All of those things get broken away.

Along with that is a level of depression. Anger and depression go hand and hand. Whatever good I've done, the positive things in my life, are distant memories. They seem so far away, and holding it together every day becomes a burden. It's a very hard job. I have to remind myself constantly of who I am.

I get to a point where I think, "Fuck it! I'm fine here. I have really stupid lawyers. I can pay. I have money! I can get someone to FedEx me the medicine I need. I'm in a good little place here. I have my own little shelter. I can hang out."

At the same time, I don't have a whole lot to go back to on the outside. I've lived a pretty lonely life for the most part. I haven't really had a home for five or six years now. My life is a series of constant moves from job to job, like a shark, and I just keep moving forward. That's all I do. I never sleep, I don't do anything except work. Now my contract is up and I don't have a job.

I'm not in a relationship, either. I'm not sure what I'm going to do. Maybe I'll hang out here for three months. Imagine seeing me three months into it, a year at the most? I may not leave the Dominican Republic. I may decide that I want to be here the rest of my life. I'm a street hustler by trade, that's my thing. Maybe that's the life I want to live. There was a part of me that felt good in that environment.

I feel comfortable in the midst of this. I'm at the point now where I can imagine myself saying, "Maybe I don't like that guy. Maybe I want him taken care of. I mean, fuck it, make him disappear. So, we're going to kill some people, man, they don't matter. They're dogs."

This change in my mindset scares me.

If I get the language barrier out of the way, I'll bet you I can be a thriving businessman in the Dominican Republic. People like doing business with me. They like my approach. I have the correct skill set.

Being comfortable in this prison is very real to me. That and being so sick is leading to a state of depression. I sit on the floor and stare at the wall in front of me and I'm... gone. People come up and try to talk to me and the other guys say, "No, no, leave him alone. Don't say anything to him." They can read me. Absolutely. There are times when guys want to do Spanish and I tell them I'm exhausted. I can't do it tonight. My brain...

"*Mentales, mentales.*"

"*Ah, sí... sí.*"

When I think about it, some of the nicest people I've ever met in my life are inside that prison. They are concerned about what is going on with me. There is a level of caring that's phenomenal.

"Here let me give you a clean shirt to wear. Here's some food. Please, please. I'm worried about you. I don't want to see you like this."

Sunday, July 5

Sunday is always a huge visiting day. Me and Jeff hate visiting days. We can't be in our cell at all during the day because everyone's family is there and everyone's screwing his wife and/or girlfriend. We have to sit out in the hall. We hate visiting days so much that eventually we pay a guard to let us hang out in the grassy area where they play softball. No one comes to visit us.

One day Jeff gets this idea and says he wants his mom to come visit him.

I say, "God, you're an idiot!"

"No, no, I want my wife to come down!" Like she needs those images to remember for the rest of her life.

"When we get out, we're going to have steak and we'll do this and this and I can't wait! This is the longest I've gone without any sex in my life."

Jeff had a vasectomy right before we left for the DR so he says, "I don't know if it's going to work or not. I haven't had a chance to test it out, man. I got to find out."

I have a condom in my backpack that he takes. He says, "This is going to be the victory condom! If we ever get out of here I'm going to use this condom with my wife."

The lawyers show up on Sunday afternoon. After they fuck up in court on Thursday, they say,

"Oh, I'm sorry, I'm sorry..."

We talk a few minutes about our next court date on Thursday, July 9th.

I'm sick as hell. I'm on my ass and they keep showing up. Why not? They're getting paid for it. I give everyone near me the Stare of Death. The lawyers want to have meetings with us and Diego. The lawyers give (my) money to Franco and tell him to take care of us and this really makes me mad.

I'm done. I'm gone.

I say, "Nothing that comes out of your mouth is important. The next thing I want to hear coming from you is 'Goodbye' as we're leaving the DR. I don't care about anything else you have to say."

That's when they start to talk to Jeff and not to me because Jeff will entertain their shit and I've had enough of it. Of course, I know how reliable Jeff is in repeating a conversation, but I don't care.

Then Franco asks if he can send us pizzas.

I say, "Oh, that's great. I don't want to eat. I'm upset. Get away from me. Get the fuck away from me." I go back to my room.

A couple of hours later, we get called up front again!

When we get there, Franco is standing there with a fucking pizza! Take a guess who paid for that pizza? It sure didn't come out of their money. And guess what happens when they send pizza? We have to walk it back through all of those halls where guys would kill one of us for a slice and then, when we get back to Area X, all the guys in our syndicate want a piece.

The irony of carrying a single pizza past the animals, and them smelling it, so we can give it to the guys in our syndicate who have enough money to get their own pizza if they want one, is not lost on me.

I tell Franco, "You've just made my life fucking harder."

Franco ignores that and says, "If there's anything you need, just ask."

"Franco, I'll tell you what I need that would make all of this so much easier to deal with. Do you really want to bring me something I need?"

Franco says, "Absolutely. That's what I'm here to do, to make life easier for you guys. Tell me what you need. I'll get right on it."

"OK, Franco, listen up. Are you listening?"

Franco nods his head.

"I. Need. My. Fucking. Medicines! Do you got that Franco? Is that clear enough for you? Do you still have the list my mother made of what I need?"

Franco is obviously miserable but he nods again.

"Say it out loud, Franco. Am I clear?"

He squeaks out a "Yes."

"Good. Then it shouldn't be that hard. And, by the way, I don't need enough medicine to last a week. I need enough to last a month. Am I clear?"

I never see any medicine the rest of the time I'm in prison.

Every day after that Alex is like, "Dude, do you guys want steak? Do you want fish? Your lawyers told me to call them if you need anything."

Basically Alex wants steaks and he wants us to call the lawyers and ask them and I'm thinking, "fuck you." Who do you think is going to pay for it? It's so stupid. I don't need this.

Wednesday, July 8

I'm up really early Wednesday. We're supposed to go to court tomorrow and that's on my mind. I can't sleep so I go over to the area where I have coffee with the old guys in the mornings. Jeff's up, too, and comes with me. I'm sitting there and a tiny spider comes crawling along on the cinderblock window. I get up and walk over to see it better. It's right in front of my face. I've never seen anything like this in my entire life. Suddenly, this spider jumps about six of its body lengths on top of a small fly.

Then this little fly and the spider start tussling it out. I say, "Jeff, come here and check this out, man. Isn't this cool?"

We stand there and watch this struggle between the spider and the fly and my face is maybe a foot away. I've never seen anything like this before. Eventually, the spider drags the fly through the cinder block and is gone. I've asked people since, "Have you ever seen a spider catch a fly? Not like in a web but he's coming along and jumps on it and attacks it?" They always say, "No."

Later that morning, the lawyers come to the prison to tell us the hearing has been rescheduled to the next Thursday, July 16th. Before anyone can explode, they quickly explain that a plane carrying the largest shipment of cocaine the Dominican authorities have ever seen, crashed somewhere on the island and the public and the authorities want to make a public display of anyone accused, or convicted, of drug trafficking.

The second issue is that one of the lawyers in the firm used to be a judge. To give us our best chance of getting out, they want to get us in front of a judge this guy knows. These are unfortunate issues but I think the way the lawyers want to handle it makes sense. So the following Thursday, July 16th is our next court date.

Sunday, July 12

Our lawyers show up the Sunday before we go to court on Thursday. They've got a translator with them but I don't have anything to say because nothing has changed in my opinion. I'm standing there and I feel and look like shit.

The lawyer asks, "What exactly happened the day that you got arrested? Please tell us the story in Spanish." Diego tells the story. I sit there and listen.

Jeff says, "What are they talking about?"

I'm translating what Diego is saying for Jeff while Diego is talking. Then he turns to me and he says, "You know what I'm saying, right?"

I say, "Yeah. Go ahead."

Then the translator asks Diego if I know Spanish and Diego says, "Yeah, he knows Spanish."

"What?"

Diego says, "He can understand us. I'm not making anything up. You can ask him."

Originally they said, "No, we're not going to say the drugs are Diego's. We're going to say the police set you up and we don't know anything about any drugs."

Now they say, "Okay Diego, we want you to say that the drugs were yours. Can you do that?"

Diego raises his voice and says, "I've been telling you this!"

Here's the problem when they do that. Now, the lawyers are telling Diego to say the drugs are his rather than Diego getting up and saying it on his own. He doesn't trust the lawyers.

"I don't trust none of your lawyers, man. I have to look out for me, now."

Do you see what I'm saying? All they did was fuck up everything I had in place and I'm pissed.

I look at them and say, "What the hell are you doing? You told him that you're not going to use this defense because it's not going to look good in court and now you're going full circle and using this as our defense."

Our defense comes down to two things:

1. The drugs are Diego's, and
2. I'm really sick.

This is our defense now. This is what they're counting on to get us out.

I say, "These stupid fucking lawyers. I've been telling our families this the whole time and they're not listening to me and this is what it comes down to."

The lawyer doesn't say it to me because if he starts telling me this shit I look at him like I'm ready to snap his neck.

The lawyer tells Diego specifically, "You need to say they were yours and they were for your personal use. Then there is no trafficking charge and the worst they have is a personal use charge. It's the only way out. That way we can change it and go to minor possession and then you're out."

"How long–how much do I have to do for this?"

"Well, a year at the most."

Then Diego says, "I ain't going to be here for a year. I got a business and I lose money every day and I have kids."

He's already losing money. He's lost his whole business arrangement with *La Perla Hotel* because of his current situation.

I'm pissed because they still haven't brought me my medicine. They want me sick in front of the judge.

"Make sure you cough like you do right now."

I look at them and I look at Diego, "Do you see what's going on?"

And Diego goes off on the lawyers. "That's why I want him out. He needs to go. Look how sick he is. You think this is an act?"

I tell Diego to say, "Do you want me to die in front of the judge? *Esta muerte en La Casa de Justicia?*" Do you want me to die in the house of justice?

My Spanish hit the fucking lawyers right between the eyes and the lawyers are like, "Oh shit. This guy right here knows Spanish."

Diego says, "I been telling you. You need to listen to this guy. He knows his shit."

Instead, the lawyers go to the guy that will listen to them without arguing–Jeff.

Jeff tells me, "The lawyers want to talk to me and then they want to talk to Diego. And then they'll talk to you." The lawyers never talk to me–ever. Then, when the strategy changes, Diego is getting nervous about it, "What the lawyers want me to do is a set–up. I'm not going to go that route. It's not my idea, it's theirs."

And I'm thinking, "Oh, God."

And then everything that I had in place is gone. You sonofabitch. I want to kill these lawyers. I tell my dad, "I swear to God. I want to beat the shit out of these stupid fucks. This is what they've done."

I've been telling my dad this over and over and he says, "You have to be kidding me. The lawyers announced a new strategy with Diego taking the fall?

You have to be kidding me. You've been telling me all along that this was the strategy."

So he goes off on Jorge, I think. My dad tells me about the conversation later.

My dad tells Jorge, "You're telling us you're a legitimate businessman and you pull this. You pull that. The entire time my son's been telling you this and you haven't learned anything about him. He got you the passports..."

I don't know how the conversation ended but I'm glad my dad had it out with Jorge, the invisible lawyer.

I had a plan and it's all there and ready to go.

Now it's even more dramatic. More people have gotten involved. More people are writing letters in both English and Spanish and submitting them to the court. Everyone is doing whatever they can to help me and Jeff. People are genuinely concerned.

Now Jeff and Diego are saying to me, "We need to go over our story. We need to know that it's exactly the same. We need to find a quiet time to talk about it." After all of the time I spent trying to get them to sit down and go over the story. I'm stressed out by now. I'm not even talking to Jeff for the most part. These are the days when I'm speaking Spanish almost all day long to everyone I'm dealing with.

I'm so sick at this point. I know I have bronchitis and I'm beginning to think it has progressed to pneumonia. My mind and body are going into shut–down. I'm getting closer and closer to not being able to get out of bed or eat. I carry an empty water bottle around so I have something to spit into every time I cough up phlegm.

People are looking at me like I'm the walking dead. "He's Samson, man, they cut his hair and look what's happening to him." The guys keep calling me Samson because my hair was long and my muscles were huge and now I'm sick and I'm losing all this weight and I'm getting smaller and smaller each day since they cut my hair. I'm sick and everyone is really concerned.

"Diego, you need to get this guy out of here; look what's happening to him. He's going to die. He's not getting the right medical care. Who the hell are these lawyers that you got?"

Every night the guards do a roll call of all the people going to court the next day. I'm so miserable Wednesday night, that I go to bed early. Jeff and Diego can handle this. They show up for roll call, say "ere" when the guard says your name, and everyone goes to bed. Tomorrow is the deciding day. We either get out, or we settle in for at least three months, possibly three years.

Thursday, July 16

We get up in the morning and do the whole routine. A guy named Juan is going to court with us. He speaks English. He lived in New York and he's a very nice guy. What happened to him was someone killed someone else with a gun that he had owned. He had it registered and had permits for it but he no longer owned it. The police show up one night and arrest him as part of the incident.

Juan comes from a very well off family and they visit him. He has tons of visitors every visiting day and they are handing out money left and right. Juan gets taxed hard–more than we pay. He's a very sincere, caring guy. He's very worried about me and Jeff. He's upset by what happened to us. Again, it's more animosity toward Diego.

"Anything you need, you let me know," and he introduces us to his family and to his girlfriend or wife, whoever she was, and he tells them about what happened to us and he says, "My family is very bothered about your situation."

Juan is going to court with us that day and he's a very positive guy. I like talking to him and I would be friends with him very easily on the outside. So we go out front to the Holy Mary statue and we wait and wait and wait.

At one point I say, "Is everything taken care of, Diego?

Jeff says, "Well, there's a problem."

"What do you mean there's a problem?"

He says, "Last night when they came around to do the roll call of everyone going to court in the morning, they didn't say Diego's name. They said everyone else's name but they didn't say Diego's name."

This is the next morning when we're standing and waiting for the bus to go to court. We've been awake for hours by now.

I say, barely controlling my anger, "And so you're telling me this now?"

He says, "What can I do? Diego's checking it right now."

"Well, did you call the lawyers yet?"

"No"

I look over at Diego who is talking to a guard holding a clipboard and say to Jeff, "What the fuck is going on? We all have to go to court together. We can't go by ourselves. You should have been on the phone last night as soon as they didn't call his name. Why are you waiting until now, when the bus could be here any minute, to do something about this?"

I'm so frustrated with everything and I'm finding out about this right now?

Diego comes back, "No, I'm not on the list."

I say, "You get on that phone and you call that number and someone better fucking answer." It's early in the morning and no one's awake yet.

"You start calling. When's the lady coming?"

Diego says, "She doesn't get in until 9:00."

"You have to figure out a way to get on the list."

"Well the court has to put me on the list."

"Get ahold of Franco. Call and call and call."

I say, "Jeff call your mother and tell her to call all the lawyers and find out what the fuck is going on."

So that's it. It's an "everything that can go wrong will go wrong" story. Anxiety is setting in.

I say, "Sonofabitch. We're going to be here another week, another month, they didn't get Diego's name on the list. We can't go to court. We're going to spend a whole day in court and nothing's going to happen and then we'll turn around and come back. Fucking shit."

I say, "Get on the phone. You have to make sure Diego is on a list somewhere." If he's not on the list, we're going to be here awhile, we're not getting out.

I'm barking instructions, "Call this, call that. We have two phones, use them both right now. Jeff start calling. Diego, start calling. Get with the guards."

They are working on all of these things, too. Jeff says, "They're supposed to call us back."

I say, "No. We don't wait for a call-back. You start calling now. Every time I look over, you two better be on the fucking phone."

Jeff says, "Why do you have to be such a dick, man?"

"Why the fuck weren't you doing something about it last night?"

"I don't know."

This is how it is for me. Then the lady who makes the list at the prison shows up.

"Diego go talk to her and figure out what's going on."

"She can't do nothing until the court calls."

"Well the court needs to call her."

"The court doesn't get in until 9:00."

I tell Jeff, "You get with the lawyers right now. Call Franco and tell him to get his fat ass down to that courtroom and make sure Diego's on that list right now. I don't care what it takes. Get that done now."

Chaos is going on all around. We're waiting on the bus to show up. Thank God the fucking bus is late.

We're sitting there and we're panicking. We're waiting and they're doing roll call and finally a guard says, "All right, I'll put you on here."

We're getting paired up and handcuffed and I say, "Diego, you'd better get on that fucking bus. You get on that bus one way or the other. I don't care what we have to do."

So Juan is with us and he's handcuffed to himself! He is not handcuffed to anyone else. He's got that much money. He's paying enough. He's spending money like it's going out of style.

He says, "My friend. Today we leave."

"I don't know, man."

"We're going to go today, man."

I taught Jeff the Lord's Prayer during our time in prison. He didn't know the Lord's Prayer. So I taught him that one. Through this whole time, Jeff is reciting it over and over, and he says Hail Mary's and he smokes like a freight train and so it's one cigarette right after another. It's such a stressful situation. We only get one appeal and then we serve our sentence of one to three years. All I can think of right at that moment is, "Oh God."

Diego says, "They say they got me on the list."

I say, "Okay, make sure that they've got it taken care of."

"They've got it taken care of."

All of a sudden the bus pulls up and it's a brand new bus! It's not the old shitty one that we always ride. We get in and the seats all the way back are nice. They're hard plastic but they've got a little bit of cloth on the plastic. The windows open and close–you can open and close them yourself.

We open up the windows and we're joking with the guards. I tell them, "Oh, this is where all our money went. You went and got a new bus for the Americans with all the money we gave you for our trips."

All the guards start laughing, everyone is laughing. "We got a new bus for the Americans!"

"Thank you. I'm glad to know that our money was spent well." And the guards crack up laughing and finally we get everyone on the bus and we're ready to go.

We're sitting on the bus and this is sounds so crazy, but I swear it's a true story. Juan sits in front of us, then it's me and Jeff, and Diego sits behind us.

We're sitting there waiting and a hummingbird flies in the window right above me and Jeff and Juan! It stops for a moment and then turns around and flies out.

The guards say, "It's a sign! You're going to leave. *"Tu fue, tu fue!"* You leave. "It's the free bird."

Jeff says, "It's the free bird. We're going to leave."

And Juan turns around and says, "My friend, we will leave together. Today we will leave. We are getting out of prison today."

And I say, "I don't know about that..."

The guards are excited for us. And now here we are. Me, Jeff, and Juan believe we have been wrongly convicted for things we didn't do. We're targets. So this bird flies in and flies out and it was crazy.

The guards are saying, "You're going to leave today. Today is when you leave."

We find it astonishing later, how much the guards want us to get out as opposed to our stereotype of guards and police officers handling criminals.

"You're going to leave today!"

It's the system. We hear things like: You guys shouldn't be here; they have held you for too long; the Americans need to go; you're good guys and nice, over and over. All the guards are like, *"tu fue, tu fue."* Today is your day, you know?

Everything is going through my mind while we ride through town. I think back on all the people I've talked to on the phone and how many people care about me back in the States. The anxiety is still there.

What am I going to say in front of the judge? I'm struggling because I kind of want to get up there and be my true self and say something like,

"What's been proven by incarcerating us? For what? And if those charges were correct and that amount of narcotics was found, what is achieved by arresting Americans? The amount in this case is not enough for these charges and for the country to stand behind that and say this is what we believe–we believe these Americans did it. And then to charge us with drug trafficking because we're tourists and we're not Dominicans. I don't know. What's been gained by all of this? For you as a country and for your justice system? What? At least in my country the small volume would have been a misdemeanor to begin with and there never would have been incarceration because nothing has been proven in this case."

That's running through my head as well as everyone's concern for me and all the people that are praying for us.

"Think. Think, Corey. Think. You have to have everything covered. What's the possibility of this happening and that happening? What if we get to court and the lawyers aren't there? What if they say this? What if they say that? What if they change their minds?"

Diego is a loose cannon. Who knows what he's going to say? No one ever knows what Diego's going to do. Diego is Diego. You don't know what you're getting.

He's already said, "I'm not doing it because the lawyers are telling me that's what I have to do."

We pull up to the courthouse. We get off the bus. We start walking around and we see the same guards that handled us before. We're supposed to get escorted by the police and the guards to the court and we walk around through this little garden area to the door. We already know where we're going so we start walking and the guard yells, "Hey! Get up front where the Americans are." It looks bad. So we all walk in and sit down in the same places on the benches.

It's the same court that we were in before with that weird ass mural on the wall. We look at it all the time. We're waiting for the lawyers to show up. Waiting for everything.

The girl's there and she's looking at us. Diego is talking to her and she says, "God, he looks very sick; he doesn't look good. What happened to him?"

Diego says, "They made him sick living there."

And she says, "Tell him I still want to have drinks with him." I don't know what she really says. That's what Diego tells me she says. Who knows what she said?

The lawyers show up with the translator and we don't know when we're going to go and so we're sitting there waiting and it's a very anxious situation. We don't know anything. The lawyers are there, but they're all talking amongst themselves and not really talking to us.

Diego's lawyer is there. He's talking to him about the court proceedings. Diego says, "What happens if I do this?"

I don't know what all they're talking about. I don't trust these guys. Diego is babbling away. His family is there, his mother, his father-in-law, and some other family members are there. So we're all waiting.

Other cases are going before us. Finally they call us. We go up and they take the handcuffs off and we sit in front of a three-judge panel. For most cases, two people go up, but with our case, we fill up the whole row.

The funny thing is that these judges wear these hats. Judges and lawyers wear robes and then the judges wear these hats and they have a ball on top of it and it looks hilarious–I guess it goes back to Spain or something. I don't know. They wear these square–round hats with a little ball on top.

The lawyers wear black robes over their suits and it looks so freaking hilarious. It must have started in Spain or another country. It's a hold over, but that's what they wear. Me and Jeff always find this hilarious and we're cracking up. We saw this the first time we went to court but it's still funny. They're all sitting up there with those things on their head, and me and Jeff are like, "What the fuck is that?"

The first time we see them Jeff says, "Dude, it would be cool if we could get two of those hats and take a picture with it. That would be so funny." I'm cracking up, laughing at them, because it's hilarious looking at them with these hats on.

Our judges are a female, a male with gray hair, and another male with dark hair. The trial is a complete circus when we get up there. There's a huge commotion. They have to arrange everybody and the translator has to sit there so he can translate for us. Initially, it's a problem because translating what the judge is saying to us is too much back and forth so the judge has the translator tell us, "Why don't you guys sit down and I'll sit next to you and talk to you so we can get going. It's the same shitty translator we had the last time and he's horrible. This is our life in the balance. It's another wild ride.

The first thing that happens is our lawyers read off all the grounds for appeal that they want to cite. Violations of this, this and this.

Reading the body language of the judges, I'd say the female judge seems very concerned for us; the judge with the gray hair looks concerned for us; and the judge with the dark hair won't make eye contact with us.

Our lawyers call the girl up. She sits on a chair on a little stand.

Someone steps up with a Bible and starts the, "Do you swear to tell the truth..."

She says, "Yes."

The District Attorney didn't want her there but the judge ordered her to appear so the lawyers have her here to testify. After the preliminaries of getting her name, address, etc., our lawyer starts by asking her, "You were charged with these guys?"

"Yes."

"And you've been released. Is that correct?"

She says, "Yes."

Then he asks her various questions trying to find out if she signed a plea agreement with the police to get out.

He says, "Did you sign anything for the police to get out of prison?"

The judge says, "Where are you going with this?"

"We're asking if she signed any papers. Was there any deal that the police may be involved with?"

The judges are getting frustrated with our lawyers because they are harping on this and the judge interrupts the questioning by saying, "You can't ask that question."

Me and Jeff find out later that our lawyers went to the girl's house. They found her in the neighborhood and asked her if she would come and testify for us. She said yeah, she would. I don't know if they had to pay her. I am sure they did.

The lawyer asks her what happened the day of the arrest and she repeats exactly what she said in court the first time.

"This is what happened, this is how it went down."

"Did you see any drugs?"

"No, I never saw any drugs."

Our lawyer says, "The police officers claim there were drugs in the car."

"I never saw any drugs."

Her story corroborates ours from the beginning. It is exactly the same. The only thing that she got a little bit backwards was she said there were two mopeds with one cop on each one when there was actually one moped with two cops on it. It was a fairly minor deviation in the facts and no one caught it. Other than that, her testimony was exactly the same as it was the first time. So she steps down.

From there the lawyers begin arguing the merits of the case saying, "You violated the rights of these Americans, this right and that right. The police state that the arrest took place under the bridge. You've heard from the witness. She says it occurred on the bridge. That is contrary to the police report." And from there, they are actually doing legitimate lawyer stuff. They are citing all the things that were wrong. It was much different and much better than what we got out of Marco.

We didn't get our rights read to us and no one provided any means of translation. They held us without charging us and they held us longer than the law allows, and a lot more problems. They are citing all of these things and how they pertain to me and Jeff. Bam! Bam! Bam!

One of the male judges says while he's flipping through our documents, "Well, there are many documents to confirm the identity of Mr.___ and Mr.___."

He's reading through all of them.

"We have letters from all of their jobs, Mr.___'s diploma, pictures of Mr.___'s children. Everything reaffirms their character and who they are. They are asking for grounds for appeal of the conviction based on all of these items. Essentially, these guys are not guilty of the crime they were convicted of. They are not drug traffickers. They are working professionals and they were here visiting."

Then Diego's lawyer gets up and he says, "My client's rights were violated because they searched his vehicle without a warrant, there are inconsistencies in the police report..." and he goes down a list of violations. "My client does not have any history of arrest..."

Now it's the District Attorney's turn. He stands up and says, "Here are the documents of the evidence that we found in the case. We stand behind our case and we believe this is the truth. These are the individuals involved."

They can't find the arresting officer. He's disappeared and, in the end, they say a female officer arrested us and found the drugs. It's like the original guy said, "I'm outta here." He's going to let a female officer take the fall for it. It's changing constantly.

Then he reads off the narcotics volume. Now the volume of cocaine is down to 2.2 grams. This is significantly below the legal limit for personal use of 2.9. It's a different volume again. He shows pictures of what he says are the drugs that were found in the car to the judges. And that was it as far as the prosecution went.

A judge says, "Would the defendants like to say anything on their behalf?"

So Diego gets up first and begins telling version number three of his story of what happened. Basically, he says, "Yeah, I was working late the night before, and in the morning, I took some drunk tourists to the airport. If there were drugs in the car, that's where they came from. I don't believe these guys had any drugs on them at all and in no way, shape or form did I jeopardize these guys. They had nothing to do with it."

He rambles on and on about, "If there were drugs there, they came from someone else, other clients," and he begins trying to tell his version of the story.

Never once does he say, "Yeah, they're my drugs and I had them on me and they're for personal use," like the lawyers thought he was going to say. Me and Jeff glance over at the lawyers and the looks on their faces as Diego was talking were not good. They are not making eye contact with us at all.

It's classic Diego so who knows what he's going to say. In my mind, I'm still thinking we're going to have to get ourselves out of this. Nothing has changed that we didn't expect. No surprises. Finally the judge has to cut him off. He has diarrhea of the mouth, babbling on and on.

Now it's Jeff's turn to talk.

When he stands up, I'm thinking, "Oh my God, please. Please help me."

Jeff does an awesome job. He talks very slowly and very concise. He gives time for the translator to translate and the translator is doing a shitty job, too. We start running into problems and we're realizing that the judge with the gray hair understands English. He knows if the translator isn't translating right, and he actually tells him this during the course of Jeff's statement, and it gets worse.

Jeff is telling them roughly about his job, "This is what I do. There is so much at stake. I work in a very secure environment. We have to have government security clearance for our jobs. They do random drug testing. We can't do drugs."

And he says this thing that I'm so glad didn't get translated, "The places where we work are known terrorist targets." And the translator looks at him and says, "What are you talking about? Terrorists? Like 911, Al Qaeda? Those terrorists?"

And I'm thinking, "Oh shit! Did Jeff just say we're terrorists like 911? Oh shit. Please stop, Jeff, stop. Stop. Stop."

And he goes on to say, "We didn't come here to do drugs. We came to tour the country. We hired this guy as our driver and our tour guide. And in no way, shape or form did we want to get involved with drugs while we were here. We have to go back to work."

That's kind of the gist of it. I think one of the judges asks Jeff a question, I can't remember. He asks both of us questions.

Now it's my turn and I get up there and I basically state who I am, my profession, places I've worked. I work on government projects in places outside the U.S. I have great responsibilities, including reporting to the federal government regarding the operation of sensitive installations that require monitoring. I get monitored physically on a daily, weekly and yearly basis. Being in good physical condition is part of my job. Anytime there is an incident, we get drug tested and my employers take it seriously. In no way am I allowed to have any participation in or use of drugs because I would lose my job. It is a requirement for my position.

I say the hotel we stayed at recommended this man as a driver for us. If we had any idea that there were drugs in the car we would have never gotten into the car to begin with. All we were attempting to do was to get a ride back to our hotel. We've been arrested and now we're in front of this court for these charges that were brought against us. There is no way that I would jeopardize my job, my career and my education by handling or being around any drugs of any kind.

The judge asks me some interesting questions. He says, "Has the U.S. Embassy contacted you? or "Are you in contact with the U.S. Embassy?" The translator kind of throws me for a loop here.

I say, "Yes, we have been in contact with the Embassy."

"Are they aware of your situation?"

"Yes, the U.S. Embassy has visited us at the prison."

Then the translator says, "Is this the mission of the U.S. Embassy?"

And I say to the translator, "'The mission of the U.S. Embassy?' What do you mean, 'the mission'? What are you talking about, 'The mission of the U.S. Embassy?'"

The translator keeps saying, "mission."

I turn to Diego and I say, "What is he talking about? 'The mission?'" He shakes his head.

Finally, I say to the judge who asked the question, "I don't understand the question."

Then he says, "Is the U.S. Embassy here today?"

This is a very delicate topic. We discussed this previously. There is a two-fold situation here. I'll see this afterwards but right now I'm thinking on my feet. This is all split second.

I look over my shoulder in the courtroom and I say, "I don't know. Every time the U.S. Embassy comes, it's a different person."

We sit back down and I'm thinking, "What the fuck was that all about?"

I have a chance to think this through after we sit down. There were two things at stake when he asked me that question. I remember hearing that the U.S. Embassy will take an interest in your case if they believe that you were wrongly convicted. They will contact you and take certain, limited, steps to help you–like when Chandler researched what we were being charged with and told us. If the U.S. Embassy doesn't take an interest in your case and doesn't show up in court, it means they think you're guilty of what you're charged with.

To understand the other thing you have to understand the country a little bit. Because our case is so odd, there is a concern that it may be a test of the Dominican justice system. The DR adopted U.S. laws and is a free democratic nation. The United States could be using the U.S. Embassy as a means of gathering information about how those laws are being enforced. Maybe that's what the judge meant when he used the word "mission." I knew when the U.S. Embassy questions came up that there were several ways to answer them and I had to make sure I got them right.

The judges take a recess to deliberate and me and Jeff are sitting there. I'm thinking, "We're fucked. Diego told story number three and the judge is questioning me about the U.S. Embassy?"

Our lawyers won't say a word to us. They get up, walk away and talk amongst themselves with our translator. They won't even make eye contact with us.

I'm thinking, "Oh, fuck."

They're sitting over there and I want to say to one of the lawyers, "MF, dude, you're supposed to know one of these judges, you have to call one in."

It's going to take a miracle to get out of this. We're going away, me and Jeff. We thought the lawyers had it and now we're going away. It was all right there—the emotions.

Then, all of a sudden, this guy comes walking up to us and he says in English, "Man, you guys are in some fucking shit!"

We turn around and he says, "Yeah, man, your translator was fucking you over."

And all the other people in the courtroom when we turn around are like, "Yeah, man," because a bunch of these people in the courtroom speak English and Spanish, and there are a large number of people in the courtroom while we're up there.

He tells us his name is Manuel and he says, "What the hell? You guys are professionals. Man, what the fuck did you guys get yourselves into?"

We tell him this is what happened to us and he says, "Holy shit man. You guys got some serious problems right now. Man, if you guys needed a translator you should have said something. I would have come up here and talked for you guys. Your translator didn't do you any favors." He says this in perfect English.

And I'm looking at him and looking at our lawyers who won't even make eye contact with us. I'm thinking, "We got fucked over again."

"You guys from the States?"

We tell him we are and he says, "Man, dude, your lawyers fucked you over. How did you even get to this court?"

We're like, "Oh, man, you don't even want to know." Diego is sitting right next to them while this is going on.

"Shit man, this is your driver right here?"

"Yeah, man."

"How do you know this guy?"

I explain how we ended up with Diego.

"Shit man, you should a called me, man. I would have driven you around town to make sure you didn't get in any shit. You guys are really fucked up. How did you guys end up over there on that bridge?" We find out later he went to college in the states to a pretty good school.

He was asking us over and over, "Is this where he took you? Is that where he took you?"

Diego is like, "Yeah, I was taking the girl home. She lives there."

The girl is sitting there and the courtroom is full of people. When I turned to look over my shoulder to pretend I'm looking for the U.S. Embassy, it was a full house.

All day I'm praying, "God give me wisdom in this. Give me wisdom in this. Please God." We're sitting there, and me and Jeff are praying.

I say, "What the hell was the embassy question about?"

Manuel says, "I have no idea. What was the fucking embassy question about?"

No one knows.

We sit there and they're back there for 20 or 30 minutes. None of the lawyers will talk to us. They look at Diego and shake their heads because he was supposed to own it. Really nice, but that was the closest he was going to get to owning it.

He didn't say, "It was mine," he said, "I had other people in the cab."

Manuel says again, "Man your translator fucked you over."

I say, "Goddammit. I knew it."

At a certain point I was picking up more. I know enough Spanish by now that I knew that guy wasn't saying what was coming out of my mouth.

What can we do? Tell the judges we'd like a new translator? Can I get Rocky from the prison to come up here because he does a much better job? How about all of these people in the courtroom? Do any of them really know English?

The judges come back out and I'm thinking, "Oh shit. Here it comes now."

The judges look at us and we look at them and we're like deer in the headlights. The judges sit down. We stand up and they're going to read the verdict. One of the judges starts talking and the translator is trying to translate.

The judge reading the verdict says, "During the law of such and such and blah, blah grounds..."

He recites the points of our lawyers' appeal and the translator can't keep up. He reads the verdict and we don't know what's going on. The translator isn't translating anything that makes sense. All of a sudden he says something and Diego throws his arms in the air and he says, "Ha!" and he hugs me and Jeff.

We stand there like, "What's going on?"

Diego says, "We did it! We did it!" and we say, "Did what?"

The translator still doesn't make sense. When he's done, everyone in the courtroom is yelling, "Yay, yay," and clapping for us, even the other prisoners, and we're standing there and we don't know what's going on.

We're confused and they're dragging this on and we're like, "What the hell?" and we have this dumb look on our faces and people are coming up and they're hugging us. We don't even know who these people are.

Manuel comes up and he says, "Yeah, he granted you guys' a bond."

"Oh, we got a bond?"

He says, "Yeah, but it has conditions on it. You got a conditional bond."

"What does that mean? What's going on?"

"Roughly, you got a zero money bond," Manuel explains to us.

Even if it's true, I'm thinking, "We got bonded out. Great. What could happen next?"

Everyone is happy and smiling except me and Jeff—we aren't smiling. We still don't know exactly what's going on or what a conditional bond is.

Manuel says, "You have been released. 'Immediate release' is what he said but awaiting further trial or further investigation."

"So, what does that mean?"

"Well, you have to stick around and check in every two weeks with the District Attorney until your case comes back up again."

I'm just standing there, stunned.

Then Manuel says, "Don't worry. You can stay at my house. You're more than welcome. You can get a job here or something. With what you know how to do you can get a job here easy. We'll get you a visa to work and hang out until your case goes through again."

What we find out is that cases never go back to court again. We got bond because at that point in time there's no money left to be made. The District Attorney isn't going to turn up any more evidence. If they did, the system would get even more backlogged because everyone gets bonded out. The system can't keep up with how much it already has and if everyone went back to court again it would be chaos. Basically, a zero dollar bond is the closest thing to "not guilty" that you're going to get.

We got a zero dollar bond so we can leave the prison. Diego has to pay a bond of like 10,000 pesos ($320). It wasn't that much considering what I paid for him to have food and a place to sleep. The lawyers are supposed to go through all of the procedures and get the papers signed so we can get out.

Manuel says, "They have to do your paperwork here and take it back to the prison and then you can be released. Right now you've been released from the court system but you have to get released from the prison system."

Diego's mother-in-law goes and gets us food and drinks and the guards take us out of the courtroom and take the handcuffs off of us. We sit out in the little garden for an hour or so. We eat lunch. We talk to Manuel about our job and stuff and then we give some money to the police officer for taking us out there. We usually don't get to do that. We're looking for Juan but we don't see him.

They came and got Juan while the judges were deliberating so he doesn't know what happened. He had to go upstairs to court, I guess.

So we're having our lunch and everyone's happy for us, even the other prisoners. "Way to go, man. Way to go. I got five years but I'm glad you're getting out." It's kind of weird how the culture is.

When they read the verdict and let us go, the outpouring from the people in the courtroom, their happiness for us even though we are strangers, is amazing. Ladies we don't even know hug us. They are happy for us. Even the guys that got convicted are excited for us. "You got out, way to go man! Very good for you."

Manuel used to be an electrical engineer. He worked all over the Midwest and he did a bunch of patent work. He worked in the States for years and he came back to the DR to relax, take it easy, and live the slow life.

"It's easy here, man. It's real relaxed. I like it here."

He runs a print shop inside the courthouse area. It's this whole giant area and he has a small printing, like copying and scanning business I guess, inside this building.

He says, "Yeah, they said there were some Americans in court so of course everyone came down to listen to your case. You guys can stay with me if you want to. You should get out tomorrow. I'll take you to the beach in *Puerta Plata* man," because I told him where we had planned on going.

Then he says, "Come with me. I don't want you to take a taxi. We're not going to take a taxi." We're all laughing our asses off.

Diego says, "Very funny."

And Manuel says, "We'll have a blast. We'll go down and meet some girls."

"Meet some girls" is code for something else, which is common there, obviously.

"You can be my guests. Here's my number. Give me a call when you get out."

The people in the Dominican Republic are still very good people in the midst of all this.

Manuel says, "It's all business down here. It's just business." We hear this over and over again. Jeff has his number and Manuel says again, "Give me a call."

Jeff has his cell phone with him and his mom calls and he says, "Yeah, this is what happened. Our case was overturned and we can leave the prison after the lawyers get our paperwork processed."

I'm not smiling. I'm not happy. I'm emotionless. I'm still cold. Jeff is the same way and I say, "Man, you've learned that lesson already, Jeff. Don't start that."

He says, "Yeah, you're right."

"Nothing has changed until we set our feet in the United States."

Who knows what's going to happen between now and then? According to our bond, we can't leave the country. Instead we're supposed to go on with our lives here so we can show up at the court every two weeks and give them some more money. The assumption is that eventually, they will bleed us dry and then they'll let us leave.

Finally, Juan comes in and he's smiling. He says, "You guys good?"

"Yeah, we're good. Not guilty!"

"Yeah, me too!"

And Juan hugs us and says, "My friends. We will be on the street tomorrow. We'll be out this weekend." And he's all excited, so we're all happy.

Then we wait around. What usually happens is the courthouse finishes all of their court procedures for the day and when they're done, all of us convicts, still handcuffed together, sit in the courtroom until the bus comes. We wait forever for the bus to come that Thursday.

Even though we're free to go, we're still the property of the prison. The court says we're free, but the prison has to get papers from the courthouse to say we can go. Until then, we're still a prisoner as far as they are concerned.

So we wait for the bus and me and Jeff are talking.

"What are we going to do when we get back to the prison?"

I say, "Oh man, I'm not going to say a word."

Jeff says, "You can't do that."

I say, "We don't have to worry about it. Diego will tell everyone." Diego will do all the talking. He always does.

The bus pulls up and we go out and it's packed again. We walk around and get on. There are two ladies sitting on the front seat. We stand and as we go, the guard kicks the ladies out of the seat and he says, "Sit down, *por favor.*"

I say, *"No necesito."* I tell him it's not necessary for us to sit. We'll stand so the ladies can sit down.

He says, "No, no, no, please sit down."

So we sit down and ride back to prison and everything is running through my head and I'm thinking, "Fuck, what now?"

What's going to happen next? How are we going to get out?

If we don't get out tomorrow, on Friday, it will be Monday. I'm overwhelmed right now with everything. Everything that could go wrong almost did go wrong.

Diego almost didn't make it to court. What he said in the courtroom was completely different from what he said before and I thought we were screwed.

It was truly a freaking miracle that we got out. Nothing went according to plan. I'm glad I answered the question about the U.S. Embassy right. I don't know where they were going with that. The translator was horrible.

Diego says, "The judge with gray hair understood English." I nod. He understood what we were saying, I think. Thank God he did.

I'm thinking about all the documents that people sent in on our behalf about what we did for a living and all that. Everyone we needed a document from was more than willing to supply it for us. They wanted to help us out—former employers, people I worked with, it was mind blowing. All the different companies I've worked for, and all the different people, so many stuck up for us.

Now I'm really on edge because this is where something bad could happen. The warden and the guards, along with the other inmates, know we're getting out and people could make trouble for us. This is their last chance to make money off of us.

I tell Jeff, "There's nothing to celebrate right now. We're going back to prison. Everything has gone wrong so far, so until we get out of here there's nothing to smile about."

We go back in the prison and a guard says, "So what happened?"

Juan is like, "They let us go."

"They released you?"

"Yeah, they released us."

"Good for you guys!" Everyone is happy for us.

He says, "How much was your bond?"

"Nothing. A zero money bond."

My roommate, Javier, says, "Can you believe that shit?"

He asks what happened in court and I kind of tell him and he says, "These lawyers. I tell you man. About time. They should have done this a long time ago. You should have never come here."

At this point in time I find out from my dad how much we spent to get out with all the lawyers and prison fees. We paid roughly $25,000 dollars a piece. A piece, not together. And that number will never go away from my memory and how I struggle with that and what happened. It was my money. Thank God, again, that I had it!

Fidel says, "Do you know that you could have lived at the finest resort in all of the Dominican Republic for two years–the nicest one–the highest end in all the Dominican Republic for two years for that amount of money!

My aunt would have paid it. She wanted to pay, but my dad wouldn't let her. He said, "No, he has plenty of money to take care of this. It's not a problem."

We get back to our cell and my phone has all kinds of messages and texts on it. I answer all of them and tell them what's going on.

I say, "We got out. Everything went wrong in court. It was a miracle that we got out."

I send my dad a text, "Not guilty but still in prison."

Nothing about my attitude has really changed. Nothing is going to change until we're not in this country anymore.

One of the lawyers calls me and tells me that their plan is to get us out by noon the next day, Friday, or by two o'clock in the afternoon at the latest.

Friday, July 17

Friday morning we get up and I have everything packed in my backpack. I have all of my stuff ready to go and Jeff gets up and has his stuff ready and now we wait. We're waiting to hear from the lawyers that they're on their way.

We've been told that we have a 24-hour window of opportunity—at the most—to leave the country without being caught. That's how long it usually takes the paperwork to reach the police. Once they have our mug shots and court papers establishing the fact that we were released on a conditional bond, they can start searching the airports and boat docks to try to intercept us from illegally leaving the country. And if they do, it's a mandatory 20 years in prison. BOOM!

The court and police started that process this morning. Today is our window of opportunity. But with as much publicity as we've had, and as many police and inmates who know about our situation, even today is dangerous. Every hour that goes by is another hour that some police snitch in the prison could inform them that we're leaving. If we don't get out of the DR tonight, escape will be even more difficult, perhaps impossible. If we don't get out tonight, we are facing months or years of being forced to live in the DR and continue to pay into the system. I'm trying not to go there in my head.

Me and Jeff compare how much money we have so we know what we can do if we need to bribe someone. We wait all day to go and we're not happy. We're not smiling. We're waiting for them to show up with the paperwork. I have a bad feeling about it.

I was right; nothing goes according to plan. Friday noon goes by. Two o'clock passes and the lawyers are still not here. I send a text message, "Still in prison," to my dad and we go back and forth about what's taking so long.

Four o'clock rolls around and that's usually the cut-off to leave the prison. The warden has to sign the papers and he's not going to hang around all night.

I tell my dad, "Well nothing's going to happen now. We're going to be here through the weekend."

I say to Jeff, "Dude, we're stuck through the weekend in this place."

Jeff is like, "Okay." I think he's finally resigned to the whole situation. It takes him a month, but he's there now.

• • •

We get all of these status reports during the day.

Jeff says, "I got a text saying they're on their way after getting the papers from the courthouse signed by the judge. There are papers here in the prison that need to be signed, too."

Everything is BS to me at this point in time. It doesn't really matter. Until we walk out of that gate nothing matters.

So, here we go. It's late. It's probably close to 5:00 and we're like, "Damn." We know the last flight out of the country on Friday night is at 7:30. The family researched this weeks ago. Who knows where it's going? We just have to get out of the country. That's all we need to do. Anywhere that's U.S. soil.

So we're waiting and it's quickly getting later and later, and all of a sudden Jeff comes in and he says, "All right, they're coming."

With all this random stuff going on throughout the day about what is going on, I look at him like, "whatever."

So now he says, "They've got the papers and they're on the way."

Well, the warden and guards are going to leave. They're not going to stay late.

I tell Diego, "See if we can pay the warden and the guards to stay later to sign our papers. We'll pay them even if the papers don't come." We're sitting there and we're not the only ones, everyone is waiting with us.

Finally they come get us and Juan. We give Diego money to pay the warden and guards to stay. Diego thinks he's getting out also.

Now we're waiting up front and all the guys from the syndicate are with us while we're out there waiting to go.

"The Americans are going to leave. They're going to leave now, finally." Everybody wants to be involved and say good–bye.

We go to the front, and we're waiting, and dammit! Franco shows up and he's bullshitting with the guards instead of coming inside so we can get the papers signed and give the warden some money.

He doesn't know what he's doing. He hands out money to everyone, not the people who are supposed to get it. He's talking to the dumb–assed guards, the low–level guards. He doesn't know who's who.

He's not waiting with us to talk to the warden and give the warden and his guys the money they expect so we can leave.

I'm thinking, "You sonofabitch." Who knows what could happened?

My dad told me earlier that they sent each of us $1,000 cash U.S., by Western Union. They sent it so we would have roughly $1,000 on us when we arrived in the States.

We get up to the front and we're waiting and we're waiting and everyone's going through processing and like you have to pay the processing guy so I give him 200 pesos. I have two, one hundred–peso dollars and one 500–peso dollars on me and 2,000 pesos after that. I give the guy 200 pesos to get us going. They process everyone except us.

We're the last ones and Franco's out there bullshitting with the guards and he needs to be over here where the warden is to speed up processing our paperwork. Everyone's trying to milk every last penny they can out of us to get out.

So we have to pay our way from the inside out. We pay these guys and they start processing us. It's getting dark outside and I'm thinking, "We're not going to make it; we're not going to make it."

Finally, we're the last ones to go. Their computer system is so slow. I don't know if it's on the Internet or not. Probably not. We try to get our information right about who we are so they'll release us. We do this dance. Now we walk around the corner to the warden's office.

In the meantime, there was a fight in one of the syndicates. Some guy in one of the syndicates broke another guy's pool stick that he used for the mini–pool table that they have in their syndicate area. So all of them are in the warden's office dealing with this issue.

The guy that broke it is saying, "Yeah, it's my fault. I did it."

The warden says, "How long are you here for?"

I guess he's got about ten years and he's asking to get transferred somewhere else and he has to go sit in the box. They have this little box thing like in the movie, *Cool Hand Luke*. You have to sit in the box when you do things like this.

He says, "I don't care if I have to sit in the box."

The warden says, "Will you pay for this?"

"Yeah, I'll pay for it."

This is our second or third warden, by the way. Our original warden isn't there anymore. When we come walking in this lady says, "We're done with this. We're just waiting for them to sign your papers to go and I need you to sign some papers, too."

Diego is with us the whole time and he says, "Yeah, they haven't got my papers."

I say, "What do you mean they haven't got your papers?"

I don't want him to have his papers but I don't say that. I don't want to pay his way out.

He says, "I don't know. They've got you a copy with this and this signature on it but mine didn't come through."

"I don't know man." I'm still dead to the world. I'm not happy about anything. I have internal anxiety but I'm a hardened poker face player by now. And we're sitting there waiting for the warden to deal with this disciplinary shit with these other guys.

This is going on in Spanish. I'm pulling out words where I can. Everyone's speaking Spanish. Even I'm speaking Spanish with the people who are processing our paperwork.

"*Sí, Americano.*"

They know a little English and it's funny how that works. It's a game, constantly.

Finally the warden comes over to sign our papers. I'm still sick. I'm coughing and blowing my nose and I look like shit.

The lady asks, "What's wrong with you?"

I sit there and Diego says, "Oh, he doesn't speak Spanish."

"He doesn't speak Spanish?

"They're Americans."

"Americans?"

This warden is so clueless. He looks at us when we come walking in. I don't think we've ever seen him before, and he had no idea that he had some Americans inside. What a piece of shit country this place is.

The warden signs the papers. He hands us our release and we walk out of his office. We're released. All the guys from the syndicate are there and they're saying goodbye.

"Hey. We're leaving."

And they're talking to us in Spanish. They're saying good–bye.

Diego says, "What's going on? How come I'm not leaving?"

I say, "I don't know, bro."

I'm trying to get out of there. Franco, the guy who is supposed to take us to the airport, is there. One of the prison guards needs to do an evaluation on us before we leave. He has a little checklist and a clipboard.

"Okay, are you injured in any way?"

"No."

He doesn't speak any English and it's all in Spanish and he recites some bullshit. It's the same guy who made us do the stand-up, sit-down thing when we first came in. So he's talking and I'm doing some hand gestures behind my back. Everyone is laughing their ass off. *Tigre Americano!* Everyone is cracking up. I'm not laughing but everyone else is cracking up.

So finally we're going to leave and everyone is saying goodbye and hugs and everything like that and Diego says, "All right man, I'll see you guys."

And BOOM! like that we walk through the gates and we're on the other side. I have my backpack and I look over and we're walking out and Diego's still in there like I planned.

Once I knew we were being released, I struggled whether to tell the Columbians to take care of Diego or not. Do I let the Columbians take care of him? He's nothing without us. I go back and forth and all I can think of are all of the people that are concerned for our safety and are praying for us. Was I willing to carry that with me the rest of my life?

I let it go. I let it go.

We hop into the SUV. It's 6:30 and the flight leaves at 7:30 and we need to get all the way through town and to the airport. If we miss this flight...

"Oh shit."

The phones are going crazy right now.

We're not sure if my phone has been tapped. I think it has, but we're not sure. So anyway, we race down the highway in the SUV and neither of the two guys driving us speaks any English. Franco doesn't speak any English.

Before we leave, my dad tells me, "Franco is very scared of you. He's talking about how big you are. You're much bigger than him and he's very scared to be around you." He's talking about me, not Jeff. Jeff is bigger than me but Franco is very scared of me. Even though I'm sick and getting weaker and weaker. Interesting.

The lawyers tell me this, too, and they're asking me, "Please be nice to Franco because he's very scared to be around you."

My dad is cracking up. He says, "It didn't take me long to figure out that you must have given him the Stare of Death."

"Yeah, he's gotten that a lot."

"Well, so you know."

I say, "Okay."

We fly down the highway trying to get to the airport in time. Me and Jeff are changing our clothes and all we have is our passports and the money we have from prison.

Franco's on the phone, and our lawyer, Jorge, talks to Jeff initially, "This is what's going to happen next. Franco is going to take you to the airport. Call him when you get through or if you don't make your flight. He's going to wait for you to make sure you leave the country okay.

"He'll drop you off, but he'll wait at the airport so you can call him if you need anything else. You have his phone number."

"Okay, whatever."

My Spanish is so good by now that I understand what he's saying.

He says, "Okay, did Franco give you money?"

"No he didn't give us any money."

He says, "Put him on the phone." So he gets on the phone with Franco.

Franco got 1,000 dollars worth of pesos, not U.S. dollars, out of the bank and Jorge is upset with him. Jorge's talking loud enough that I can hear them both.

"No. You were supposed to give them U.S. money."

Franco is telling Jorge, Yeah, I had to pay some of the guards. They hand up and Franco says, "You're on Spirit Air. Here's the flight and the confirmation number."

They're making the reservations while we're en route to the airport. This thing is last minute. So, okay, we're hauling ass. I write it down. I'm thinking we're going to land somewhere and not have our phones. There's no way we can call anyone when we land.

And fucking Jeff says, "We're not supposed to take our phones with us in case they're tracking us," or something like that. I should have punched him in the face when he's telling me this stuff. He always gets the information wrong.

He says, "We can't have any suitcases so don't check any bags on the flight."

I say, "Okay."

Jeff gets on the phone with Jorge while we're in the car and says, "Yeah, I get it. I get it," and Jeff gets off the phone.

I say, "We can't take any bags?"

He says, "No, he says we can't *check* any bags, take them with you." He calls Jorge back and says, "Oh yeah, you're right."

According to Jeff we can't take our phones, but Jeff takes his.

I was so pissed.

It takes almost 45 minutes to get to the airport. The whole time I'm staring out the window watching the Dominican Republic speed by. It's beginning to get dark but I can see the city miles away and people standing outside the rundown cement boxes they call home. I can't believe we are almost out of this country and away from all of the horrible things we experienced. But still, I can't forget how wonderful most of the people we met were. I'm so sick and my stomach cramps up worse than usual. I don't talk to anyone. I just pray over and over, "Please get us out of here, God, please."

We get to the airport and we have everything. We walk up there. It's a Spirit gate. Like shit! This flight takes off in 20 minutes. We're panicking.

This is a very high-risk activity that we're doing right now. Supposedly, we have a 24-hour window to leave the country before they post our information, but it's been more than 24 hours since the court let us go the day before. With it being this late in the day, who knows? Nothing in this country works like it should. After that, if someone scans our passport and something pops up, it's back to prison.

So we get inside and we're standing in line. The lady is sitting there and she's taking names and Jeff's name is on the list, but mine is not. I say, "Ah, shit" and I give her the confirmation number and she says, "*Sí, sí, esta bien, bien.*" Go ahead, keep going through the line.

So I get on the phone with my dad, "are you sure you got this number right? Are you sure about this confirmation number? Because the number was wrong on the money–remember that?"

So we get to the front and I tell them my confirmation number and he says, "No, it's not here."

I say, "No, it has to be there."

He checks it again and he says, "Oh, here it is."

"Oh, great."

Jeff has already bolted. I'm thinking, "You MF! Wait for me."

So the man says, "Where's your passport?" I give it to him and he scans my passport.

"Here you go. Here are your customs forms to fill out."

It's all in Spanish but we're in a hurry. We're trying to be cool about it. We go through Security. We give them our passports and there are police officers everywhere so we're trying to be cool. Franco's there, hanging out off to the side. We fill out all the information on the little slip and get through Security.

Franco gives us 500 pesos, a 500-peso bill. We have to pay when we go through customs because we've been here longer than 30 days. We have to pay $100. It's a weird thing, I don't know. We each have just enough to cover it.

So the guy looks at each of our tickets. We have our boarding pass. They have our passports and we start walking through Security. And here's the Security thing. I throw my bag on the conveyor belt. I have liquids in my bag and it goes right through Security! It was the most lax thing I ever saw. No wonder this is the drug trafficking hub!

We go right through. We have our stuff and walk around the corner and now we get to Customs and fill out a lot of paperwork. They scan our passports, again. All of a sudden a lady stops Jeff. He's in front of me.

She says, "You need to go over and see this lady."

And I'm thinking, "Oh, fuck."

I have to play it cool and calm, man, play it cool and calm. This other lady that we're waiting for shows up. It's me and Jeff. We're looking around and looking around. Everyone else is going though Customs.

She looks at our papers and says, *"Ah, es no."* She changes the date of when we arrived in the DR to five days later so we don't have to pay the 30 days, $100 fine. We thank her.

She says, *"De nada, fue, fue."* Good-bye.

Now we're going through and we're super friendly and happy. We walk through customs, around the corner, and we realize we have a long way to walk to get to the gate and the plane is almost ready to depart.

I say, "Oh shit! Our flight!" We have to get to the gate and we try not to walk too fast and draw attention to ourselves. We're walking, walking and come around the corner right before the gate, and all of a sudden, BOOM! The flight is delayed two hours!

I say, "Oh shit." Now we're going to be here until at least 9:30.

Me and Jeff are standing there and I say, "I've had flights delayed before but I've never had a set time period for how long it's going to be. Two hours. I've never heard, 'it's delayed for two hours.' Usually, the flight's delayed and they drag you along, but no, this flight is delayed two hours."

Me and Jeff find a place to sit and we're like, "Oh, God."

I'm thinking, trying to figure it out. Then I start wondering, would it take the police two hours to get our paperwork back at the prison and get out here to arrest us? Paranoia is setting in.

"Oh, man."

We're sitting there and sitting there and I say, "I'm going to go get something to drink, man, I'll be right back."

I go down to a little snack bar area to get something to drink. There's a girl in front of me and I'm not sure what I look like, well, I know what I look like. She's in front of me and the lady behind the counter rings up her total and the girl only has U.S. dollars. She has a U.S. hundred dollar bill that was too large and the girl says, "I don't have change for anything that large in U.S. dollars."

The girl needs pesos, right? I have a 1,000 peso note and I say, "Es nada, con amiga." And I give the girl working the cash register a 1,000–peso bill and I'm getting two sodas, two Gatorades. The girl is getting a sandwich or something like that.

The girl at the cash register gives me my change and the girl with the sandwich is offering the cashier her credit card.

The girl at the cash register says, "Oh, it's all right. He paid for it."

The girl is like, "You paid for it? Uh, muchas gracias."

There's this little bar/restaurant thing, so we go wait in the bar and watch a baseball game. Jeff orders a Presidente beer and I get like a Coke or Pepsi or water or something like that. We're both scared to eat because we have dysentery. And we're nervous and we're sitting there watching the game and I'm sitting there watching over my shoulder every time a security person walks by or a police officer walks by. Waiting and waiting at the airport.

The phone rings and Jeff answers it. He's the only one with a phone now. And whenever he says, "Here, talk to Corey," it means the person on the other end of the phone only speaks Spanish. Otherwise he talks the whole fucking time.

"Hello."

It's Franco and he asks if we're through the checkpoint. We were supposed to call him when we got through but we forgot.

I say, "Sí, Sí no problema. El Control de Seguridad es buena."

I'm talking to him in Spanish and telling him we're fine. No problems. We're waiting on the flight.

He says, "Buena suerte, mi amigo."

I say, "Gracias." We hang up and that is it.

The phone is dying and I'm thinking why the fuck did I give Franco my phone?

Franco wants me to use his phone so I'm thinking my phone has been compromised because they constantly send all the information and these big text messages through Jeff's phone, not mine. When I use my phone, after I dial and I start talking, I can hear this big click. I've talked on phones that were tapped before, especially cell phones, and it's easy to do. This was a while ago when I had a friend that had legal problems. Every time I talked to him I would hear that click. My phone started to click, too, so I talked to my parents in code. We figured it out.

I'd be surprised if they tapped the phone because I don't think the country is that technologically advanced. To this day, our paperwork says we were in La Victoria prison. No one ever knew where we were. None of the information was correct so I'd be surprised if it was that organized. I should have kept my phone.

Finally the plane arrives. Jeff is flying first class. I don't know why, that's just what he did. His parents bought him a first class ticket.

"I'm flying first class, baby."

"Okay, whatever." I couldn't have cared less as long as the plane gets me out of the Dominican Republic.

I sit down in my seat and buckle my seat belt. I'm on the aisle and there's an old man sitting next to the window. A few minutes later, a young, very attractive blonde stops and points at the middle seat.

"That's me," she says.

I unbuckle the seatbelt, stand up and move into the aisle so she can sit down. It's a momentary distraction while I keep an eye on everyone getting on board. All I see are tourists, nobody in a police uniform. I'm still afraid someone from the prison let the police know we're leaving the country.

Now we're taxiing, now we're waiting for take off.

I'm whispering, "Please take off, please take off," and when it finally does, I'm praying, "Oh, thank you, God," over and over.

Once the plane reaches cruising altitude, the blonde with the bluest eyes I've ever seen turns to me with this big smile and says, "I'm so glad we're finally out of the Dominican Republic. I've had the worst vacation of my entire life!"

And I say, "Oh, really?"

She says, "Yeah, you're not going to believe it!"

Honest to God–this really happened!

Epilogue

Corey and Jeff made it back to the States safely and after receiving medical care, Corey returned to his normal, unstoppable self. They remain close friends and see each other frequently.

Dominican Republic Human Rights Report 2016

These excerpts are from the Country Reports on Human Rights Practices for 2016 as reported by the United States Department of State • Bureau of Democracy, Human Rights and Labor.
For access to the entire document, go online to
https://www.state.gov/documents/organization/265794.pdf

DOMINICAN REPUBLIC 2016 HUMAN RIGHTS REPORT EXECUTIVE SUMMARY

The most serious human rights problem was widespread discrimination against Haitian migrants and their descendants. In 2013 the Constitutional Tribunal ruled that Dominican–born descendants of individuals residing in the country without legal status, most of whom were of Haitian descent, were not entitled to Dominican citizenship and retroactively revoked their citizenship. The naturalization law, promulgated in 2014, helped restore citizenship rights to many of those affected, although the majority remained without nationality documents at year's end.

Other human rights problems included extrajudicial killings by security forces, overcrowded and dangerously substandard prison conditions, arbitrary arrest and detention, lengthy pretrial detention, weak rule of law, and impunity for corruption. There were also reports of chronic violence against women, including domestic violence, rape, and femicide; trafficking in persons; discrimination against persons based on sexual orientation or gender identity; and inadequate enforcement of labor laws.

The government took some steps to punish officials who committed human rights abuses, but there were widespread reports of official impunity and corruption, especially concerning officials of senior rank.

Section 1. Respect for the Integrity of the Person, Including Freedom from:

a. Arbitrary Deprivation of Life and other Unlawful or Politically Motivated Killings

There were numerous reports that the government or its agents committed arbitrary or unlawful killings. The National Human Rights Commission (NHRC) reported more than 180 extrajudicial killings by police forces through September. The Attorney General's Office reported 74 extrajudicial killings through June.

b. Torture and Other Cruel, Inhuman, or Degrading Treatment or Punishment

Although the law prohibits torture, beating, and physical abuse of detainees and prisoners, there were reports that security force members, primarily police, carried out such practices. The law provides penalties of 10 to 20 years' imprisonment for torture and physical abuse and sentences of up to 30 years for aggravated cases.

The NHRC reported that police used various forms of physical and mental abuse to obtain confessions from detained suspects. According to the NHRC, abusive methods used to extract confessions included suffocation by covering detainees' heads with plastic bags, hitting them with broom handles, forcing them to remain standing overnight, and hitting them in the ears with gloved fists or hard furniture foam so as not to leave marks. The Attorney General's Office stated it did not receive any formal complaints of torture during the year. In August the Attorney General's Office officially instructed local prosecutors to monitor prisoner treatment and allegations of torture.

Prison and Detention Center Conditions

Prison conditions ranged from compliance with international standards in "model" prisons or correctional rehabilitation centers (CRCs) to harsh and lacking adequate space and medical care in "traditional" prisons. Threats to life and health included communicable diseases, poor sanitation, poor access to health–care services, a lack of well–trained prison guards, and prisoners attacking other inmates. These problems were exacerbated in traditional prisons, which were severely overcrowded.

Physical Conditions: Gross overcrowding was a problem in traditional prisons. The NHRC reported that on average there were approximately 15,000 prisoners in traditional prisons and 10,000 in CRCs, a ratio constant over the past several years, as traditional prisons had not been phased out. La Victoria, the oldest traditional prison, held more than 8,000 inmates, although it was designed for a maximum capacity of 2,500. La Romana Prison was the only prison where facilities for male and female inmates were separated, but collocated.

Police and military inmates received preferential treatment, as did those with the financial means to rent preferential bed space and purchase other necessities.

According to the Directorate of Prisons, military and police personnel guarded traditional prisons, while a trained civilian guard corps provided security at CRCs. Reports of mistreatment and violence in prisons were common, as were reports of harassment, extortion, and inappropriate searches of prison visitors. Some prisons remained effectively outside the control of authorities, and there were allegations of drug and arms trafficking, prostitution, and sexual abuse within prisons. Wardens at traditional prisons often controlled only the perimeter, while inmates ruled the inside with their own rules and system of justice. The Attorney General's Office reported it received 15 complaints of prison abuse, determined four had merit, and prosecuted them.

Health and sanitary conditions were generally poor. Prisoners commonly slept on the floor because there were no beds available. Prison officials did not separate sick inmates. All prisons had infirmaries, but most infirmaries did not meet the needs of the prison population. In traditional prisons inmates had to purchase their own medications or rely on family members or other outside associates to deliver their medications. Most reported deaths were due to illnesses. From late February to March, a cholera outbreak in La Victoria resulted in 75 positive cases and four deaths. The National Tuberculosis Control Program reported that the Ministry of Health, in conjunction with the Attorney General's Office and the Directorate of Prisons, instituted a program to control the spread of tuberculosis in 32 prisons.

According to the Directorate for the Control of Sexually Transmitted Diseases and HIV/AIDS, 2 percent of the prison population was HIV-positive. The directorate reported that all prisons in the system provided on-site HIV/AIDS testing, treatment, and counseling services. According to the Directorate of Prisons, all prisons provided HIV/AIDS treatment, but the NHRC stated that, while CRCs were able to provide HIV/AIDS treatment, none of the traditional prisons was properly equipped to provide such treatment. In the case of the CRCs, some prisoners with mental disabilities received treatment, including therapy, for their conditions. The government did not provide services to prisoners with mental disabilities in traditional prisons. Neither CRCs nor traditional prisons provided access for persons with disabilities.

About the Author

I have wanted to be an author since I was very young. My father was in the Army and I grew up across the United States, Japan and Germany. While we lived in Germany, we traveled to other European countries. All of these experiences gave my natural curiosity and imagination fertile ground to grow on.

My first book was about a Martian invasion. In addition to the story, I illustrated it with green-eyed purple Martians done in colored pencil. I bound it in a clear plastic cover with a yellow slide-on piece to hold the pages together. I was eight.

When I'm not writing, I'm in my artist's studio working in acrylics, pastels and mixed media. I have a lot of ways to stay creative and I'm never bored. I owned a business for 23 years but have been retired for almost 10. I love being retired and being able to write and paint whenever I want to.

Because of my health, this book took me several years to write and get to the point where it could be published. It first came out as an e-book in February 2016. I'm thankful for services like Amazon and CreateSpace that allow good writers to get published without the difficulty of trying to find an agent or get a contract with a large publishing house. Where would we be without the Internet? I know my life, for one, is larger because of it.

Thank you for reading *Unjustly Accused*. I hope you enjoyed it.

You can take a look at my other print and e-book books on my website at, **www.SusanLStewart.com** or visit my author page located on Amazon at **amazon.com/author/susanlstewart**

Amazon reviews are so important to a book's success. Would you please take a moment and write a review? Thank you so much!

27544849R00162

Printed in Great Britain
by Amazon